Weight Watchers®

Success
Every Day

Weight Watchers®

Success
Every Day

Macmillan ✴ USA

MACMILLAN GENERAL REFERENCE

A Simon & Schuster Macmillan Company

1633 Broadway

New York, NY 10019-6785

Library of Congress Cataloging-in-Publication Data

Weight watchers success every day.

p.   cm.

Includes index.

ISBN 0-02-860392-3

1. Reducing.   I. Weight Watchers International.

RM222.2.W328   1995

613.2'5--dc20   94-24253

CIP

Manufactured in the United States of America

10 9 8 7 6 5 4 3 2 1

W eight Watchers has written this book of meditations to help you fulfill the promise in every day and to offer support and encouragement on your weight-loss journey.

In these pages you can explore some of the many challenges that you may encounter along the way and share the experiences of others who are traveling this road with you. These are reflections on how stress, negative habits, fatigue and even boredom can be subtle deterrents to positive actions. You will find reflections on how optimism, courage, physical activity and laughter can boost your confidence and enhance your self-esteem, reinforcing your commitment to go on. There are practical hints for dealing with real-life situations and remaining focused on your goals.

It is our hope that this little book will help make your trip a little smoother.

For best weight-loss help, we recommend that you attend Weight Watchers meetings, follow the Weight Watchers Food Plan and participate in a program of regular physical activity. For the Weight Watchers meeting nearest you, call (800) 651-6000.

"It's not that some people have willpower and some don't. It's that some people are ready to change and others are not."

JAMES GORDON, M.D.

If you are hurting your body by consuming too much food or alcohol, by smoking or with another negative habit but can't seem to make any changes yet, don't berate yourself for a lack of willpower. It's hard to make headway on problems until feeling well becomes more important than the activity that harms you. In some self-help groups, this is known as "being sick and tired of being sick and tired."

Dr. Gordon suggests that those who have not yet reached this stage ease up on themselves. Instead, he advises developing complete awareness of what you are doing. So if you're eating ice-cream sundaes when you want to lose weight, you should remain completely focused on that activity. Observe that the first few spoonfuls of ice cream are enjoyable, but the next 20 are less so. Or if you want to quit smoking, notice that the first puff is satisfying but the rest of the cigarette gives you a dry throat.

There's nothing wrong with having habits. We rely on them to get through each day. Healthy habits include brushing your teeth, getting up at the same time every day and driving carefully. But when habits are unhealthy, try to find ways to eliminate them. Paying closer attention to all your habits will bring you another step closer to success.

⤳ *Tip for the Day* ⤲
Observe how you feel before, during and after you indulge in a bad habit. Do the negative emotions outweigh the positive ones?

*"It is only possible to live happily ever
after on a day to day basis."*

MARGARET BONNANO

A normal inclination is to compare ourselves and our progress with that of others. Some may have relatively little trouble losing weight and keeping it off, while others may have frequent plateaus and very slow weight loss. Because we're all unique people with different bodies, we're bound to meet with success in individual ways. Doing the best we can one day at a time is the only way to cope.

When Mimi decided to lose weight, she was 22 pounds overweight, bored with being a housewife and ignorant about nutrition and exercise. It took her eight months to lose weight, sometimes at a rate of only $1/4$ pound each week. She says that knowing her tendency is to lose weight slowly and accepting that fact made weight loss easier. By being patient and not losing sight of her objective, Mimi reached her weight goal. But equally important, she has kept the unwanted weight off for more than 20 years and now has a successful career as an older model.

If you are discouraged about the pace of your weight loss, review ways you might be slowing down your progress. Are you controlling your portions and getting enough physical activity? If you are doing all the right things, congratulate yourself and don't compare yourself with anyone else. After all, it's not important how quickly you reach your goal; what matters is finally getting there and learning the behaviors along the way that will keep you there.

Tip for the Day
*Remind yourself that changing your body and your life is something that
can be accomplished only one day at a time.*

"It is impossible to walk rapidly and be unhappy."

Dr. Howard Murphy

Ever since ancient Greek times, doctors have recommended that their patients walk to ensure good health and long life. Many physicians are also convinced that walking banishes the blues. One American psychiatrist is so wedded to this idea that he arranges to meet his depressed patients at a local track where they can walk and talk together. "You can't be depressed if you are moving," he explains.

Experts agree that successful and long-term weight loss is accomplished only through behavior modification, healthy eating and regular exercise. Because it is easily accessible, walking is often recommended as the first exercise to try. If you haven't worked out for many years, however, even short distances may be daunting. At first, Anne could walk only a quarter-mile without stopping, but now she walks three miles at a good clip every morning before breakfast.

Brisk walking is a wonderful way to exercise and banish the blues at the same time. Carve time out of every day to walk. Try parking in a distant spot and walking to the store. Or take the stairs instead of the elevator. Staying active will not only reduce cravings and burn calories, it will give you an emotional boost too.

Tip for the Day
Reduce your reliance on a car or public transportation
and take a walk today.

*"Fear is a question: What are you afraid of, and why?
Just as the seed of health is in illness, because illness
contains information, your fears are a treasure
house of self-knowledge if you explore them."*

MARILYN FERGUSON

One woman who was unsuccessful in losing and keeping off weight battled the same 70 pounds over and over until she decided to deal with her worries about success and failure in personal situations. She was so afraid of not being liked and saying no that she punished herself by eating. After she addressed her concerns in therapy, learning that being happy meant being true to herself and not to anyone else's wishes, she was able to stay on a healthy eating and exercise plan. This resulted in reaching and maintaining her weight goal.

Is fear preventing you from making an important change in your life? Are you afraid that losing weight will make you stand out more in social situations? Or are you afraid that taking time for regular exercise will make others think you're selfish? Whatever project you've been putting off because of your fears, take steps to address those fears now. Talking to a friend, writing in a journal or consulting with a professional can be an excellent way of seeing if your fears are warranted or groundless. Use one or more of these outlets to give your emotions less power over how you behave and the life choices you make.

Tip for the Day
*What is your biggest fear? Write a few sentences
about how the fear developed. What would really happen to you if
your fear were ever realized?*

"Things are seldom what they seem,
skim milk masquerades as cream."

Sir William Schwenck Gilbert

When you were young, you were probably admonished by your parents and grandparents to drink your milk because it was good for you and it would make your bones strong. Many fall out of the habit as they get older, including milk in their meals only if they happen to pour it over cereal or use it in coffee or tea. Some even develop an intolerance for lactose—the sugar naturally found in milk—and assume that they can never have milk again without feeling uncomfortable.

Including low-fat or skim milk in your meals is important because it provides essential nutrients and makes for a well-rounded diet. If drinking a glass of milk is unappealing, it can be used to prepare pudding or yogurt, or it can enrich soups and other drinks. And if lactose intolerance is a problem, there are lactose-free milk and tablets available that eliminate milk's unpleasant side effects. Milk also has physical benefits, as it helps to combat osteoporosis.

Ask yourself if you are getting your full quota of milk each day. If not, think of alternative ways to include it, such as in yogurt or cheese. After all, if milk can keep you strong and healthy while satisfying nutritional requirements, it deserves a place of honor in every kitchen.

⮞ *Tip for the Day* ⮜
Incorporate milk and other dairy products into
your meal plan today to ensure that you get your daily quota of
calcium and other nutrients.

"Man is what he eats."
LUDWIG FEUERBACH

To be successful at long-term weight loss, a regular program of daily exercise is essential. And if you know how to supply your body with the correct nutrients and energy it needs, you can make the difference between having a positive and enjoyable workout or struggling through it.

During sleep the body burns up its energy stores, so before your morning workout you may want to have a glass of fruit juice to restore your glucose levels. If you plan an afternoon workout, eat easily digestible carbohydrates like sweet potatoes, whole-wheat crackers or fruit no sooner than an hour before exercising, and be sure to keep the body hydrated with enough water. At all meals it's important to eat foods that are effective energizers, especially low-fat protein sources like split peas, wheat germ, black beans and lentils and complex carbohydrates like brown rice, corn, rolled oats and whole wheat.

What you eat has a great deal of influence over how successful you are, particularly when it comes to exercising effectively. So give yourself the greatest chance of success during your workouts today by eating for optimum energy.

↪ *Tip for the Day* ↩
Avoid high fiber or hard-to-digest foods right before exercising because your body will have to work digesting food instead of furnishing your muscles with energy.

"[Television is] the triumph of machine over people."
FRED ALLEN

There are two times when your metabolism sinks so low that you are barely burning any calories—when you sleep and when you watch television. Researchers say that sitting in front of the television induces alpha waves that mimic the sleep state. The body is almost inactive. Given this information, think about how you can combine or replace TV-watching with worthwhile activities.

One popular way to make television time productive is to ride a stationary bicycle or walk on a treadmill while watching the news or a favorite program. Or, use this time to pamper yourself: soak your feet in a basin of warm water, get a massage or do your nails. Other useful activities to combine with viewing include working on a knitting or needlepoint project, doing stretching exercises and lifting weights.

Although a healthy lifestyle consists of as much vigorous activity and movement as possible, it's almost inevitable that you will spend some time each day watching television. Keep in mind as you settle down for this activity, however, that you don't have to allow your body to sink into torpor. If you have the urge to eat while in front of the set, keep cut-up vegetables, air-popped popcorn and sparkling water nearby. With some ingenuity, you can make even this sluggish period turn into a benefit for you.

⟋⟍ Tip for the Day ⟋⟍
*Think of ways you can combine watching television with an activity that
will make your day more healthy and productive.*

*"Hold a picture of yourself long and steadily enough in your
mind's eye, and you will be drawn toward it."*

HARRY EMERSON FOSDICK

Many successful athletes visualize winning performances so that
when the moment of competition arrives, they already have
prepared themselves to be self-confident and assured. One
skater who continuously found herself losing to her rival, even
when she was better trained, said that it wasn't until she could
mentally see herself winning that she actually felt empowered
to go out and skate well enough to be the champion.

Use this powerful technique to make yourself a winner at
weight loss. Spend a few minutes each day visualizing your body 10 to 20 pounds thinner and see yourself being
comfortable and at peace around food. Imagine yourself turning down tempting foods and being satisfied with nourishing
foods. See yourself wearing flattering clothes and a hairstyle
that accentuates your best features. Let these pictures linger in
your mind as long as possible. Make sure that you have the
feeling that you absolutely *will* be this person, not that you
might be.

Take some time today to fill your mind's eye with positive
pictures of yourself. If you can do this regularly and with strong
conviction, you can follow anywhere your mind has taken you.

⟋ *Tip for the Day* ⟍
*Visualize yourself succeeding at a specific and important goal today.
Fill the picture with a lot of realistic details, holding that image
as long and steadily as possible.*

*"I write entirely to find out what I'm thinking, what
I'm looking at, what I see and what it means. What I
want and what I fear."*

JOAN DIDION

When you join Weight Watchers, you learn that it's essential
to write down meal choices so you will have a concrete plan of
action for the day. Not only does this eliminate the problems
that can come from last-minute rushing to create a healthy
meal, it is also a reminder that you can eat substantial servings
of good foods. In doing so, you can feel satisfied and reach a
weight that is healthy and acceptable.

Writing can also help in other ways. Research has shown
that people who spend several minutes writing down their feelings each day are happier and have greater self-esteem than
those who don't. The process of listing your concerns, fears
and joys can help you see patterns in your life that may be
contributing to your feelings about food. It can also show you
how emotions are powerful triggers for behavior.

After you complete your meal plan, record in a journal how
you feel this morning. Are you anxious about a situation that
may cause you to want to eat? Are you depressed because a
relationship isn't working out? If you can identify feelings that
might lead to overeating and safely vent your emotions in a
daily journal, you'll not only help your program, you'll have an
inexpensive and effective way to take care of your mental health
too.

→ *Tip for the Day* ←
*Write your meal plan and next to it jot down your feelings
about the coming day.*

"Laughter is by definition healthy."
DORIS LESSING

When you're sad, frustrated or worried, there's no better antidote to your problems than a good laugh. Laughter is a way of saying that there's no obstacle too difficult for you to overcome. It communicates to others that you don't take yourself too seriously. Laughing also attracts people to you because others want to be around someone who is happy.

While genuine laughter is good for your soul, it's also been proven to be good for your body. Researchers have found that laughter enhances breathing. It also reduces levels of stress-related hormones. When we're more relaxed, we are more flexible, creative and loving. Can it help you lose weight? No one knows for certain. There's no question, however, that feelings of well-being and optimism can assist you in reaching your goals.

There are many ways to bring more laughter into your life. You can watch funny shows, post zany cartoons where you'll see them and learn a new joke every day. You can also make a point of laughing at yourself or making a collection of your own bloopers. Humor is a powerful tool that can bring healing and joy into your life, so the more you can create and foster it, the greater will be its benefits.

❧ *Tip for the Day* ❧
Learn a new joke today and tell it to someone.

"Perhaps I am a bear, or some hibernating animal underneath, for the instinct to be half asleep all winter is so strong in me."
ANNE MORROW LINDBERGH

When winter arrives, it's not uncommon for the shorter days and colder temperatures to wreak havoc with exercise plans. If you habitually enjoy a morning or evening walk, this season's lack of sufficient daylight can prevent you from getting out for several months. And quite often you can lose your enthusiasm for exercise during the winter because you don't wear revealing clothes and thus have less incentive to tone your body.

If you find yourself making excuses not to exercise during the winter, you need to change your routine so you can maintain your fitness schedule. Some exercise consultants advise having a more varied regime than normal to help beat boredom. Recommended indoor activities include jumping rope, step aerobics, slide aerobics, mall walking and even country line dancing. To beef up your weight-loss work, consider investing in a punching bag or doing shadow boxing during an aerobics routine. Other reliable standby activities for the winter months include stationary biking, walking or jogging on a treadmill and following along with a taped or televised fitness program. And if you enjoy being outdoors, try hiking in snowshoes, skating or cross-country skiing to keep your body moving.

Don't allow the winter months to stall your fitness progress. Certainly it can be more difficult to find energy and initiative when darkness arrives early, but with some creativity and determination, the winter can be an exhilarating time of new fitness routines and rededication to achieving the weight-loss and exercise goals you set for yourself.

Tip for the Day
If you have found yourself making excuses not to exercise because of the season, challenge yourself to do something new. Call a local YMCA and ask about swim classes or buy a new fitness video. Then ask a family member or friend to join along with you.

"A surprising number of people start weight-loss programs believing all they need is 'willpower' and a container of cottage cheese."

EMME SOKOL

Undertaking new activities usually requires the necessary supplies that will help you achieve your goals. For example, in school you supply yourself with textbooks, notebooks and pencils. When you are learning a sport, you purchase the equipment and clothes needed. The same is true when you decide to lose weight and develop a healthy lifestyle; you need the right tools to aid your efforts.

Measuring spoons, measuring cups and a food scale are helpful items to have on hand. Useful kitchen appliances include a wok, blender and microwave oven. A journal to record your progress and emotions while eating and comfortable shoes for walking are also important. The right plate can help too. Research shows that pale, solid colors appease the appetite and several small servings of food are more satisfying than one large one.

Make sure you have the necessary and helpful equipment to make healthful living as easy as possible. Brainstorm about ways you can make meal preparation efficient. Buy items that will streamline your efforts. You'll remain committed and motivated if you treat weight loss as if you were going to school or learning a new skill.

Tip for the Day
Make a checklist of items that will help you in the kitchen and buy at least one of them.

"Anger as soon as fed is dead—'Tis starving makes it fat."
EMILY DICKINSON

Whenever Angela was angry at someone she would head straight for a fast-food restaurant or her refrigerator and sate her emotions with greasy, fattening food. "I was the classic people pleaser," she remembers. "I could never stand up to anyone so I just stuffed my face and went along with whatever anyone else wanted."

In order to lose weight and maintain weight loss, it's essential to develop strategies that will prevent you from eating out of anger. Give yourself permission to express your anger. Experts suggest a constructive way to vent anger is to state your needs calmly and without insulting the other person. For example, instead of offending your spouse about your in-laws, simply give a concrete instance of an incident that bothered you and say how it made you feel. In that way, the focus is off the other person and on your feelings.

Physical activity is a good way to handle angry feelings too. A brisk walk around the block will give you a chance to practice saying aloud statements that will help calm an upsetting situation. Take note of aggravating situations and people that trigger overeating. Practice saying aloud statements that would change the outcome of some upsetting situations. Role playing with a friend or therapist and writing in a journal can also lead to positive changes. The more you learn how to channel your anger in an appropriate way, the less likely you'll be to hurt yourself through overeating.

↭ *Tip for the Day* ↭
Write down two recent interactions that made you angry and caused you to eat inappropriately. If you had to relive them, what would you say or do differently that would enable you to vent your anger more constructively?

*"Man is the only animal whose desires increase as they are fed;
the only animal that is never satisfied."*

HENRY GEORGE

When Tracy was pregnant, she gave herself license to eat for two and admits that eating became a comfortable pastime, not a physical need. When she reached 190 pounds—up from her starting weight of 135 pounds—she realized she couldn't discern true hunger from emotional hunger. After joining Weight Watchers, she discovered how to eat normally and understand her body's natural cravings. As a result, she has lost 55 pounds and says that she has a new and healthier life.

Kathleen had a similar experience. When she reached age 40 with forty extra pounds, she realized that she ate by the clock, not because she was hungry. After starting a routine of nutritious and healthy foods, she lost her craving for sweets. She was able to listen to her body for the first time in years. She says she actually desires low-fat foods and that heavier dishes like fried chicken aren't appealing any longer.

As you change your food choices to include fruits, vegetables and lean sources of protein, you may be surprised to find that you can more effectively satisfy your hunger with these types of foods than what you may have chosen before. You'll also discover that by making wise meal selections, you'll provide yourself with the energy you need to achieve all your goals.

➤ *Tip for the Day* ➤

Pay special attention today to how you feel before and after meals. Are you hungry at mealtime? Do you feel a comfortable sense of fullness without being stuffed when you're done?

"We cannot swing up a rope that is attached only to our own belt."

WILLIAM ERNEST HOCKING

Sometimes you might be too proud to seek help for something that's bothering you, whether it's your weight, your relationship with your spouse, or a difficult project at work. There are many reasons why you might prefer to isolate yourself: maybe you were raised to be independent, or perhaps you're afraid to allow others to see your vulnerability, or maybe you're just frightened of the possibility of failure.

Being successful at weight loss requires support. Most things in life are easier when you have the support of people around you. When you're down, they can hold you up. When you're low on motivation, they can encourage you. In fact, many who have lost weight attribute their achievements to the strength they derived from others and the knowledge that they weren't alone in trying to change themselves.

If you are trying to lose weight without outside help, question your motives for doing so and remind yourself of the many advantages of being involved in a support group: friendship, a feeling of community and shared goals and interests.

Tip for the Day

Experience the power of group dynamics. Sit in on any meeting devoted to a single interest or topic such as a writers' club, garden club or amateur joggers group.

"Every time I think I've touched bottom as far as boredom is concerned, new vistas of ennui open up."

MARGARET HALSEY

Many people find that the first day or so of being snowed in or restricted to their home for another reason is refreshing. Given an excuse to slow down, you might nap, catch up with reading or writing or clean a closet that has needed attention. If this enforced rest goes on for more than a day or two, though, its novelty can wear off and you can run out of things to do. If you're not careful, you might turn to food to alleviate boredom.

When cabin fever strikes and the refrigerator looks like a good place to take refuge, consider some of these ideas from experts. First, try to find a cooperative project that can be done with several household members, like cataloging photographs or rearranging the furniture. Next, don't let the weather keep you from exercising: have a jump rope or aerobics tape ready for inclement days. Finally, try cooking an unusual dish or doing something out of the ordinary to break the cycle of doing the "same old, same old."

Be creative if you're confined to the house today. Do everything in your power to avoid letting the situation lead to overeating. Remember that boredom is a temporary condition that eventually goes away. With some ingenuity and patience you can expand your horizons while still keeping to a healthy fitness plan.

Tip for the Day

Have one household project ready to tackle when bad weather strikes.

"Trouble is only opportunity in work clothes."
HENRY J. KAISER

When Gail began to have vision problems and headaches, she assumed it was related to stress, a recent move and the responsibilities of raising two small children. After a number of tests, however, Gail was diagnosed with multiple sclerosis and was told by her doctor that if she weren't so overweight, she wouldn't be in such pain. Humiliated and depressed, Gail then joined Weight Watchers, determined to address her weight problem in a sensible way.

Gail eventually lost 52 pounds and became an inspiration to many others along the way. While a diagnosis of a progressive and incurable disease may have caused others to become pessimistic, what Gail accomplished as a result of her troubles shows that you don't have to let anything stand in the way of succeeding. Gail says that learning to survive and thrive despite her challenges has given her the confidence to pursue her dreams. She now works with people who have physical and emotional challenges, especially mentally disabled adults.

Don't allow troubles to deter you from your goal of reaching a certain weight, achieving a fitness goal or going after a professional dream. While many situations may appear upsetting, you might be surprised to find that they contain valuable lessons to help you cope with difficult events in the future. And if you adhere to a program of exercise and nutritious meals instead of drowning your emotions in junk food, you'll always have enough energy to cope with whatever befalls you.

≈ *Tip for the Day* ≈
*Instead of looking at trouble as an excuse to eat, look at it as an
opportunity to strengthen your abilities to reach your goals.*

"The most sympathetic of men never fully comprehend woman's concrete situation."

SIMONE DE BEAUVOIR

When Harold, a forty-two-year-old accountant, decided to lose weight, his wife was delighted that he was beginning to take better care of himself. She supported his efforts and praised his every success. But as Harold got closer to his weight goal, her attitude changed. He says she felt threatened by his renewed zest for life and was even jealous of his new wardrobe and handsome look. It wasn't long before she began subtly to sabotage his efforts. For example, she let their membership at the health club lapse and made zucchini bread one evening because she thought the bread would count for both bread and vegetable portions.

Harold's wife isn't unique. Researchers have found that when people lose weight in programs that emphasize changing coping strategies and identifying triggers for emotional eating, spouses and partners are often the biggest saboteurs of their mates' efforts. One researcher reported that a woman who lost 30 pounds was rewarded by her husband with a two-week tour of French restaurants. This "reward" led her to regain her weight.

To be successful at weight loss, it's important to be aware of who is and is not supportive of your efforts. Resolve not to let anyone else's jealousy or mixed emotions affect your program. Point out incidents of sabotage—direct or indirect—when you spot them. Over time, you'll probably find that the more determination you have to reach your goal and transform your life, the easier it will be to overcome obstacles when they arise.

❧ *Tip for the Day* ❧

Ask someone who is close to you to be supportive and encouraging of your weight-loss efforts by accompanying you to a support group or joining you in your exercise.

"Inside myself is a place where I live all alone and that's where you renew your springs that never dry up."

PEARL BUCK

Many of us live lives that are so jam-packed with commitments that we have little time to ourselves. If we aren't busy at work, we're coping with parenthood, helping aging parents, pursuing volunteer commitments or just keeping up with daily errands and chores. In this type of hectic world, it's difficult to find the time to just sit back and do nothing. But when life is this busy, that's exactly what we need to do to regain balance in our lives and recharge our batteries.

Meditation is one of the easiest and most effective ways to develop a rich inner life and relieve stress. Meditators say that just two ten-minute sessions of focused breathing each day are sufficient to re-energize yourself, remove worry and regain perspective on life. One woman says that she meditates every day before lunch. This practice helps her get in touch with her emotions and reminds her that food is supposed to nourish the body, not divert her from problems or comfort her when she's down.

Spend some time in quiet contemplation today away from ringing telephones or the demands of others. Take note of how you are feeling. Are you happy, sad, anxious or depressed? Do any of these emotions trigger hunger pangs or a sense of emptiness? As you increasingly incorporate a meditative peacefulness into your days, you'll discover that being in touch with your inner self won't just help you stay on your weight-loss program, it will also impart feelings of serenity. This will help you be successful in every area of your life.

✎ *Tip for the Day* ✎
Meditate for at least ten minutes today when you know you'll be undisturbed.

"For better or worse, the workplace has become the eatplace."

GABRIELLA STERN

Due to increased pressures at work and the changing nature of some companies, the office is no longer a place where you might eat only your brown-bagged lunch. National research shows that the number of meals brought into offices from restaurants has risen 30 percent, and it's not just for a midday meal. Studies show that many workers are now eating two—and even three—of their daily meals at their desks.

It's critical that you prepare yourself to follow a healthy eating and exercise regimen at the office as well as at home. This means planning ahead to ensure that unexpectedly late hours don't leave you hungry and prone to vending-machine snacking. If you know you are going to be stuck late in the office, pack healthy treats to forestall cravings or bring a prepared dinner to reheat in the office microwave. Another good way to handle late-night meal dilemmas is to prepare several nutritious meals at the same time and freeze them. When you get home, simply pop one into the microwave.

Don't allow long or unexpected hours at work to cause you to eat poorly. Have a plan for the times when you are forced to eat more than one meal at your desk. Try to make it as pleasant as possible. Keep some nice utensils available and always have condiments or herbs in a drawer that you can use to dress up a spur-of-the-moment dinner. Although you may not always be able to have your meals *where* you want, you can always find ways to make sure it's *what* you want.

⌒ *Tip for the Day* ⌒

Think of two ways you will deal with having a meal at work, even if you're not prepared. Find the location of the closest deli or grocery where you can buy a salad or nutritious entrée.

*"Happiness: a good bank account, a good cook
and a good digestion."*

JEAN-JACQUES ROUSSEAU

Many people who lose weight find that having a newly trim
body and active lifestyle bring surprising moments of happiness that at one time they may not have thought possible. Here
are some that have been cited by men and women who have
been successful at weight loss:

"Being able to wear a pretty dress, not an ugly sack."

"Dancing at a wedding instead of standing on the side."

"Being able to walk to my seat at a football game."

"Fitting comfortably behind the wheel of the car."

"Finding a seat at the movie theater."

"Playing outside with my children and not getting
exhausted."

"Passing a window on the street and liking the
reflection."

If you are temporarily stalled in your weight-loss progress
or you want to be spurred on, think of some of the
emotional and physical benefits you have already received from
losing weight. While some of these examples may seem minor,
the cumulative effect of these moments of happiness will bring
you the joy and energy needed to remain committed to living
a healthy and well-balanced life.

Tip for the Day

*Think of one surprising moment of happiness you've had as a result of
beginning a sensible weight-loss plan.*

"The undertaking of a new action brings new strength."
EVENIUS

Virginia spent an unhappy childhood being ridiculed by classmates because she was overweight. When she got older, though, she decided to stop crying about the insults and instead to apply her energy toward losing weight in a sensible way. Now many pounds lighter, she says that no one has to be an ugly duckling.

Virginia brings this same message of determination to the meetings where she is a Weight Watchers leader who has maintained a 105-pound weight loss for several years. She emphasizes that anyone with the courage to try can lose weight. Instead of relying on your wishbone, she stresses, it's essential to depend on your backbone to achieve your goals.

If you are trying to work up the energy to go to a Weight Watchers meeting, keep in mind that simply beginning your task will give you the enthusiasm to take even more beneficial actions. As Virginia's story demonstrates, success doesn't come to those who make wishes, it comes to those who take steps to make those wishes come true.

Tip for the Day
Take one step toward a goal in your life and notice how that one action
energizes you to build upon it.

"The discovery of a new dish does more for human happiness than the discovery of a star."

ANTHELME BRILLAT-SAVARIN

Dull meals lead to feelings of deprivation, which often precede an episode of overeating. For this reason, it's essential to be as creative as possible when preparing meals. Many sources can inspire you to make great meals. The food section of the local newspaper, featured segments on the news, magazines and cookbooks, which are usually one of the largest sections at a bookstore, will all stimulate your culinary skills.

Here are some ideas to help create an entrée or side dish that is interesting and healthy.

- Use flavored vinegars to add punch to dressings or sauces.
- Mix grated cheese with bread crumbs to cut down on fat in toppings.
- Flavor plain yogurt with fruit spreads, extracts and spices for dips and sauces.
- Instead of adding cream to soup, try pureed vegetables for thickness and flavor.
- Make chili with ground turkey in place of other ground meats.

Use these tips as a jumping-off point to new and tasty creations. These will make meals on your weight-loss program a delight. With the advent of new cooking techniques and the wide availability of fresh foods and spices, you can always create your own themes and vary them according to your desires.

≈ Tip for the Day ≈
Take a standard dish you prepare often and alter some of the ingredients to create a new taste sensation.

"Providence has hidden a charm in difficult undertakings which is
appreciated only by those who dare to grapple with them."

ANNE-SOPHIE SWETCHINE

When Leslie was young she was uncoordinated and overweight.
As an adult she joined a weight-loss program and became slender. But she still carried around feelings of
inferiority about her physical shortcomings. When a friend
challenged her to enter a triathlon, she was intrigued
despite her lack of skills. Leslie agreed to try, though, and after
months of training in swimming, bicycling and
running, she entered and finished the race.

Leslie said later that completing the race gave her a feeling
of accomplishment that heightened her self-esteem. Most important, she realized she could apply the same
determination to other situations and achieve similar
successes. This is unquestionably true. Whenever you set a goal
for yourself and meet it, you have that achievement to be proud
of, and you know that you possess the skills necessary to be
persistent in going after your dreams.

Don't shrink from setting difficult goals for yourself
today. Whether you are aiming to lose weight, change your
career, confront a problem head-on or learn a new hobby, set
your sights high. The process of overcoming one
obstacle at a time along the way will give you more
confidence than anything else in life can ever supply you.

Tip for the Day
Spend several minutes visualizing yourself reaching a goal
you have set for yourself, and then say aloud, "I can
be successful at anything I put my mind to."

"We don't know who we are until we see what we can do."

MARTHA GRIMES

At one time Dawn was like many other aspiring actresses. She waited tables to make money and went to endless rounds of auditions in the hopes of getting a role. After being repeatedly rejected because of her excess weight, Dawn joined a weight-loss program and lost 22 pounds. As a result of her success, Dawn has set even loftier goals for herself professionally. She says that losing weight taught her to go after what she wants, whether it's ordering food in a restaurant to be prepared in a special way or putting together her own theatrical production.

As you lose weight and discover feelings of success, use those emotions to motivate yourself in other areas of your life too. After all, if you can change your exercise and eating patterns, how hard could it really be to try out for the church choir? And if you can realize a lifelong dream of wearing a smaller size dress than you did in high school, what makes you think you can't give an outstanding speech?

Don't limit yourself in any area of your life today. Use your success in changing your behavior as a springboard to go after your dreams and to develop unbounded confidence in yourself. You'll discover that once you can honestly recognize what you've accomplished in the program, you'll probably see yourself in a new and more flattering light.

Tip for the Day
Congratulate yourself for the strides you've made in
being healthy and think of other areas of your life where you'd like to
apply the same energy and enthusiasm.

"[Clothes are] always the reflection of one's self-respect."

ANONYMOUS

When you aren't proud of your body, your tendency might be to wear ill-fitting clothes to hide your flaws. What this often means is that you wear shapeless suits and dresses. You wear coats in hot weather and rarely shop for new or stylish items, telling yourself that you are too fat or ugly to deserve to look nice.

If you are following a sensible eating plan, though, you are on the road to achieving the body you want, one that will give you joy and energy. Instead of waiting until you reach your weight goal, update your wardrobe now. You may not yet have the waist size or cheekbones you want, but the sooner you groom yourself well and stop acting ashamed of your body, the greater will be your self-esteem.

Check out your closet today. Is it filled with "fat clothes" that are drab and unflattering? If so, clean it out. Make a point of adding one item every week that will help to celebrate the new you. Whether it's a vest, a hat, updated makeup or a fitted skirt, present yourself in a way that will enhance your new shape. You will communicate the feelings of self-confidence and enthusiasm that are necessary to achieve your goals.

Tip for the Day

Discard a piece of clothing that reminds you of your fat days and replace it with something for the new you.

"We don't get offered crises, they arrive."

ELIZABETH JANEWAY

As much as we would like to have problem-free lives, everyone experiences crises that test their coping skills. Many people turn to food in times of extreme stress because it can provide a temporary distraction, replenish energy and induce a feeling of calm. Unfortunately, eating in response to a crisis usually results in weight gain, which creates its own cycle of depression and anxiety.

Because stress is often a common precursor to overeating, we offer some useful tips to manage stress better and deflect the desire to overeat: First, when a crisis occurs, it's important to calm down and assess the situation correctly. This can be accomplished through deep breathing and visualization of tranquil scenes. Once the mind is quiet, the crisis may not seem so overwhelming. Second, exercise is a good technique to release stressful energy and has the additional benefit of improving your mood. Third, to further remove the possibility of emotional eating, keep prepackaged meals on hand so that the time spent preparing and handling food is kept to a minimum.

If you have always eaten in response to crises, develop a plan that will eliminate the urge to overeat. You may think this is unnecessary if your life is fairly placid now, but being prepared for challenges is a major part of triumphing over them. Remember, it wasn't raining when Noah built the ark.

⤔ *Tip for the Day* ⤔
*Think of realistic ways you can respond to a crisis so that it
will not trigger emotional eating.*

"The shoe that fits one person pinches another; there is no recipe for living that suits all cases."

CARL JUNG

When Cecile finally decided she wanted to lose weight and feel physically and emotionally better, she turned to her friend Arlene for advice. Arlene, who ate a strict macrobiotic diet, extolled the virtues of her program, saying that she had lost a great deal of weight and successfully kept it off for years. Consequently, Cecile completely changed her cuisine and attempted to eat just like her friend, but it worked only temporarily. Feeling deprived and bored, she gorged herself on her favorite foods and soon regained all of the weight she'd lost.

Be attuned to your personal likes and habits before trying to copy someone else's way of life. For example, if a friend is a vegetarian but you love meat and fish, you'll never be successful on your friend's program. And if your spouse is a devoted jogger but you prefer low-impact aerobics, you might get injured or dispirited if you slavishly copy his or her workout.

Remember that you are unique. How you choose to live your life should reflect your likes, dislikes, proclivities and temperament. If you go against your innate traits—either by trying to eat like someone else or take a job because your friend recommends it—you're bound to disappoint yourself and create a recipe for living that fails. Only by knowing whether the shoe fits you and by creating the circumstances in which you can wear it will you achieve the success you desire.

⟳ *Tip for the Day* ⟳

Develop your own recipe for success. Pledge to yourself that you will follow a healthy lifestyle that is tailored to your specific needs.

> *"Whatever is reasonable is true, and whatever is true is reasonable."*
>
> GEORG W. HEGEL

Before a person can successfully lose weight and keep it off, it's important to address some of the myths that can hurt our efforts. Here are some misconceptions that need to be abolished:

- *The less you eat, the more weight you'll lose.* Not true. The less you eat, the more likely your body is to think it's starving; it will hold on to every single calorie while your metabolism simply gets slower and less efficient.

- *You shouldn't eat between meals.* Planned snacking can maintain your blood sugar level and decrease feelings of hunger between meals.

- *Too many sweets make you overweight.* Actually, complex carbohydrates should make up the bulk of your diet. Sugar and sweet foods aren't the only culprits; it's also excess fat that makes you gain weight.

- *You should weigh yourself every day.* Not only are daily fluctuations normal, but a person who begins to develop muscle may become thinner, but weigh the same or even more.

- *Your diet is more important than whether or not you exercise.* Study after study has shown that the people who are most successful at weight loss are those who also exercise regularly.

➽ *Tip for the Day* ➽

Carefully scrutinize your beliefs for unfounded myths and operate only from what is reasonable and true.

"There is no such thing as a little garlic."

ANONYMOUS

One of the best ways to make food zesty and interesting is liberal use of herbs and spices. But these substances do more than dress up food, they can have a medicinal effect as well.

Garlic, for example, does more than make your breath and cuisine aromatic. It has also been shown to lower cholesterol by as much as 23 to 27 points. Another herb, kudzu, has been shown to reduce the desire for alcohol. Green tea, popular in China, is now linked to lowered levels of liver, pancreatic, breast, lung, esophageal and skin cancers. It also lowers the risk of cardiovascular disease, decreases blood sugar levels, inhibits viral colds and flu and prevents gum disease, cavities and bad breath. In addition, dandelion tea can ease fluid retention, thyme can eliminate coughs and lavender can help with insomnia.

Learn as much as possible about the health-inducing properties of the seasonings you use in your meals. Many books, magazines and videotapes are now available on this subject, so understanding how to make your meals delicious as well as healing has never been easier.

❧ *Tip for the Day* ❧

Visit a health-food store or read a holistic magazine for new insights on how to boost your vitality in natural ways.

"One must not lose desires. They are mighty stimulants to creativeness, to love, and to long life."

ALEXANDER A. BOGOMOLETZ

Jo was once 185 pounds overweight and she remembers how difficult it was to get through each day. Before entering a turnstile, for example, she had to decide whether or not she could get through it safely. She remembers feeling overwhelmed by these routine occurrences because they made her feel so helpless.

Jo eventually met her weight goal after joining Weight Watchers and then began to help others develop the skills and attitude to have the same success. One thing she emphasizes in the meetings where she is a Weight Watchers leader is that anyone who is trying to lose weight must create continual incentives, such as buying clothes in smaller sizes, so that there is always something to work toward. She reminds members that they often buy bigger clothes as they gain weight, so doing the same thing as they get slimmer makes sense, and it will keep them motivated.

If you aren't making progress toward losing weight or meeting some other goal in your life, encourage yourself with incentives. Buy a belt in a smaller size, make an appointment at a spa or purchase a new piece of exercise equipment. You'll find that keeping your motivation fresh will help you set and achieve your goals.

Tip for the Day

Think of one small item you can buy that will push you toward reaching a goal, like a colorful exercise outfit or a pair of hand weights.

*"Exercise alone provides psychological and physical benefits.
However, if you also adopt a strategy that engages
your mind while you exercise, you can get a whole host of
psychological benefits fairly quickly."*

JAMES RIPPE, M.D.

Because carving out time for yourself is difficult, it's a good idea to find activities that achieve two goals at the same time. The new trend of "mindful exercise" combines meditation with physical movement. The idea is to provide the body with physical exercise while also giving the mind an "inner workout."

Two examples of mindful exercise are yoga and t'ai chi. Or, you can create your own mindful exercise by doing a low-intensity workout, such as walking, while listening to soothing music or repeating a comforting or familiar word or phrase. The key is to leave the chatter of the mind behind while becoming conscious of the body's movements. The benefits of eliciting this type of relaxation response are many. Studies have shown that mindful exercise induces immediate and positive emotions such as enthusiasm, alertness and self-esteem, as well as reducing anxiety and depression. Physical benefits include strengthening the body against ills like high blood pressure, cancer, heart disease and osteoporosis.

If you are in a time squeeze, consider mindful exercise as a way to reap the physical and psychological benefits of activity and meditation in one session. By doing movements that both strengthen your body and heal your mind, you can efficiently achieve your health and fitness goals.

⋙ *Tip for the Day* ⋘
*Try to combine walking with listening to soothing music, or use the stationary
bicycle while repeating a comforting phrase.*

"I simply cannot understand the passion that some people have for making themselves thoroughly uncomfortable and then boasting about it afterwards."

PATRICIA MOYES

Lee began to dread going to work every morning but she wasn't sure why. Finally, when her aching shoulders and back drove her to a chiropractor, she realized that she sat in an uncomfortable chair all day. Now she has a contoured chair with armrests and support for her lower back. Not only has this eased the tension in her shoulders and made her more comfortable, she's more productive, too.

It is important to cater to our comfort occasionally when we are trying to reach goals. One way to improve your chances of weight loss, for example, is to make mealtimes pleasant by having a comfortable seat, a nice view and as serene an environment as possible. We should strive to be comfortable while we exercise so that we aren't tempted to abandon our program. Wearing constricting leotards or poorly fitting shoes gives us an excuse to give up.

Sometimes being too comfortable can lure us into complacency about areas of our life that need to be changed. But making sure that we feel relaxed and sure of ourselves at other times can be very conducive to growth. Try to improve your environment today, knowing that if you are comfortable, you are also happier and more productive. Having a good balance in this area will make life more pleasant, and it will undoubtedly make you more successful.

Tip for the Day
Wear comfortable clothes today and take note of whether they make you happier and more energetic.

"We know that every woman wants to be thin. Our images of womanhood are almost synonymous with thinness."

SUSIE ORBACH

At an early age, most girls absorb the message that to be thin is to be successful. This is communicated through magazines, television shows, beauty pageants and dieting articles that suggest the idea that a skinny woman is a desirable woman. To try to accommodate these unrealistic ideals, many women attempt starvation but wind up overeating instead. This creates an emotional eating cycle that is difficult to break.

To lose weight and maintain the loss, the weight goal must be appropriate to each person's height and frame. In the process of working toward this goal, many women begin to understand that the skinny ideal isn't just unhealthy, it's impossible. It's far better for the body to adjust gradually to eating and fitness routines that will make you slender and comfortable, not skeletal and ravenous.

Remember that being very thin doesn't necessarily make you healthy. If you eat balanced meals, exercise and take care of your body, you'll settle at the weight that is right for you. You can let go of the unrealistic expectations that contributed to your overeating and shame about your body in the first place.

⸙ Tip for the Day ⸙
Ask yourself if you are following a weight-loss program because you want to look and feel healthy, or whether your goal is to get thin no matter what.

"Coffee was a food in that house, not a drink."
PATRICIA HAMPL

One of the lists that many Weight Watchers members eagerly turn to is "Additional Items." This is because quantities for these items are not specified; you are simply encouraged to have them in "reasonable" amounts. But some people use this recommendation as a license to overindulge. They think that because coffee has negligible calories it's acceptable to have as much as desired. Many people also feel this way about decaffeinated diet soda and tea.

It's important to remember the word "reasonable" when drinking these beverages, though. Drinking too much can have negative side effects. For example, too much caffeinated coffee can cause jitters, insomnia and hunger pangs, as well as have a laxative and diuretic effect. Overindulgence of anything, even if low in calories, defeats the purpose of feeling and satisfying genuine hunger because constant satiety prevents you from being in touch with the real needs of your body.

Be careful not to overdo items like coffee in your weight-loss efforts. If you find yourself reaching for soft drinks, coffee and tea throughout the day, ask yourself why and what your real needs are. Being moderate with all things, even decaffeinated coffee, will not only help you learn to eat healthfully; it will also enhance other aspects of your life.

Tip for the Day
Keep track of how many cups of coffee, tea and soda you drink today. Make a commitment to cut down if you find yourself always reaching for a cup, even if you aren't hungry or thirsty. Be sure that you are drinking enough water.

"Medication without explanation is obscene."

TONI CADE BAMBARA

Taking medications from time to time is a fact of life for most people; some even require it on a regular basis. Nancy found that weight loss enabled her to stop taking blood-pressure medication, but she still needed insulin to manage her diabetes. She continued her weight-loss routine along with daily monitoring of her blood sugar and a supervised course of medical treatment. Another weight-loss program member wanted to quit smoking without undoing her work in the program, so she used the nicotine patch under medical supervision.

To be a well-informed patient, it's imperative that you understand the effects of various medications, particularly if you are making an effort to lose weight at the same time. For example, while the birth-control pill is a safe contraceptive, it is associated with occasional side effects such as nausea and weight gain. Some antidepressants also result in dry mouth, constipation and weight gain, while others can induce abdominal pain and weight loss. The nicotine patch, blood-pressure medication and antiseizure drugs can have side effects ranging from lightheadedness and irritability to impotence and lethargy.

If you are taking any type of medication, ask your doctor about its effect on weight and appetite. Know if you should expect your weight to go up or your energy to decrease. Becoming empowered as you lose weight means more than taking responsibility for what you eat; it means taking the best possible care of your body.

∽ *Tip for the Day* ∽

Look in your medicine cabinet and take note of the different medicines you take. Do you know exactly what they can do to your body and whether there are certain foods and beverages you'd be well advised to avoid while on medication?

"[Sleep is] the golden chain that ties health and
our bodies together."

THOMAS DEKKER

Since the invention of the light bulb, round-the-clock television programming, red-eye flights and a global economy, the world has shifted from a daytime working environment to a twenty-four-hour one. While this has ushered in more convenience in many ways, it has also prompted concern among health officials that sleep deprivation is a major hazard, resulting in more traffic accidents, less attentiveness at work and an increase in sickness.

For the person who is trying to lose weight, sleep deprivation can wreak havoc in many ways. If you're tired, you are more likely to turn to snacks and caffeinated beverages for energy. It's also easy to skip exercise in favor of a nap because you're simply too exhausted to work out. Chronic fatigue can also result in the body becoming especially susceptible to illness, which can impede achieving health and fitness goals.

If you are shortchanging yourself in the sleep department, here are some suggestions to help you get more rest and feel more energetic. First, figure out how much sleep you need to feel your best and then calculate how sleep deficient you are each week. Move your bedtime back at least a half-hour until you get used to retiring earlier. Don't view sleep as a luxury; it is a necessity. If you can routinely get the rest you need, you'll find that not only will you feel better, you'll also have the willingness and enthusiasm to tackle and succeed at your weight-loss and fitness goals.

≈ *Tip for the Day* ≈
Track your sleeping patterns for a week and analyze whether you are getting
enough rest to promote optimal fitness and healthy eating habits. Make at least
one change in your lifestyle if you are chronically tired, such as cutting back on
caffeine or skipping a late television show.

"[Common sense] is the best sense I know of."
LORD CHESTERFIELD

To lose weight successfully and create a lifestyle that is health oriented, one of the things you must do is to use your common sense. There are many ways people neglect common sense when attempting to lose weight. One is in not reading nutrition labels, or deciding to eat a product only because it claims to be light or low cholesterol but might be high in fat. Also, some foods that advertise themselves as "high fiber" neglect to add that it takes multiple servings to achieve those fiber standards.

Some people also make the mistake of thinking that a product that is low in fat means that it can be eaten liberally. One woman who frequently indulged in fat-free cookies as part of her weight-loss program ended up gaining weight, which she says brought home the message that calories, not just fat, are important in achieving weight loss.

Common sense also must be applied to fitness routines. If you are overly enthusiastic about starting an exercise program, you may injure yourself and cause more harm than good. Use caution and seek a doctor's approval before undertaking any new or vigorous activity, particularly if you haven't exercised for many years. If you are experiencing unusual aches or pains, it's smart to do an alternative activity until you are pain free.

Use your head and apply common sense to your nutrition and fitness plans today. You know your body better than anyone else, so heed its signals. If a food claim appears too good to be true, trust your judgment. If you can stick to the guidelines of a sensible weight-loss program and follow your best instincts, you'll undoubtedly meet with success.

Tip for the Day
Can you think of a food you overindulged in recently because it claimed to be low fat or fiber rich? If you had heeded your better instincts, would you have eaten it in the first place?

*"I truly feel that there are as many ways of loving as
there are people in the world and as there are days in
the life of those people."*

MARY S. CALDERONE

When Janet was 60 pounds overweight, she acknowledged that
months, even years, went by without her being asked on a date.
Consequently, whenever someone asked her out, she was a
bundle of nerves and felt anxious about intimacy. Janet eventually lost weight and received the attention she desired from
men, but she found herself still grappling with feelings of discomfort about her body.

Experts say that if you were overweight for a long
period, take time to develop self-confidence and readjust to
dating as a slim person. Instead of being desperate to please
someone else, you need to ask yourself if you think the relationship is appropriate for you. Take a "go slow" attitude toward intimacy if you're unaccustomed to physical closeness.
Remember that you can demonstrate love through hugging,
being honest with someone else and sharing quiet moments.

If dating strikes terror in your heart because you're frightened of intimacy, explore your feelings in a supportive
atmosphere with friends or a professional counselor. Try
activities like dancing or yoga that will help you become more
comfortable with your body. As your self-confidence increases
with weight loss success and you become used to the "thin
you," you'll find that being able to express and receive love
and affection becomes easier.

∽ *Tip for the Day* ∽
*Do you shy away from being touched? Think of an activity that will make this
easier, such as touching a friend in a supportive way or hugging someone you're
fond of.*

"Page one is a diet, page two is a chocolate cake."
KIM WILLIAMS

The quotation given above refers to the contradictory messages conveyed by many women's magazines. Since the 1960s there has been an elevenfold increase in the number of diet-related articles in women's magazines. Yet at the same time, these magazines have continued to tout the joys of desserts, rich dishes and hearty eating.

To lose weight and keep it off, it's important to know how you are subtly encouraged to eat. Tempting recipes and mouth-watering pictures of food are one such inducement. Some stores even have the aroma of fresh bread or chocolate piped in because it makes people hungrier.

Be conscious of the many stimuli in your environment that encourage you to eat. Notice the advertisements, television commercials, packaging of foods and layouts of the supermarkets you shop in. Note times when you feel hungry and ask yourself if it's real hunger or whether it's the result of one of these stimuli. The more you are aware that you are being encouraged to eat, the less likely you'll be to succumb to false hunger and temptation.

≈ *Tip for the Day* ≈
*Walk through the supermarket carefully, noting how you
feel after walking through each section. Take note of the kinds of
products placed at eye level. Be aware of products displayed prominently at the
ends of aisles where you may be most tempted.*

*"Eating habits are like a mother tongue you learn as
a child and never forget."*

SANDRA HABER, PH.D.

For many people, poor nutrition was instilled in childhood because their parents modeled unhealthy eating and exercise habits. For example, one woman who is attempting to shed 25 excess pounds blames her problem on her mother's cooking, saying that her mother always steered her toward rich and cheesy foods throughout her childhood and early adulthood. Another woman who is battling extra pounds says that she feels compelled to finish every meal with a sweet because she grew up watching her mother do the same.

When you reach adulthood, it's time to separate from your parents and take responsibility for your own eating behavior. While it's helpful to recognize that you always clean your plate because you were told to as a child, you must take actions now as an adult to steer your eating onto the right track. Similarly, if you grew up in a house where a parent was constantly counting calories and going on and off restrictive diets, make an extra effort now that you've grown up to ensure that your own weight-loss efforts are balanced and sensible.

Be mindful of the lessons you learned from your parents about food and body image, but remember that you have the ability to create a healthy lifestyle now. Carving out your own adult identity is an important step in finding satisfaction and peace because you'll be more likely to reach the fitness and weight goals you set for yourself. And you can pass along better lessons to your own children.

∽ *Tip for the Day* ∽
*Are you still doing something unhealthy you learned from a parent, like
finishing others' leftovers, that is preventing you from succeeding at weight loss?*

"A compliment is a gift, not to be thrown away carelessly, unless you want to hurt the giver."

ELEANOR HAMILTON

When people begin to see the results of their commitment to living healthfully, they are often unprepared for the compliments they receive from admiring family members and friends. Susie, who hadn't been told she was pretty for many years, didn't know what to say the first time a man complimented her slender figure and told her how attractive she was. She says she embarrassed herself by blushing and saying something inane.

It's important to learn how to accept compliments graciously because well-earned praise reinforces motivation and self-esteem. Instead of downplaying a compliment by saying things like, "Oh, this dress isn't all that pretty," or "I haven't really lost much weight," smile and acknowledge your success. Thank the person complimenting you and say you're pleased with the progress you've made, or say that you're fond of what you're wearing, too. This type of response will build your self-confidence, and it will make the person who complimented you feel appreciated too.

Analyze how you handle compliments. Do you act surprised and unworthy of the attention, or do you thank the person for his or her thoughtfulness? As you go through your day, try to remember that positive attention is something to be enjoyed. It's important to learn to accept attention and compliments in a way that will make both the giver and recipient feel good.

Tip for the Day

Practice saying thank you with a smile, and restrain yourself from adding unnecessary comments that detract from the compliment.

"As with most fine things, chocolate has its season. There is a simple memory aid that you can use to determine whether it is the correct time to order chocolate dishes: Any month whose name contains the letter a, e or u is the proper time for chocolate."

SANDRA BOYNTON

For people who love chocolate, there is never a time when it's not appropriate—or enjoyable—to eat it. Fortunately, with the right planning it's easy to have the foods you love, like chocolate, while still losing weight. And with Valentine's Day fast approaching, it's a good idea for everyone to come up with "safe" ways to enjoy this wonderful sweet when you're celebrating the sweethearts in your life.

If only the real thing will do, try eating individual M & M's or shavings from top-quality chocolate bars on yogurt or in a hot drink. Reduced-calorie chocolate pudding or frozen treats can also satisfy a chocolate urge without undoing your good efforts. In addition, unsweetened cocoa powder can also be added to a variety of foods, from plain yogurt to cottage cheese to milk. And some of the new chocolate toppings are both sugar free and fat free.

Just because you're losing weight doesn't mean you can't indulge your sweet tooth with a little chocolate from time to time. When you do it, however, plan your meals carefully to accommodate the treat and focus completely on your food while you eat it so that you can savor every bite. If you do this, you'll find that chocolate, indeed, is always in season.

  Tip for the Day
Experiment with chocolate flavorings so that you can make even your morning cup of coffee a chocoholic's dream.

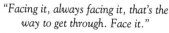
> *"Facing it, always facing it, that's the*
> *way to get through. Face it."*
>
> JOSEPH CONRAD

To lose weight you must reach a point where you face the fact that you are destroying the quality of your life with unhealthy eating and exercise habits. This is the most important step anyone takes in dealing with weight management problems—facing them and not backing away from the challenge of changing what makes you uncomfortable. For that reason, simply joining a weight-loss program is a major and helpful action toward reaching your goal.

If you have successfully faced the fact that you need to do something about your weight, why not use that same courage to change something else in your life that is frightening you? For example, if you suspect your child's caregiver isn't doing a good job, confront the situation directly instead of hoping you're wrong. If you're in a relationship that isn't perfect, have an honest talk with your significant other and don't sugarcoat your concerns. Or if your car is making strange sounds and you're afraid it's going to break down, make an appointment to see a mechanic today.

The key to success in life isn't *intending* to do something— it's actually *doing* something. So make a point of facing something you've been avoiding out of fear or embarrassment. Summon up the same courage you used in joining a weight-loss program to do it. You might be surprised to discover that if you confront thorny issues, conquering them isn't as difficult as you might have thought.

Tip for the Day
Face something today that you've been avoiding.

"A good marriage is one which allows for change and growth in the individuals and in the way they express their love."

PEARL BUCK

When Julia got married, she remembered her mother's admonition that the best way to a man's heart is through his stomach. So she set out to please her husband with her prowess in the kitchen. Consequently, both of them steadily gained weight during the first few years of marriage and Julia's slender body on her wedding day became a distant memory.

Julia fell into the all-too-common newlywed trap of equating marital happiness with gourmet meals. Researchers say that the average woman gains 5 to 28 pounds after marriage, partly due to heartier eating habits and partly to neglect of regular exercise in order to spend more time with her spouse. Experts say that effective ways to counteract these bad habits include making more low-fat dishes, not trying to match your husband bite for bite and finding time to exercise together, perhaps playing tennis or taking a nightly walk. And when the demands of pregnancy and motherhood create more eating traps, it's essential to make your nutritional needs a top priority. Do not allow other burdens to be an excuse for improper eating.

There are many ways to express love in a marriage. Cooking and overeating don't have to be among them. Try to find windows of time when you can pursue nonfood-related activities with your family. Share the Sunday crossword puzzle, play a favorite board game or take a walk in the country. Change and growth in a marriage usually feel uncomfortable at first, but if the changes you enact result in greater vitality and well-being, your love will grow too.

Tip for the Day

List some of your favorite activities with your spouse or significant other. Do they involve food, or do you have a shared appreciation for other pastimes?

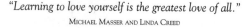

"Learning to love yourself is the greatest love of all."
MICHAEL MASSER AND LINDA CREED

You may often put unrealistic conditions on what makes you successful, or when you will finally feel comfortable with yourself. If you are overweight, you might think that you can't love yourself until you reach an acceptable weight. Or if you're working on a project at work, you may think that you're capable only if the project gets rave reviews. Similarly, if you are a parent, you might consider yourself successful only if your children turn out exactly as you want them to be.

Learning to love and accept yourself needs to start today, not at some future time when external conditions are met. If you don't love yourself right now, being slender or getting elected to a prestigious post or making a lot of money won't bring you the happiness you think it might. Until you accept yourself today, you'll keep setting higher and higher goals for yourself that will guarantee that you'll never be happy with who you are.

If you are still withholding self-acceptance because you aren't at some arbitrary point in your life, such as a certain weight, remember that loving yourself just as you are is the most positive thing you can do for yourself. Think of something that you love about yourself—your attentiveness to a grandparent, your ability to complete projects or your sense of humor—and use it to counter negative feelings that crop up. The more you can do this, the greater the gift you can give to yourself.

≈ Tip for the Day ≈
Focus on a trait of yours that you treasure. Remind yourself that this and other things about you make you special, not necessarily your weight or outward appearance.

*"Curious things, habits. People themselves
never knew they had them."*

AGATHA CHRISTIE

None of us is overweight because we *choose* to be that way. Quite often weight is gained gradually because of a sedentary job, childbearing, a change in our metabolism or some other factor. Whatever your reason, you may also have acquired habits that aren't serving you well. Losing weight will mean acknowledging and changing those behaviors.

Sheryl says that she started to gain weight in college because of bad eating habits, constant pressure and hectic deadlines. Brooke was slim until her late twenties, when her habit of late-night snacking caught up to her. After joining a weight-loss program, both women recognized how they had unconsciously adopted unhealthy habits and they learned how to substitute new ones, such as snacking on healthier foods.

Scrutinize your habits today for behavior that is preventing you from being successful. Do you measure your food carefully, then snack on the excess without realizing it? Do you absentmindedly lick the spoon after making something for your children? Do you always take advantage of free samples at the supermarket? If behaviors like these are conspiring to derail your food plan, do something to change your actions.

⇔ *Tip for the Day* ⇔
*Think of a habit you'd like to change or eliminate, and then
list several ways you will actually go about it.*

"Green is the fresh emblem of well-founded hopes. In blue the spirit can wander, but in green it can rest."

MARY WEBB

You may have a favorite color that makes you feel pretty or energized when you wear it, a color that conveys a message about who you are and how you want to be perceived. Wearing red may help you to appear authoritative or in control, while muted colors like pink or yellow send signals of softness and more approachability.

Just as colorful clothing affects your moods or other people's perceptions of you, the color of your surroundings can influence your feelings about food. Eating in a room that is predominantly red has been shown to increase appetite, which is why so many fast-food restaurants have red color themes. On the other hand, light green has a calming effect and makes you feel more contented, which is why so many hospitals have green walls in recovery and patient rooms.

Use the power of colors to help you feel successful today. Dress yourself in hues that convey optimism and self-confidence. Be aware of how other people's outfits and your surroundings subtly influence you, too. Take notice if some colors stimulate your appetite, so you can avoid those kinds of triggers on days when your motivation needs a boost. Knowing how to use color to maximize your chances of achieving your goals is but one more way you can create a healthy lifestyle.

∽ *Tip for the Day* ∽
Put on an outfit today that conveys confidence, optimism and success.

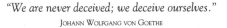

"We are never deceived; we deceive ourselves."
JOHANN WOLFGANG VON GOETHE

When you join Weight Watchers, you are taught which foods will work best to help you achieve a healthy, fit body. It's also very important, especially in the beginning, to weigh and measure food so that you don't inadvertently serve yourself portions that are too generous or too meager. Measuring is essential because you learn to "eyeball" the right serving size if you are dining out or don't have access to measuring tools.

Annette initially tried to follow the program without using measuring cups, measuring spoons or a scale because she thought she knew how big four ounces of meat was and what one cup of vegetables looked like. When her weight didn't budge, her leader suggested that she examine her portion sizes more carefully. Annette discovered that she had been allowing herself twice as much food as she'd thought. Once she followed proper portion sizes, she began to lose weight.

Be sure that you practice honest eating today and measure your portions. If you have to dine out often, practice at home by measuring amounts of food similar to the meal you anticipate eating. Later, at the restaurant, you can remember the appropriate serving size. Your achievements in losing weight depend on how vigilant and determined you are, so give yourself every opportunity to adhere to the program and you'll be certain to achieve the weight-loss goals you set for yourself.

❧   *Tip for the Day*   ❧
Weigh and measure your food carefully today. Take special note of serving sizes so you can accurately calculate portions when you are dining out.

"We distinguish the excellent man from the common man by saying that the former is the one who makes great demands upon himself, and the latter who makes no demands on himself."

José Ortega y Gasset

Losing weight and developing a healthy lifestyle are not necessarily things that come easily to anyone. Usually you will have to change long-standing eating habits, restaurant preferences, relationships with people who may not be supportive of your goals and behaviors that don't serve you well. To do these things, you must frequently make great demands upon yourself and endure some initial discomfort. The results, however, should more than make up for the pain.

Here are some ideas for demands you can make of yourself to help you break long-standing bad habits:

- Before you are seated at a restaurant, ask that any unhealthy or fattening foods be removed from the table.
- Don't accept the key for the hotel minibar when traveling. If you don't have the opportunity, you won't indulge in something you shouldn't have.
- Go to the movies armed with cut-up vegetables or fruit to avoid visiting the snack bar. Air-popped popcorn and rice cakes also make tasty treats. (Check theater rules.)
- At the airport, avoid newsstands that sell fattening treats in small packages. Instead, buy a small serving of nonfat frozen yogurt.

~ *Tip for the Day* ~
Make at least one demand of yourself today that will help you create healthier habits.

"Nothing ever goes away."

BARRY COMMONER

It's tempting to think that reaching your weight goal means that you never have to worry about food or being heavy again. But countless people who have successfully stayed at their weight goal say otherwise. If you aren't prepared for the freedom of eating larger portions and if you suddenly stop weighing and measuring your food, you may be startled to wake up one day many pounds heavier than you thought you were.

Dana has gone from a size 22 to a size 10 and lost 65 pounds in the process. But, she says, achieving that goal was easier than maintaining the weight loss. She says that attending regular support groups helps her stay committed to a healthy lifestyle. Another woman who has successfully achieved a large weight loss manages her weight through daily efforts. She says she takes one day at a time and reminds herself often that she's always vulnerable unless she's vigilant about her eating habits.

Be aware today that achieving your weight goal is just another important step you take in creating a healthy lifestyle. You need to eat several meals each day for the rest of your life, so temptation may always be with you. But if you stick with the habits that helped you lose weight, you'll keep your newly slender figure.

Tip for the Day

Remember that you must always be vigilant about food, even when you have achieved your weight goal. Maintenance requires as much care and attention as weight loss did.

"Why do strong arms fatigue themselves with frivolous dumbbells?
To dig a vineyard is worthier exercise for men."

MARCUS VALERIUS MARTIALIS

There was a time when people labored for survival, exercising their bodies naturally because machines didn't exist to make the effort for them. These days machines do much of our work. Our transportation is rarely on foot, labor-saving devices make everything easier and people must make a point of finding ways to break a sweat. It's no wonder that each generation of children is less active and more obese.

Because of our society's evolution to more sedentary ways, we must find ways to bring as much vigor into our daily activities as possible. Try shoveling snow instead of using a snow blower. Do some strenuous cleaning around the house instead of hiring others to do it. Take your children for long walks instead of drives. Use stairs instead of elevators whenever possible. Using arm weights while doing routine activities is another way to provide fitness benefits.

Remind yourself today that our current way of life doesn't lend itself to fitness and think of at least one way to burn off more calories and tone your body. Finding ways to talk on the phone while standing or stretching, or walking to pick up your children at school instead of driving can get your body more accustomed to the level of activity we were created to perform.

       Tip for the Day
Add a new activity to your day that will help tone your body, such as stirring a recipe by hand instead of with a mixer.

> *"There was a definite process by which one made*
> *people into friends, and it involved talking to them and*
> *listening to them for hours at a time."*
>
> REBECCA WEST

One of the best ways to keep yourself motivated to attend Weight Watchers meetings, especially when you've reached a plateau with weight loss, is to develop friendships with the people you meet there. Instead of just seeing the meetings as a time for a weigh-in and a lecture, meetings can become a wonderful place to share stories with people who are struggling with the same issues.

Carrie says that some of her best friends are other single women like herself whom she has met at her Weight Watchers meetings. They often have similar concerns and interests outside of losing weight, she says, and she has fostered these friendships through walks and meeting them for coffee. Because these bonds enriched her emotional life, they made going to meetings more enjoyable.

At your next meeting, strike up a conversation. Ask others how they are or what their week was like. The more you can connect with other people and find similar interests, the more likely you'll be successful at weight loss.

Tip for the Day
Call a person you've met in the program and
offer to meet them for a walk.

"Sorrow was like the wind. It came in gusts."

MARJORIE KINNAN RAWLINGS

All of us have had waves of sadness overcome us at times. But how we react varies greatly from person to person. Some will weather these down periods with relative ease. For others, however, sadness can bring great cravings to eat because they use food to anesthetize upsetting feelings. If this describes a familiar pattern, it's wise to develop strategies to prevent it from undoing your efforts to lose weight in the future.

Ellie's first bout with the blues came after the birth of her son. She remembers periods of uncontrolled crying over minor matters, as well as haphazard eating patterns because of the baby's unpredictable sleeping schedule. Nancy's overeating skyrocketed after the death of her husband, as friends and neighbors consoled her with gifts of food, which seemed to take the edge off her sadness. But when you use food as a buffer for your feelings and in so doing create a weight problem for yourself, you are only ensuring that you'll remain down.

Develop strategies for dealing with the cravings that often accompany the blues. Perhaps you have a pastor or counselor you can call. Try using a journal as a better outlet for your feelings. Be aware of the stresses that may arrive in "gusts" and have a plan ready to implement so that sorrow never has to interfere with achieving your weight goals.

❧ Tip for the Day ❧
List three ways you can use immediately to address a period of feeling down, such as ridding the house of tempting foods or making an appointment to seek counseling.

"Poets are regular people who live down the block and do simple things like wash clothes and stir soup."

NAOMI SHIHAB NYE

To break the habit of emotional eating, it's important to come up with alternative activities that help enrich your soul and express your feelings. One way that has been helpful to many is penning their thoughts in a journal, particularly in the form of poetry. Because there are no rules about what poetry is, there is no right or wrong way to express yourself. Poetry doesn't need perfect sentence structure, capitalization or even punctuation. Poetry is simply an expression of your inner emotions.

If you have not tried poetry as an outlet, pick a subject that is on your mind and write down the thoughts that come into your head. Don't censor yourself; just focus on being honest. And don't write for anyone else's eyes. This is your private world and you are free to create something that brings pleasure to only you. If you are still balking at trying poetry because you don't think you have a poet's demeanor, remind yourself that poets aren't a special breed—they're doing laundry, stirring soup and changing diapers just like you.

⟨⟩ *Tip for the Day* ⟨⟩
*Write a short poem about how you perceive yourself or
things that bring you joy.*

"A hobby a day keeps the doldrums away."
PHYLLIS McGINLEY

Once food is seen in its proper perspective, you'll find that you have a lot more free time. Instead of spending hours cooking, eating and then resting after overeating, you will have new-found time that can be used for hobbies or other purposes, such as learning to play an instrument, taking up a sport or writing poetry. Not only will these kinds of activities keep you away from food, they're a wonderful way to make new friends.

When Ruth began to lose weight, she decided to learn how to sew the new clothes that would fit her changing figure. After several months of weekly lessons, Ruth began to branch out into creating window treatments and handbags. Now Ruth has a hobby she loves that reinforces her success at weight loss and gives her a focus away from food. She also has a skill she's proud of and that constantly presents her with new challenges.

If overeating has been your main hobby in the past, make a point of spending a few minutes doing something that brings you pleasure but isn't work-related. Whether it's crossword puzzles, flower arranging or going to a flea market, finding the time to indulge your interests and relax on a regular basis is an important part of learning how to live a balanced and happy life.

Tip for the Day
Make a list of three hobbies you'd like to pursue. Plan ways to incorporate at least one of them into your life this week.

"A human being must have occupation if he or she is not to become a nuisance to the world."

DOROTHY L. SAYERS

One of the most depressing and stressful experiences a person can have is losing a job. When you are unemployed, time weighs heavily and food looks more tempting than usual. In fact, turning to food for comfort is common, according to one vocational consultant, who says that 50 percent of her clients gain weight after losing their jobs.

One of the main reasons people overeat when unemployed is because, in an uncertain world, food is the one thing they can control. But as the pounds pile on, the comfort of food turns into guilt and depression, which only adds to the stress of being out of work. To combat this tendency, experts advise finding another area of life to have control over. Try starting a needlework project or building a bookcase. Avoid making food a reward for completing a task. Maintaining a routine, such as adhering to a regular exercise schedule, can also give the day structure.

If you're unemployed—or even if you're just bored and have time on your hands—take steps to ensure that gaining weight doesn't add to any challenges you're already coping with. Make nutritious eating a top priority, and exercise at least one hour each day. The more you can feel in control of these important areas of your life, the greater your feelings of self-confidence and optimism will be—qualities that will undoubtedly help you in your job search or in attaining any goals you set for yourself.

❦ *Tip for the Day* ❦

If you are unemployed, make sure your day is filled with routines that help you to feel organized and in control.

> *"Tomatoes and oregano make it Italian; wine and tarragon make it French. Sour cream makes it Russian; lemon and cinnamon make it Greek. Soy sauce makes it Chinese; garlic makes it good."*
>
> ALICE MAY BROCK

Some people think that losing weight or restricting their food intake means eating dull meals that lack pizzazz. They might also assume that they cannot visit ethnic restaurants with foreign cuisines because they won't be able to enjoy themselves *and* lose weight. But if you are knowledgeable about foreign cuisine and you are prepared ahead of time to order dishes that are light and healthy, almost any type of restaurant can support you in achieving your weight-loss goals.

During the Chinese New Year in February, it's customary to celebrate with a meal featuring a whole fish because it signifies abundance and prosperity. This type of dish can successfully be incorporated into a weight-loss plan when the fish is poached and paired with stir-fried vegetables flavored with ginger. For an Italian meal, whole-wheat pasta and a garlic-tomato sauce will keep you on a healthy track and help you to feel like you are eating with international style. Many other cuisines feature grains and legumes, which are wonderful low-fat sources of protein.

Be creative with your meals today and remember that you can create a varied meal plan and still lose weight. With a good cookbook and the right spices, you can travel around the world in your own kitchen.

❧ *Tip for the Day* ❧
Pick an ethnic cuisine you enjoy and plan a meal that features dishes from that country.

"The body is shaped, disciplined, honored, and in time, trusted."
MARTHA GRAHAM

A sensible weight-loss program consists of several basic components, one of which is developing a sound and regular exercise program. As part of this plan, it's wise to consider including resistance training. Resistance training is an anaerobic exercise that stresses muscle groups for a short period of time. It is a way of using weights to increase lean body mass, burn calories and build muscle density. Resistance training has many important benefits, not just helping to restore the muscle tone of your youth. For example, muscle burns calories more quickly and efficiently than fat. And fit muscles are trim and firm. If you tone your muscles while you lose weight, you'll be able to wear smaller sizes sooner.

Some women fear that using weights will make them look bulky and unattractive. These fears are unfounded because average workouts don't produce body-builder results. It also isn't necessary to train too frequently. Professionals say that we can achieve benefits in as few as three sessions a week that work different parts of the body. One pleasant side effect for women is that not only will strength training improve self-esteem, it helps retard the onset of osteoporosis.

If you haven't yet incorporated resistance training into your exercise routine, look into ways to do so today. Contact a local gym and ask about classes or talk to a professional trainer. Many books and videos are available on this subject too. The more ways you can shape and discipline your body, the more you'll surely find that you can trust it to serve you well.

≈ *Tip for the Day* ≈
Investigate ways you can use free weights, rubber bands or weight training machines to enhance your fitness program.

"It's choice—not chance—that determines your destiny."
JEAN NIDETCH

Sometimes we feel like life has dealt us a bad deck of cards. We're stuck in a job we dislike and go home to a relationship that has soured. We look in the mirror and we're unhappy with what we see. We're overweight, we look exhausted, we're stressed to the max.

But we do have choices. They may not be easy ones and they may not completely solve our problems, but we can choose to make our lives a little better. We can talk to our boss or update our resumé and start to read the want ads. We can seek counseling to help us deal better with our best friend or lover. And we can start to take better care of our bodies.

If we're overweight, we can face the music and decide it's time to eat better. No matter how difficult our lives seem at the moment, we can still choose to eat foods that will give us energy and strength, foods that will nourish us without piling on the pounds. We can decide to take charge of our future right now by joining a weight-loss support group like Weight Watchers. At Weight Watchers we can choose the balanced food plan that is best suited to our lifestyle. We can enjoy the support and encouragement of people who can help us make lasting changing in our eating habits. And best of all, we will soon see a new person in the mirror, one who looks healthier, happier and, yes, thinner.

∞ *Tip for the Day* ∞
*Remember that choices can be as simple as remembering to take
your vitamins. Even small choices add up to big benefits.*

"Even God cannot change the past."

AGATHON

There is nothing that can waste time and drag down your spirits more quickly than regretting past actions and wishing you could go back and relive a certain period in your life. One woman whose fiancé broke off their engagement spent more than two years in isolation and sadness, regretting the years she'd given to their relationship, the opportunities she'd missed, obsessing about what she could have done differently to make the ending a happier one. It wasn't until her friends and family convinced her that she had to get on with her life that she became more outgoing again. Soon afterward, she met a man who later became her husband.

You may be guilty of this same type of obsessiveness around food. Perhaps you're sad that your weight and obsession with food caused you to close off certain friendships, avoid taking risks and hate yourself. Don't give the past more energy than the future. Make a fresh start today. Instead of dwelling on past overeating, failed diets or unhappy socializing, focus only on what today can bring. All of your regrets can never change the past, so choose what you want your future to be like and then make your best effort toward making that happen. If you can give up the past and train your eyes toward the future, you'll be able to make lasting change in the present.

Tip for the Day

Don't allow yourself to look back and wish you'd behaved or looked differently at a certain point. Focusing on the past only steals energy that can be better used to create a happy future.

"Look to your health; and if you have it, praise God and value it
next to conscience; for health is the second blessing that we
mortals are capable of, a blessing money can't buy."

IZAAK WALTON

Lydia remembers that before she decided to lose weight in a
sensible way, she tried to wish away her excess weight, some-
how hoping that she'd magically wake up thin one morning.
This type of wishful thinking isn't unusual. It's an attitude that
you may have carried over into other areas of your health, mistakenly thinking that if you ignored pain or other internal
warnings, they'd go away.

If you are committed to losing weight and developing an
active lifestyle, you owe it to yourself to make sure the rest of
your body is in top shape too. This means seeking professional
advice when you aren't feeling right, understanding how to
prevent diseases like osteoporosis, knowing what procedures
should be performed as preventive measures and following
through with any advice you are given.

There is nothing worse than being unhealthy and knowing
that there is something you could have done to prevent the
problem or address it more quickly. For this reason, make sure
you keep up on every area of your physical well-being today.
Read as much as you can so that you are educated about issues
that pertain to your health. You'll find that when you are careful and thoughtful about all areas of your fitness—not just your
weight—you'll have good health, the blessing that "money
can't buy."

❧ *Tip for the Day* ❧
Buy a health magazine and read an article you might not normally read,
or check a book out of the library that provides information about the
special needs of your age group.

"Part of the secret of success in life is to eat what you like and let the food fight it out inside."

MARK TWAIN

Gail went through dozens of diets where she has endured un-balanced meal plans that left her skin flaking, her nails soft and her body starving for the right nutrients. She confesses to trying grapefruit and egg-white regimens, ketchup and cottage-cheese meals and low-calorie milkshakes, all to no avail. Her history of dieting failures left her believing that the only way to lose weight was to hate what you put into your body.

When Gail joined a program based on nutritious and bal-anced eating, to her surprise she found that she was able to include all of her favorite foods, within moderation, and still reach her weight goal. She was also surprised to discover that sensible eating didn't mean eating only rabbit food. Lisa, a professional chef who lost 60-plus pounds, echoes Gail's feelings. She says that the flexibility of the plan allowed her to use her creative skills, which helped her to achieve her goal.

Make sure when planning your weekly meals that you in-clude foods that you enjoy, not just foods you think you *should* have. If you can follow Mark Twain's advice and eat what you like—but within moderation—the food may "fight it out," but you'll always be the one who wins.

⤳   *Tip for the Day*   ⤶
Find a way to adapt several of your favorite recipes to your healthy weight-loss program.

"If you think you can, you can. And if you think you can't, you're right."

MARY KAY ASH

One of the most important ingredients in any weight-loss program is its ability to instill in its members confidence that they *can* reach the goals they set for themselves. In Weight Watchers this is done through the weekly meetings, where leaders, who have already achieved and maintained their weight goals, share ideas and solutions with members, motivating them to be successful too.

One popular leader in Texas makes sure that she emphasizes that she isn't special. If she can change her life, the other members can, too. She says that she always reminds people attending her meetings that she is also a member. For people who are new to the program, it's especially inspirational to meet others who have already won the battle they are just starting to fight. One member remembers feeling unusually hopeful at her first meeting because her leader set the example that hard work and persistence could lead to lasting success.

Look in the mirror this morning and say out loud that you *will* reach your weight goal and make healthy changes in your lifestyle. If you feel negative self-talk starting, silence it with positive affirmations. Concentrate on the success you see at meetings and visualize yourself being successful. You'll discover that when you believe in yourself, there's no goal that will be out of your reach.

 Tip for the Day

Ask yourself if you truly believe that you can reach the goals you set. If you feel yourself wavering, write down positive affirmations and say them to yourself in front of the mirror.

"That best portion of a good man's life,/ His little, nameless, unremembered acts of kindness and of love."

WILLIAM WORDSWORTH

When you're caught up in losing weight and changing your life, it's very easy to lose sight of the fact that other people have important needs and desires. In fact, you may be so delighted about your weight-loss success that your days begin to revolve around planning nutritious meals, going to support group meetings, buying new clothes or exercising. And in your excitement about your weight loss and your new goals, you may unconsciously be directing all your conversations to be about you only.

If you have unknowingly slipped into this self-absorbed mode, do a random act of kindness for no other reason than you'd like to help someone else have a good day. Forget about yourself for a few minutes. Pay an expired parking meter as you walk by, or leave an overly generous tip for a good waiter. Take a warm meal to a homeless person, and brighten a sad person's day with a genuine compliment. Random acts of kindness may feel awkward or strange at first. But like any habit that is practiced diligently, remembering to think of others can become an enjoyable and uplifting pastime that helps to keep your weight-loss efforts in perspective and increase feelings of self-esteem.

～ *Tip for the Day* ～
Do something anonymous and kind today for someone who could use a lift.

"The best things carried to excess are wrong."
CHARLES CHURCHILL

Whenever Linda wants to lose weight she eats nothing but salads and diet sodas, and plenty of them. It's not unusual for her to visit a salad bar at a restaurant two or three times, filling up her plate with heaping mounds of fresh vegetables, which she'll wash down with soda and other noncaloric drinks like coffee. Because her daily calorie total remains fairly reasonable on this type of plan, Linda sees no problem with this pattern when she wants to lose a few pounds quickly.

Unfortunately, it is possible to have too much of a good thing, even vegetables. Although the calorie count may be low, allowing yourself unlimited amounts of certain foods because they're low in fat promotes the idea of overindulgence. You need to learn portion control. If you don't, you're setting yourself up for failure and weight gain once you revert to your regular meals. Filling your stomach with bulk and liquids prevents you from learning how to distinguish true hunger and satiety from emotional cues to eat.

Remember to use self-restraint when you're tempted to go overboard on artificial sweeteners, diet sodas, gum and vegetables because you think they'll make it easier to lose weight. Change your behavior so that you learn to be satisfied with moderate amounts of food. This is a valuable lesson that will enable you to have a lifetime of fitness and well-being.

∽ Tip for the Day ∽
Be alert to any signs of overindulgence today, especially on behaviors or edible items that have no apparent effect on your weight.

"Every adult ought to be taking at least 3 grams of vitamin C a day. That will cut down the incidence of essentially all diseases."
LINUS PAULING, M.D.

For over half a century, Linus Pauling was at the forefront of the movement to investigate the human body's reaction to chemicals and vitamins. When he first claimed that massive doses of vitamin C helped people reduce their likelihood of illness, scientists scoffed. But in recent years study after study has confirmed that taking vitamin C is a boon to human health.

Pauling says our ancient ancestors may have had the ability to make vitamin C, which he feels is a crucial element in fighting illness and being healthy. As the society shifted to an agricultural one, humans lost this ability but still ate large amounts of vitamin C. Now, with processed foods so prevalent, getting even one-tenth of the vitamin C your ancestors ate is difficult. Pauling suggests that taking supplements and eating foods high in vitamin C, such as citrus fruits and leafy vegetables, can reduce the incidence of modern diseases like cancer, which have risen with the onset of the highly processed Western diet.

In your meal planning today remember to include foods that are rich in vitamin C and other nutrients. It would also be helpful to read about the properties of various foods in order to understand the value of what you are ingesting. The more you can make your meals healthful and rich in valuable supplements, the better you're likely to feel.

⇔ Tip for the Day ⇔
Learn about the nutritional properties in the foods you eat.
Make sure to get at least the recommended dietary allowance (RDA)
of every vitamin and nutrient.

*"[Dreams are] a secret code, different for each person, which
you learn to decipher."*

ANONYMOUS

One place you can get valuable information about your health
is in your dreams. Sigmund Freud was one of the first to write
about how dreams can symbolically reveal illnesses of which
you are not yet aware. A psychologist with expertise in dream
analysis says that the body is often represented as a car, and
parts of the car that aren't running smoothly correlate with
your own body. One man who was living a workaholic life and
taking no time to eat or exercise had repeated dreams about
burying a vintage car from the year of his birth with all of its
cylinders in gear. He finally realized that he was on his way to
an early grave unless he cut back on his work and made more
time for his health.

Pay attention to your dreams and note any symbols that
may have to do with your health. Taking care of yourself means
heeding the input from your body and mind during the day.
But to be really successful it's a good idea to be aware of the
signals your subconscious sends, too.

⮞ *Tip for the Day* ⮜
*Keep a dream journal this week and jot down impressions
upon awakening. Do any of the images appear to be
messages about your lifestyle?*

*"Nobody should smoke cigarettes—and smoking with an ulcer is
like pouring gasoline on a burning house."*

SARA MURRAY JORDAN

Once you begin to eat nutritiously and exercise regularly, lingering bad habits can become more obvious. One of the most detrimental to health—and most difficult to break—is smoking. Some experts say that smoking may be the hardest of all addictions to end because of nicotine's stranglehold over the body. And if you began smoking at an early age, you may have decades of this bad habit to contend with.

Smoking is a killer. Tobacco is the leading cause of diseases like lung cancer and chronic obstructive pulmonary disease (COPD), and it is linked to a higher incidence of strokes and heart disease. New research shows that smoking makes recovering from muscle tears more difficult because smoke is thought to lessen blood supply to muscles and tendons. But facts like these aren't always effective in getting smokers to quit. Sometimes you have to understand the role that smoking has played in your life in order to move beyond it. One recovered smoker said he'd had to face the fact that smoking was his best friend, and that he'd need to make real friends to replace its presence in his life.

If you are addicted to nicotine, try to understand what nicotine means to you. Remind yourself often that smoking will eventually negate any progress you attempt to make in eating or exercising. Until you stop smoking, you'll continue the destruction of your "house."

⇆ Tip for the Day ⇆

*If you are a smoker, investigate smoke cessation classes. Call the
American Cancer Society, American Lung Association or other related
group for hints on how to help you break this deadly addiction.*

"Bread is the staff of life."
ENGLISH SAYING

It was once thought that bread was off limits to the person who wished to lose weight. As more nutritional information was disseminated and people began to understand the importance of a balanced diet, however, bread came back into favor. In fact, for the person who wishes to lose weight and feel satisfied, several servings of this filling, low-fat food every day are essential.

Consider learning how to make your own bread. Baking bread requires some patience, but many bakers say that the rhythm of kneading and rolling is therapeutic. And nearly everyone enjoys the wonderful aroma of fresh bread baking. Making your own bread also gives you the freedom to add ingredients that make the loaf more nutritious, such as wheat bran, wheat germ, soy flour or whole-wheat flour. Even those who don't like to cook can do this. Bread machines turn out hot, fragrant loaves in a few hours with minimal effort.

If you want to jazz up your bread allotments, make your own or buy an unusual variety you've never tried, such as flat bread or sourdough. Bread is truly "the staff of life" and is an important component of a well-rounded diet. Make sure you get enough and enjoy every bite.

Tip for the Day

Find a bakery where you can buy fresh, healthful whole-grain breads and try a new kind. Have the loaf sliced into 1-ounce slices to discourage you from eating overly large portions.

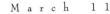

"Look in the mirror. The face that pins you with its double gaze reveals a chastening secret."

DIANE ACKERMAN

It's often said that the eyes are the windows of the soul because the expression in your eyes can easily convey happiness, dismay, excitement or enchantment. If you have spent years carrying around the burden of being overweight, it's likely that other people see low self-esteem or depression in your eyes. You may have even felt so ashamed of your appearance sometimes that you failed to meet another's gaze.

As you lose weight, you'll undoubtedly be happier and more self-confident. Your gaze will be more direct and honest. Sandra agrees, saying that weight loss gave her the confidence to look people in the eye because she finally liked who she'd become. Because your eyes play such an important role in expressing your emotions, spend some extra time grooming your brows and eye area to ensure that you make the best impression possible. For women this includes using tweezers for brow shaping and using flattering neutral shades of eye shadow to accentuate and define the lids. Eyeliner and mascara can also add drama, as can tinted contact lenses if you're feeling bold or experimental.

Be conscious of how your eyes are communicating your feelings when you are talking to others today. Part of becoming empowered means developing all of your assets to the best of your abilities. Start on your eyes and make them windows on your positive, new world.

Tip for the Day

Take care to emphasize the beauty and expressiveness of your eyes today.

"She wanted something to happen—something, anything: she did not know what."

KATE CHOPIN

Boredom is the enemy of the person trying to lose weight. When time looms large, it's easy to find yourself in front of the refrigerator looking for something to snack on. Boredom also saps energy, making it especially difficult to summon the energy to exercise, attend a meeting or get together with a friend.

There are many effective ways to beat boredom, however. Go to the library and check out books on a subject that really interests you, perhaps traveling or woodworking. Become involved in a volunteer activity that will give you new friends as well as a positive glow of satisfaction. Explore a museum or historical site in your area, take a ceramics class or schedule a makeover at a local beauty school.

If you are feeling bored, it's not because there aren't a lot of options available to you. It's because inertia or your fears of failure has put you in a rut. To break out of this pattern, think of several things you'd like to try and then enlist a friend to do one of them with you. For example, sign up for a museum lecture series, organize a day-long trip to an outlet mall or take your pet to a local nursing home where it can brighten a shut-in's day. "Something" can always happen to you, but you are the one who is responsible for bringing it about.

≈ *Tip for the Day* ≈

Make a list of three activities that you can do that will engage your mind and body. Promise yourself to do one thing on your list the next time you catch yourself thinking or saying that you are bored.

"At my age the bones are water in the morning until food is given them."

PEARL BUCK

Osteoporosis is a bone disease that afflicts primarily women in the latter part of their lives, although men too may suffer from it. It causes bones to become soft and prone to fracture and crushing. The "dowager's hump," a curvature of the upper spine, is caused by this disease. Osteoporosis doesn't appear overnight, however, and whether or not it will occur is sometimes a result of how active we have been in our early years and how healthfully we have eaten. Although some osteoporosis effects are genetically linked, there are many lifestyle choices we can make to prevent osteoporosis and its damage.

Bone loss typically begins in a woman's mid-thirties, but it can be hastened by a poor diet and sedentary lifestyle. Too much caffeine, which is found in coffee, tea, chocolate and soft drinks, raises the rate of calcium excretion. Alcohol suppresses the growth of new bone and decreases the absorption of valuable nutrients. A good diet means eating the correct combinations of food so you get enough calcium through milk, vegetables and grains.

A sedentary lifestyle contributes to osteoporosis as well. Add weight-bearing activities like walking, biking or tennis to your day to maintain strong, healthy bones. Any activity that gets you off the sofa and onto your feet will help create a body that feels strong and vital well into your mature years. And the sooner you get started, the better.

꙳ *Tip for the Day* ꙳
Think of your meals as opportunities to prevent lifestyle–related diseases such as osteoporosis.

"Let me tell you the secret that has led me to my goal. My strength lies solely in my tenacity."

Louis Pasteur

William has the best of intentions when it comes to exercising, but his downfall is his lack of consistency. Every summer he joins a Masters Swim Team and declares that he'll be a disciplined swimmer throughout the winter to maintain his fitness and toned body. Then the fall arrives and he doesn't follow through, so his good work of the summer is not reinforced.

Consistency is one of the keys when it comes to losing weight and living healthfully. If you follow a sensible meal plan during weekdays but overeat on weekends, you're not likely to get to the weight you want. If your weekly exercise routine goes in fits and starts, you may begin to think of yourself as a person who can't stick with a healthy program, a thought that can become a self-fulfilling prophecy.

Remember today that success means having the tenacity to reach toward your goals on a daily basis. If eating sensibly is a seasonal occasion, or exercise is something you do only when you have someone to walk with or when the weather is nice, you thwart your desires to have a healthy lifestyle and a body of which you can be proud.

❧ *Tip for the Day* ❧
If you find yourself stopping and starting various healthful activities, try to change your approach so that paying attention to your health can be an enjoyable part of every day.

"The best thing about a cocktail party is being asked to it."
GERALD NACHMAN

One of the things a health-conscious person dreads most is attending a party and trying to adhere to his or her weight-loss program. Charles is one such person. He says he always overeats at parties and is especially vulnerable if there's a dish he has never tried. Once he starts eating, he complains, it's almost impossible to stop.

Weight Watchers encourages people to plan ahead when they know they'll be attending a party. One tip is to call the host or hostesses and ask which foods will be served. Most party givers will try to accommodate their guests' special needs and prepare something that can be enjoyed freely, like fresh vegetables. If there won't be any foods that can be incorporated into your meal plan, use some Optional Calories or Personal Selections to eat something acceptable. It's also a good idea to call a friend in the program for support and discuss ways you can keep from overeating before you go to the party.

If a party is coming up soon, make some allowances in your meal plan so that the night won't be an eating disaster. And most important, while you're at the party, make a point of focusing on the people around you rather than the food. Although nibbling may have been your preoccupation at parties in years past, you'll discover that engaging in stimulating conversations and meeting new people can bring you far more enjoyment than any food could. Remember, a party is a celebration for people, not food.

❧ *Tip for the Day* ❧
Write down three things you will do before you go to your next party that will help you stay on your weight-loss program.

*"If you have formed the habit of checking on every
new diet that comes along, you will find that, mercifully,
they all blur together, leaving you with one definite piece
of information: French-fried potatoes are out."*

JEAN KERR

Often, people who join Weight Watchers are veterans of countless other diet programs that promised quick weight loss with unrealistic food plans or even "fat burning" pills. It's likely that none of these programs offered group support, sensible food choices or help in making positive lifestyle changes. They only offered false hope.

Weight Watchers has taken great care to design a food plan that is flexible, balanced and healthy. Certain foods like French fries aren't banned; you are encouraged to design meals that are sensible and include foods you love. With the Optional Calories and Personal Selections you can choose to have wine with dinner, cake at a wedding celebration or even pizza at a ball game. By learning nutritional balance and moderation, you can reach your weight goal without ever feeling deprived or bored.

Make sure you are taking full advantage of all the choices Weight Watchers offers you today. If you have fallen into a rut and are eating the same meals each day, talk to your leader or look at Weight Watchers cookbooks to find ways you can enliven your menus. By adding your own personal touches and following a sensible food plan, losing weight can be a pleasure, not an exercise in deprivation.

⇜ *Tip for the Day* ⇝
Incorporate one new food into your menu plan today.

*"In reality, serendipity accounts for 1 percent of
the blessings we receive in life, work, and love. The other
99 percent is due to our efforts."*

PETER McWILLIAMS

Have you ever looked enviously at someone who has a good
job, a loving family and is in good physical health? Perhaps
you wondered why that person was so "lucky." If you think
that luck can never happen to you, think again. Experts say
that a key ingredient in luck is a person's self-efficacy, or their
belief in their capabilities. These lucky people persevere after
setbacks, see challenges instead of threats and never let go of
their dreams.

One woman bought nine dollars' worth of trinkets at a flea
market and later had them appraised for six thousand dollars.
But she's not lucky; she's well informed. She spends much of
her spare time browsing in antique stores or reading and study-
ing about what she collects. Similarly, good health is not a
lucky accident. People whose weight is under control work to
maintain a healthy level. They are conscious of what they eat
and how much. They pass up desserts and other foods that are
high in calories but low in nutrition. The more you take care
of your body and become aware of its needs, the luckier you'll
be when it comes to your health.

Prepare yourself for your own good luck. Just as raises come
to those who work hard, weight loss comes to those who persevere after setbacks and who continue to believe in themselves.
The more you know what you want out of life and you prepare
yourself for that eventuality, the more luck you'll have.

⇆ *Tip for the Day* ⇆
*Instead of envying someone their good fortune today, find out what steps
he or she took to smooth the way for opportunities to occur.*

"For the night was not impartial. No, the night loved some more than others, served some more than others."

EUDORA WELTY

Stacey never had a problem with her weight until she began to work the late shift at a fast-food restaurant. Instead of eating her dinner at six P.M., Stacey started waiting until the end of work, just before she went to bed, to eat a greasy fast-food meal. It wasn't long before she was heavier than she'd ever been and unhappy about how she looked.

Stacey's problem is common among people who work late or have overnight shifts and must rearrange their dining schedules to accommodate their working hours. To cope with these unusual hours, try to stick to sensible meals that will satisfy you during long, quiet nocturnal hours. Plan ahead of time and bring to work healthy snacks that will keep you from visiting a vending machine. It's also important to make sure you get enough rest during the day so you don't use eating as a way of stimulating yourself to stay awake.

Don't let the challenges of late work hours undermine your efforts to eat right. Devise a plan that accommodates your special hours and make sure you allot enough time for group support meetings and exercise. Certainly, the night shift or other unusual working hours can make attending to your physical health more difficult. But if you are determined and knowledgeable, you can maintain a healthy lifestyle regardless of what the clock says.

❧ *Tip for the Day* ❧
If you plan to work late or be out later than usual this evening, schedule a snack or a light meal to help fight nighttime cravings.

*"If you haven't forgiven yourself something, how
can you forgive others?"*

DOLORES HUERTA

As much as you want to be perfect in your food plan,
slips often happen. For some people these can be hour- or week-
long food orgies that undo months of hard work. For others,
deviating from a weight-loss program means eating a few extra
snacks or succumbing to temptation on a stressful day. Either
way you must learn to forgive yourself for your lapses and find
ways to use your experiences to strengthen your resolve in the
future.

Weight Watchers provides a pamphlet with tips for people
who overeat and need to get back on track with their meal
plans. Some of the suggestions include first of all acknowledging to yourself that you've made a mistake and reminding yourself that it's what you do next that counts most. Next, don't
"awfulize" the problem; if it's an isolated incident, you may be
able to use Optional Calories and Personal Selections to cover
the amount. Finally, forgive yourself. What you've done has
happened to many other people. You're not a "bad" person
simply because it happened to you.

Be aware of the triggers that lead you to overeat. Learn to
avoid certain people or situations if they consistently lead you
into trouble. By doing so, you can turn your setback into a
benefit. Above all, remember to love yourself despite your
imperfections. By learning to forgive yourself, you also learn
the gift of tolerance for others.

Tip for the Day
Remind yourself that there is no slip so bad that you can't recover from it.

"Walking is man's best medicine."

HIPPOCRATES

Growing up, Susan never had a weight problem because of her family's emphasis on sound eating and regular exercise. The pounds started to pile onto her five-foot, three-inch frame when she got married. Her husband was a gourmet cook, and they enjoyed rich meals and wine often. Finally, while recovering from a neck injury, Susan ate her way up to 161 pounds because she couldn't move her body much. Disgusted with herself, she joined a weight-loss program and vowed to change her life.

Ultimately, many things *did* change in her life, including a 50-pound weight loss, a divorce and a new job. But the biggest change in Susan's life was what happened when she started walking as exercise. After following a suggestion to try walking as a way to speed weight loss and boost her mood, Susan gradually went from nighttime strolls around her neighborhood to joining a race-walking club. Now Susan is an international contender on the race-walking circuit. She credits her weight-loss program with introducing her to the joys of walking and also giving her the confidence to pursue it competitively.

You don't have to become a champion race-walker to gain the benefits of regular walks. A brisk ten-minute jaunt has the power to raise your metabolism and elevate your mood. If competition appeals to you, though, investigate local organizations that will provide you with a forum to vent your energy and achieve fitness goals. Whatever form your walks take, remember that the only thing that really matters is that you get your body moving and absorb the benefits that regular aerobic movement can provide.

Tip for the Day
Put on some walking shoes and go for a walk today.

"[Spring is] a true reconstructionist."
HENRY TIMROD

For many people, the year truly begins in the spring because the world is fresh and green; everywhere you look there's evidence that life is renewing itself. This is also the traditional time when you undertake a thorough "spring cleaning." You put some order into your surroundings, organizing kitchen cupboards, arranging tools in the basement or garage, cleaning closets and weeding out clothes and other items that you no longer use.

Spring cleaning can perform several valuable functions. If you're steadily losing weight, it's likely that some of your "fat clothes" no longer fit, so giving them to charity would be a good way to dispose of them. Getting rid of clutter helps you in other ways, too. By creating order out of chaos, you develop feelings of self-confidence. By keeping busy, you divert yourself from eating and distracting thoughts about food.

Use some of your newfound energy on spring cleaning today. Tackle a few disorganized closets and make plans to have a garage sale with a friend or give your cast-offs to charity. Use this time to bring order to your kitchen, too. Stock up on healthy food, replenish your spice rack, throw out leftovers in the refrigerator and replace missing staples. By giving your house a thorough spring cleaning, you will renew your surroundings, and you'll be renewing your spirit, too.

≈ *Tip for the Day* ≈
Renew yourself and your surroundings by discarding useless clutter. Pick one closet or cupboard and clean it thoroughly.

*"It is wonderful how quickly you get used to things,
even the most astonishing."*

EDITH NESBITT

When Lyn joined a weight-loss program she couldn't imagine ever being able to turn down triple-decker fudge cakes, fried chicken or buttery croissants. Over the next ten months of eating low-fat foods she lost more than 45 pounds. At the same time she also lost her cravings for her former treats, a change that took her completely by surprise. She says she's amazed by her newfound urges, and cringes at the thought of putting the old high-fat foods in her body.

Lyn's experience is hardly unusual, nor is it just wishful thinking. Experts say that a combination of physical and psychological factors help explain how fat lovers *can* retrain their tastebuds. If you are determined to forgo high-fat foods because they're not healthful, it's possible that you can talk yourself out of overindulging. And it's been shown that people who eliminate excess fat from their diets without substituting diet versions of foods like nonfat cream cheese or reduced-fat mayonnaise actually lose their taste for fat, possibly because it sits in their stomachs longer and impedes digestion.

If you are plagued with cravings for high-fat foods, experiment with herbs, spices and other condiments to make your dishes interesting and tasty. You can lose weight faster if you've cut back on high-fat foods, and you'll give your body the benefit of learning to want what is truly best for it.

⟡ *Tip for the Day* ⟡
*Think of three ways you can include more foods that are
naturally low in fat into your meal plan.*

"Of all the self-fulfilling prophecies in your culture, the assumption that aging means decline and poor health is probably the deadliest."

MARILYN FERGUSON

Jo Ann, a sixty-two-year-old grandmother, is a legal secretary during the day, working as efficiently and professionally as possible. Twice a week, however, she dons tap shoes and leotard and attends a tap-dancing class where she cuts loose and benefits from aerobic exercise in the process. She explains that dancing makes her feel like a teenager and that it provides an antidote to a world that often seems gloomy.

Jo Ann isn't the only person who is defying the stereotype that aging means decline and poor health. Many people find that the empty-nest syndrome is just a myth. Once your children are grown, you have freedom to pursue activities and sports that you may not have had time for in earlier years. Harold retired from a demanding career at sixty-five and found that it didn't just bring him more time, it also brought him a few extra pounds. So after joining a weight-loss program and losing weight, he decided to enroll in a theological studies course. Now he's training to be a priest and finds that his "golden years" are bringing him more fulfillment than he ever thought possible.

Don't believe that being over a certain age means being overweight, inactive or forgetful. There's no age at which you cannot undertake a course in self-improvement. Beginning the process can be rejuvenating in and of itself. You'll find that if you continue to set goals and look ahead, you'll make every age in your life a time of growth.

⇌ *Tip for the Day* ⇌
Examine your ideas about aging. Do you accept that you can learn and grow as you get older, or do you believe that it is a period of steady decline?

"Anger is a great motivator."
ANONYMOUS

Everyone has a different reason for making a commitment to losing weight and developing a healthier lifestyle. For Max, it was the shock of seeing an unflattering video of himself at a family reunion. For Maggie, it was being asked if she were pregnant when she wasn't. For Nancy, it was anger at having her weight prevent her from doing something she really liked to do—play racquetball.

It was this latter reason, anger, that drove Becky to lose weight. At five-foot-seven and 311 pounds, Becky was refused medical insurance because she suffered from ongoing weight-related problems, including high blood pressure, borderline diabetes and gastritis. She remembers feeling the rejection was a personal insult, and her anger motivated her to lose weight. As a result, her health risk was reduced and she once again was insurable. Now weighing 151 pounds, Becky says she's willing to take personal and professional risks she never would have taken before and that she doesn't experience uncertainty and self-doubt any longer.

Remember today to channel your anger as a positive force to make an important change in your life. Whether you need to apply to graduate school, refinance your mortgage or challenge an inequality in your life, you'll find that using very strong emotions like anger in a wise way can be enormously helpful in pointing you toward and helping you achieve your goals.

❧ *Tip for the Day* ❧
Pick a situation you are angry about and ask yourself whether you can use that energy to help you find a solution.

"I prefer my oysters fried;/That way I know my oysters died."
ROY G. BLOUNT, JR.

Some people are leery of including fish as part of their protein selections because they mistakenly believe that eating seafood raises the risk of getting certain diseases. Although this fear has become widespread, there is little truth to it. In fact, only raw shellfish such as oysters and clams are potentially dangerous, and even so, adequate cooking can destroy the pathogens.

There are many reasons why fish should be a regular part of everyone's diet. Fish provides concentrated amounts of protein, and it is usually low in saturated fat and calories, too. And the type of fat that *is* found in fish—omega-3 fatty acids—has been linked to alleviating symptoms of arthritis, psoriasis, migraine headaches and autoimmune diseases like lupus. To ensure the quality of the fish you eat, shop in reputable stores, buy seafood that looks and smells fresh and avoid roadside stands, where vendors don't have the same strict quality standards as fish markets or supermarkets.

If fish isn't a regular part of your meal planning, think of creative ways to introduce it in tasty dishes. Cookbooks and food magazines can provide good ideas about how to do this. With the wide variety of fish available now, making seafood a regular part of your eating regimen is easy and it's smart.

∽ *Tip for the Day* ∽
Prepare one new fish dish this week.

> *"A successful individual typically sets his next goal somewhat but not too much above his last achievement. In this way he steadily raises his level of aspiration."*
>
> KURT LEWIN

When Deirdre arrived at her first weight-loss meeting, she was depressed about her weight and wanted to get it off as fast as possible. When her leader told her it would take several months to reach her weight goal, she considered going to a program that promised faster results. But as the weeks passed, Deirdre found that setting and reaching small weekly goals enhanced her self-esteem while also teaching her behavior modification skills that helped keep her weight off for the long term.

Achieving anything worthwhile in life requires that you break down your goals into small, realistic steps. For this reason Weight Watchers encourages members to view weight loss as a long-term project consisting of many parts. For example, instead of deciding to become a marathoner you can set an initial goal of walking briskly for 20 minutes each day. And instead of focusing only on reaching your weight goal, you can reward yourself for every 5 or 10 pounds lost with a nonfood treat or a picture of yourself in new "thin" clothes.

Make sure that you have set a number of small goals for yourself, not just one big one. If it's taking too long to feel a sense of accomplishment, consider making the goals more reachable and frequent. You'll find that if you can build on your achievements and reward yourself often for your hard work, your journey to success will be more pleasant and you'll develop feelings of self-confidence and self-mastery at the same time.

Tip for the Day

Set a goal that you can reach today, such as cleaning your desk, writing a thank-you note or sticking to your weight-loss program.

"A watched pot never boils."
ANONYMOUS

When you start an important project you're probably eager to check your progress from moment to moment to gauge if you're on your way to success. For people who want to lose weight, this behavior can take the form of constantly jumping on and off the scale, trying on smaller sizes of clothing every day and obsessively looking in the mirror for signs of improvement, such as a more defined jaw line, a slimmer waist, a flatter tummy.

To be successful, however, you must take a long-term view of your project and steer clear of monitoring yourself so often that it seems to overtake your life. People who are addicted to the scale find it helpful to put away the bathroom scale and get weighed once a week at Weight Watchers meetings. Others find that keeping themselves occupied with activities and goals that have nothing to do with weight loss can prevent them from obsessing about today's weight. An added benefit of distracting yourself from monitoring your daily progress is that you're less likely to become discouraged by temporary setbacks and less likely to give up.

The best approach to take with weight loss or any other important goal is, first, to know where you want to go, and, second, develop a plan to get there. Only then are you ready to start the necessary day-to-day work that will eventually make the pot boil.

⸺ Tip for the Day ⸺
Instead of obsessing about how quickly or slowly you're progressing toward your goal, focus more on whether you're making the behavioral changes that will enable you to maintain your success once you achieve it.

"Cheerfulness, it would appear, is a matter which depends fully as much on the state of things within, as on the state of things without and around us."

CHARLOTTE BRONTË

If you look around you'll probably notice that optimists generally draw positive situations and people to themselves, while pessimists often lurch from crisis to crisis, lamenting life's woes and their inability to have anything good happen to them. People who have had trouble losing weight may fall into this latter camp because they've been unable to imagine themselves feeling or looking good. Part of the solution is learning to be more of an optimist.

One important reason to develop a cheerful attitude is that studies have shown that hopefulness helps healthy people stay healthy. People already in good health are more likely to seek out ways to take care of themselves. Experts say that one way to train yourself to be an optimist is to remind yourself that good things have happened to you in the past even when you were challenged. Learn to give yourself credit when good things happen, rather than attributing them to chance or good luck. And, make yourself view setbacks as opportunities to change, not proof that you're a failure. So if you overeat at a party or holiday gathering, figure out a plan for the next time. Turn a potentially negative situation into a learning experience rather than declaring yourself a diet failure.

Remember today that how you view the world and yourself plays a huge role in how much success you can draw to yourself. So believe in yourself today and know that you have the power to overcome whatever faces you. You'll find that the more good you see in yourself, the more good you'll have in your world.

Tip for the Day

Instead of looking for cheerfulness outside yourself today, create it within.

"For the sense of smell, almost more than any other, has the power to recall memories and it is a pity that you use it so little."
RACHEL CARSON

The next time you are feeling blue and you want a way to lift your spirits without turning to food, follow your nose. Research has shown that scents evoke powerful memories and feelings. You can change your mood simply by being in the presence of an aroma that reminds you of a happy time.

It's interesting to note that certain scents stimulate memories of childhood, making you feel nostalgic and calm. People born in the 1920s and 1930s say that fragrances of flowers and grass are most powerful in this regard, while children of the 1960s and 1970s find that the smells of baby powder, detergent and felt-tip pens makes them feel most nostalgic. The reason for these differing odors is that older Americans were more likely to grow up playing outdoors, while more recent generations had indoor memories. It's not surprising that unpleasant smells like bus fumes, dog waste and sewer gas were commonly cited triggers for unhappy memories no matter which generation a person was from.

Use your nose to lift your spirits today. Although eating isn't necessarily a good option, the smell of food cooking—especially of bread baking—works wonders on 85 percent of all people. Think of other scents that may be helpful to you, too, such as lavender, swimming pools or horses. Whatever scent you choose to surround yourself with, remember that knowing how to calm yourself naturally is a tool to help you succeed in reaching your goals.

❧ *Tip for the Day* ❧
Close your eyes and think about a time in your life when you were happy. Is there a scent associated with this memory, such as a certain shampoo you used as a child or a fragrance your grandmother wore?

> *"Time cools, time clarifies; no mood can be maintained quite unaltered through the course of hours."*
>
> MARK TWAIN

Whenever you feel angry, sad, confused or anxious, it's tempting to want to turn to something that can take away your cares and temporarily soothe you. Unfortunately, if you're overweight, chances are that food comes to mind first. If this has been your tendency, it's imperative that you learn new skills to cope with your feelings effectively without gaining weight and erasing any progress you may have made in losing weight or developing a healthy lifestyle.

One man who used to raid the refrigerator late at night says that his solution was to go for midnight jogs or get into the car and drive for an hour. If he could occupy enough time, he explained, food wouldn't seem like a good option afterward. This same technique has been invaluable for people who routinely vent their anger without stopping to think through their situation. One woman who used to be a self-confessed "screamer" now writes letters to people she's angry with and then puts the letter away for a day or so. Although she never sends the letters, she says she's happier after writing them.

If you're feeling very emotional about something and you're tempted to blow your food plan because of it, delay your gratification by getting into the car for a drive, calling a friend who's talkative or starting a long project like cleaning the attic. Chances are that you'll take your mind off food long enough to eliminate your food cravings and stay committed to your food program.

❧ *Tip for the Day* ☙
Think of two ways to divert yourself the next time food beckons and you need to distract yourself for an hour.

"We begin to see that the completion of an important project has every right to be dignified by a natural grieving process. Something that required the best of you has ended. You will miss it."

ANNE WILSON SCHAEF

Some people find that pursuing a goal is more enjoyable than reaching it. This may be the case for those who enjoy planning nutritious meals, celebrating steady weight loss and receiving compliments on their constant progress, but who feel sad or lost when their journey is ended. When this is the case, it's important to come up with strategies to ensure that maintaining a weight goal receives as much vigilance as losing weight.

It's essential to realize that a letdown period is normal when you've accomplished something important. Even though you're proud of yourself, you may feel suddenly without purpose if you don't have a set goal before you. For that reason you might want to change your sights from weight loss to increasing the intensity of your workout or learning a new professional skill. At the same time, it's important to remember that maintaining your weight goal will *still* require effort. Slacking off may lead to weight gain.

Be prepared for some sadness when you reach your weight goal or any other milestone in your life. Try to have a new goal ready for yourself to make it a little easier. Life will always be filled with beginnings and endings. But if you're prepared for a normal mourning period, your endings can always flow into fresh and exciting starts.

⟐ *Tip for the Day* ⟐

Think of a special way to mark an important achievement in your life that can be a springboard to a new journey.

"[Spring is] when life's alive in everything."
CHRISTINA ROSSETTI

One of the most wonderful aspects of turning the clock forward at the onset of spring is that it seems to create more hours of daylight. For those who are susceptible to the sadness and lethargy caused by lack of sunlight, spring also marks the end of mood swings and a resurgence in vitality and happiness.

Although the mild weather will boost your spirits, the temptation to be outside as much as possible can play havoc with meal planning if you aren't careful. If you want to exercise after work and before dinner, plan a snack to sustain you in the afternoon and have a light dinner. Or if you want to take a morning walk, make sure you plan a breakfast that fits your energy needs. Also, make sure you take sufficient time to enjoy your meal. As much as you may want to be outdoors, eating on the run encourages bad habits like unplanned snacking and careless measuring of portion sizes.

Take advantage of all the abundance and beauty that spring has to offer you today, but remember to take care of yourself. Continue to attend your weight-loss meetings and be disciplined about adhering to your planned meals. With creativity and flexibility you'll find that every season can add diversity and strength to your efforts to live a healthy life.

Tip for the Day
*Enjoy some outdoor exercise today and revel in the scent
of clean air and freshly turned earth.*

*"For me, words are a form of action,
capable of influencing change."*

INGRID BENGIS

When Roberto joined Weight Watchers, he presented a real challenge to the leader. A professional chef, Roberto had earned acclaim and monetary success creating restaurants noted for large portions and authentic Italian cooking. To keep up his gourmet image Roberto felt compelled to eat and drink heartily with his patrons and peers. Unfortunately, this lifestyle left him 75 pounds overweight. Roberto needed to learn how to mesh his desire to be healthy with his need to maintain his professional standing.

Roberto's hectic schedule and long hours made attending weight-loss meetings very difficult. The leader worked with him to create gradual changes and healthier eating habits that Roberto could put into practice himself at work or on the road. She also helped him come up with positive affirmations to help him reach his goals. Instead of using vague statements of desire, such as "Today I will be healthy," she told him to say aloud, "Today I will eat more vegetables" or "Today I will get at least ten minutes of exercise." Specific affirmations like these helped Roberto focus better on his goals despite his limited free time, keeping them in his conscious mind.

Remember to invoke the power of words as you change your eating and exercise patterns today, especially if you don't have a lot of time to devote to reaching your goals. If you can at least give your mind specific instructions on where you want to go, you may be surprised to find that you can work on your program even while you are occupied with other matters.

      Tip for the Day
*Examine the affirmations you give yourself. Could you be giving yourself
more specific instructions each day?*

> *"Whoever said money can't buy happiness
> didn't know where to shop."*
>
> ANONYMOUS

Sometimes when you are trying to break yourself of a bad habit—like overeating—you unconsciously replace it with another one. Jackie noticed that when she stopped overeating she found herself shopping compulsively to fill the void eating had once satisfied. She said her spending finally reached the point where she had to join a support group for compulsive debtors and cut up her credit cards.

Beware of inappropriate shopping conduct if you are prone to replacing one compulsive behavior with another. Do you find yourself shopping to relieve boredom, sadness, or feelings of low self-esteem? Do you buy items you don't want or need? Do you buy expensive things in defiance of someone? Do you find yourself buying things impulsively, even while feeling that you can't stop what you're doing?

Compulsive shopping may start out innocently enough, but if you allow it to go on unchecked, it could become a financial and psychological problem for you and your family. Be aware today of how you spend money and analyze whether you purchase food, clothes, or anything else in a manner in which you once ate. Just as you are learning to enjoy quality food in judicious amounts at the right times, learning how to spend your hard-earned money in a fulfilling way is also a skill that everyone should have and know how to use.

⋙ Tip for the Day ⋙
*If spending is a problem, consider putting your credit cards
out of sight for a few weeks or months. Ask yourself
if you can make a budget and stick to it.*

"Vegetables are interesting but lack a sense of purpose when unaccompanied by a good cut of meat."

FRAN LEBOWITZ

One of the most common weight-loss efforts is to limit oneself solely to low-calorie foods like certain vegetables and fruits. One woman says that she followed this type of restrictive program and felt so deprived after two weeks that she went out and ate nothing but fast-food hamburgers and fried chicken for a week—effectively erasing the weight she'd lost on the diet and even adding a few pounds more.

When planning your meals, be sure that they are balanced and include more than just generous servings of low-calorie vegetables. For although they are wonderful sources of fiber, vitamins and nourishment, vegetables often need to be eaten in combination with complex carbohydrates or proteins so your body can absorb their full benefits. Eating protein—whether from legumes, dairy sources or meat—also serves the important purpose of keeping you full longer. This eliminates the chances of suffering from hunger pangs shortly after finishing a meal.

Remember today that overeating isn't the only temptation you may face in trying to lose weight. You may be tempted to try to lose weight faster by undereating and going light on protein. Keep in mind that every successful weight-loss program preaches the virtues of balance from fats to complex carbohydrates. You will be doing yourself and your body a favor if you get your full quota from all of the food groups.

≈ *Tip for the Day* ≈
Review your meal plans to see if you are getting enough protein,
or whether you are occasionally shortchanging yourself
to try to lose weight faster.

"When you are not physically starving, you have the luxury to realize psychic and emotional starvation."

CHERRIE MORAGA

Donna and Dawn are both former beauty queens who starved themselves and resorted to unhealthy practices in order to compete at the top levels of their profession. Dawn remembers working out for five hours each day and drinking liquid algae concoctions to sink to her lowest competition weight. Donna says that to shrink her legs she'd wrap her thighs in plastic wrap and ride an exercise bike for hours.

Neither woman was able to maintain these punishing rituals, though, and soon after their pageant days ended, they gained weight and found happiness as size 12 models. Looking back they say that starving themselves prevented them from being who they wanted to be. Dawn now realizes that people are more attracted to your positive qualities and to the happiness and self-confidence you radiate than to your physical appearance. At Weight Watchers, Dawn and Donna both learned how to eat nutritiously and not be obsessed with food all day. Their new understanding of the importance of nutrition and a healthy way of eating has freed them both to pursue work that they love and to find enjoyment in other areas of their lives.

If you are starving yourself, you are diverting your energy from other, more important needs, such as being fulfilled in your profession or finding love in a close relationship. Remember that a body that is constantly deprived is a body that will never know health or happiness.

∽ *Tip for the Day* ∽

Ask yourself if you are ready to accept the fact that starvation equals serious bodily harm. Affirm to yourself today that you will eat the proper servings of nutritious food and not shortchange yourself to speed up weight loss.

"To follow, without halt, one aim: There's the secret of success."
ANNA PAVLOVA

Many people find that reaching a goal comes only after years of unsuccessful attempts to change. For example, Anne tried to quit smoking for several years before her fifth and final attempt led her to freedom from nicotine. She says that rather than feeling discouraged about her failures, she learned valuable techniques each time that helped her ultimately formulate a winning strategy.

The same may be true of weight loss. Carol joined a weight-loss program with the goal of losing 31 pounds but found herself unable to forgive herself for maintaining or even gaining during some weeks when she followed the meal plan exactly. As a result, she quit and rejoined the program several times, finally learning that her body responded best to several small meals each day rather than three regular-size ones. Carol says she succeeded because keeping her goal in mind helped her to finally accept and learn from her individuality.

Don't be discouraged if you encounter setbacks in your attempts to lose weight or reach some other goal. Each of these events will bring valuable insights that can help you in your next attempt. If you can follow, "without halt," where you want to go, success will come to you eventually.

≈ *Tip for the Day* ≈
If there is a program you've quit because you didn't succeed the first time, think of something you learned from the experience and use it to motivate you to try again.

"The most powerful factors in the world are clear ideas in the minds of energetic men of good will."

J. ARTHUR THOMSON

When Aristotle taught in ancient Greece he did so while walking up and down the pathways of the Lyceum, students trailing behind him. Ralph Waldo Emerson said his best work came to him during long solitary strolls through the countryside. Charles Dickens once walked 20 miles through the streets of London while pondering a chapter of *A Christmas Carol*. Architect Frank Lloyd Wright said his most creative work was done while working on his farm.

While exercise is a key ingredient of a healthy life, it has also been shown to spark creativity. One study showed that previously sedentary women who jogged 20 minutes twice a week scored higher on tests of creative thinking than women with no fitness routine. Why? Because once the mind enters into a state of contemplation, the subconscious sifts through information and stimulates connections and solutions unavailable to the conscious mind.

If you are stymied by a problem today, try to let go of it, using your exercise time to let your mind roam. Not only will your body benefit from the physical activity, but you may be surprised to find that your subconscious devises the solution to whatever is on your mind.

❧ *Tip for the Day* ❧
Use your exercise time to come up with ideas and possible solutions to a current challenge in your life.

"After all it is those who have a deep and real inner life who are best able to deal with the irritating details of outer life."

EVELYN UNDERHILL

In ancient times resting one day each week was an inviolable law that everyone observed. In the twentieth century, though, that is often not the case. Malls are usually jammed with shoppers on weekends, hardware stores are filled with people working on projects and overworked parents use this time to catch up on chores. As a result many people have forgotten that physical and emotional reserves need to be replenished regularly. Taking a day of rest isn't optional, it's something you require and deserve.

If you find yourself overwhelmed with the irritating details of everyday life, examine how you spend your days off from work. Are you always running—to sports games, the office, the supermarket? Are you so busy on weekends that you rarely have time to enjoy the Sunday newspaper? Do you frequently schedule appointments and errands for weekends because that's the time when you catch up instead of taking a well-deserved break?

If the answer to any of the above questions is yes, try to find a way to make your free days a period when you can slow down, contemplate your life and think of ways you can approach the coming week with more balance. When you fill your nonworking time with activities that deplete you, remind yourself that regular "down time" will provide you with the energy and enthusiasm you need to succeed in building a balanced, healthy lifestyle.

⌖ *Tip for the Day* ⌖

Cancel all unnecessary plans for the weekend and make the commitment to carve out some peace and relaxation for yourself.

*"[Advice is] what you ask for when you already know the answer
but wish you didn't."*

ERICA JONG

Like most people, you may typically ask others for advice when
you want to make a change in your life, such as losing weight.
Quite often, however, the advice you get isn't what you want
to hear because it involves more work than you're willing to
do. Such is the case with revving up your metabolism to burn
calories and body fat more efficiently. Anyone looking for advice about how to make this happen should know that the
following advice isn't always easy, but it has been proven to
work.

To increase your metabolism, here are some helpful tips:

- Increase your muscle mass through resistance training, such
  as exercises with dumbbells, elasticized bands or weights.
- Eat a healthy breakfast. A good breakfast will give you energy to start the day and minimize impulsive snacking or
  overeating later.
- Exercise for more than 30 minutes. After about a half-hour
  of sustained exercise, the body begins to use its fat stores
  for fuel.
- Stop restrictive dieting. The more you severely restrict your
  calories, as opposed to simply switching to a healthier meal
  plan, the lower your resting metabolic rate will go, triggering your body to store fat.
- Alter your exercise routine. Every few weeks you should
  shake up your exercise routine so that your entire body gets
  a workout and a greater chance to attack fat stores.

Tip for the Day

*To enhance your weight-loss efforts, choose two of the fat-burning tips
listed above and practice them today.*

"After silence, that which comes nearest to expressing the inexpressible is music."

ALDOUS HUXLEY

One of the things you learn as you lose weight is that you may have often turned to food in the past to soothe yourself and cope with uncomfortable feelings. To be successful at weight loss, though, it's imperative that you discover the roots of those distressing feelings and then come up with effective strategies to express your emotions in ways that can help you, not hurt you.

One of the most popular stress busters is losing yourself in music. There are many different ways to accomplish this: Put on headphones and turn off your thoughts with a symphony, sing along to a favorite song, or if you play an instrument, use it to occupy your body and mind at the same time. Researchers say that while all forms of music can be therapeutic, it's best to listen to musical pieces that have a regular, calming rhythm like classical works. Because of the disjointed beat of many rock-and-roll songs, experts say these can leave listeners feeling more tense than relaxed.

Consider the power of music if you are searching for ways to overcome emotional eating today. Keep a radio in the kitchen in case you are tense while preparing meals and invest in tapes or compact discs with calming music to make car rides more enjoyable. It's often said that music can calm a savage breast, so use its power to your advantage today to ensure that the power of overeating doesn't ruin your day.

Tip for the Day

Buy a piece of music you can play when you are feeling stressed, or tune your radio to a classical music station.

"Journal writing is a voyage to the interior."
CHRISTINA BALDWIN

When Karen joined a class aimed at helping people uncover the reasons they overate, the teacher encouraged her students to keep journals of their emotions, fears and innermost secrets. Although not a writer, Karen soon found the process of making a journal entry each morning to be cathartic and revealing. She says that at first her journals were filled with a record of calories and how fat she felt. Now she says her journal is her "best friend" and that she regularly writes about her pain, her joy and her challenges. By doing this she has learned to turn to her journal instead of a doughnut for comfort.

Writing in a journal has many benefits, not the least of which is staying busy doing something besides eating. Studies have shown that people who write about their feelings every day have better mental health than those who don't. The price is right, too. All you need is a notebook, a private place to store it and a regular block of time when you can chronicle your feelings. Some busy professionals keep their journals at work, where it's easier for them to take a few quiet minutes, while others find that writing at night is an effective way to review the day.

If the only time you write is to plan your meals, try to branch out by writing about other things. Explore topics such as when you first felt uncomfortable about your body, when you first turned to food for solace and whether your self-esteem is dependent on your weight. If you can make recording your feelings a daily habit, you'll not only find food less alluring, you'll also have rich inner reserves upon which to draw in difficult times.

∽ *Tip for the Day* ∽
Set aside five minutes today to write about any happiness,
sadness or even anxiety you are feeling.

> *"Imagination is the beginning of creation.*
> *You imagine what you desire, you will what you imagine*
> *and at last you create what you will."*
>
> GEORGE BERNARD SHAW

One of the most powerful tools you have to help you achieve your goals is your mind. Researchers have shown that people who can visualize themselves succeeding at a task are more successful than those who don't. Creating these mental images can actually cause your brain to form new neural connections that stimulate your ability to learn and retain information.

You can use the power of visualization to help you achieve your weight-loss goals as well as the dreams you have for yourself in other areas. Find a place where you can relax comfortably and take several uninterrupted minutes to let your mind drift. Imagine how you want your body to look, how you will move after reaching your weight goal and how you will dress. Do you look happy? Do you see yourself at peace with your body? Are you wearing flattering colors and figure-enhancing clothes?

If you do this exercise every day, trying to feel like you are already the person in your reverie, you'll send your subconscious messages that will help change your behavior in important and beneficial ways. The more you use this technique and others like it to create a positive self-image, the more your actions will be directed in ways that bring you success.

⇌ Tip for the Day ⇌
Take five minutes to visualize yourself in the body you want.
Vividly imagine yourself eating healthfully and
enjoying a new and active lifestyle.

"My favorite thing is to go where I've never been."
DIANE ARBUS

One of the best ways to ease tension and have fun is to take a trip to a new or unusual location—either a day trip or an extended vacation. For the person who is unaccustomed to being assertive, traveling can be a valuable experience. One woman who rewarded herself for losing weight with a trip to Italy said that dealing with visas, currency, schedules, tickets, transportation, maps and luggage made her feel independent, self-confident and brave.

Trips may also help you to appreciate what you already have. One woman who visited Asia was humbled by how little some people had to live on and how happy they were with their few possessions. Another woman who hiked through a destitute country said she'd never take a warm meal for granted again. And almost everyone who returns from a vacation trip—even a day-long escape to the seashore or a nearby town—is refreshed and renewed, returning with more enthusiasm for the tasks left behind. This may be related to a job challenge, trying to lose weight, or being a better parent.

Taking regular respites is more than a noncaloric way to broaden your horizons and enrich your life. Children who see that their parents need time to be alone with each other develop a greater appreciation for the importance of the parent-parent connection and enhance their own self-reliance. Start saving money now for a trip or a brief getaway to recharge your batteries and get a new perspective on life. Traveling doesn't have to be expensive, but its rewards can be invaluable.

≈ *Tip for the Day* ≈
Take advantage of airfare promotions and hotel discounts to plan a trip that is rejuvenating but doesn't break your budget.

"Illusions are art, for the feeling person, and it is by art that you live, if you do."

ELIZABETH BOWEN

Although there is no substitute for losing weight and exercising to make your body look trim, you can create the illusion of being at least five pounds thinner by having the right posture. Fashion models and ballerinas, women whose professional success often depends on looking slim and streamlined, are taught to exhibit perfect posture.

To give the illusion of being thinner today, practice walking with your pelvis tilted slightly forward, chin up and shoulders back. One way to encourage this type of alignment is to stand close to a wall with your hands at your sides. Lean back until your head, back and shoulder blades are touching the wall. Finally, slide your body slightly downward on the wall, keeping your back as straight as possible against the wall.

As you go through your day, remember how your body felt when erect and straight against the wall. Correct your posture whenever you feel yourself slumping at your desk or while you walk. Another way to align your body is to do yoga poses that emphasize the body's fluidity. Whatever course you take in creating an image of slenderness, remember that losing weight and toning your body are still the best ways to achieve the figure you desire.

Tip for the Day

Throw your shoulders back as often as you can today. Notice how different your body feels when you sit or stand erect and tall.

"[Painting is] a stratagem by which you conquer life's disorder."

ALFRED BARR

If you are looking for a quick way to brighten your environment, exercise your body and give rein to your creative impulses, grab a paintbrush. One woman wanted to give her bedroom a happier feeling after she changed her lifestyle and lost weight. She satisfied her urge for a brighter environment by buying a can of paint and painting her walls a sunny yellow. "It's the most inexpensive therapy I've ever had!" she says.

Although doing your own interior decorating may seem intimidating, it's very freeing to be the master of your surroundings. In a few hours you can transform a bedroom into a welcoming respite, give new life to a child's room or make a bathroom a colorful oasis. There are many ways to personalize your work too. Sponge on the paint for a soft effect, create flowery scenes or do some stenciling. Paint doesn't need to be limited to inside the house, either. A great way to welcome spring and demonstrate your creativity is to paint flowerpots and fill them with your favorite plants and herbs.

If you enjoyed painting as a child, you'll probably enjoy it as an adult, too. Bring some color into your life today by painting a picture, a wall or other item. Not only will you bring some new order into your life, you'll be celebrating your healthy new lifestyle in a colorful way.

Tip for the Day
Find something you'd like to paint—a flowerpot, mailbox,
door or room—and buy the necessary supplies so that you
can embark on a fun project.

"Blessed are they who heal you of self-despisings. Of all services which can be done to man, I know of none more precious."

WILLIAM HALE WHITE

Weight Watchers leaders help members understand the Food and Activity Plans, inspire them to keep coming back and guide them to smart choices that will enable them to succeed in reaching their weight goals. Leaders also have another, less tangible role. By celebrating members' achievements, sharing their own struggles and proving that anyone can succeed if they have the determination, they boost self-confidence and help members learn to believe in themselves.

Mary says that at her first meeting she was feeling "cranky and resentful" about her weight, but listening to her leader speak about her own 75-pound weight loss inspired Mary to return the next week and eventually become a leader herself. One of the things Mary stresses in her meetings is that she gained and lost weight repeatedly and considered herself a failure. But once she learned to forgive herself, she could continue to persevere until she succeeded.

Keep in mind today that being successful consists of more than just losing weight. It also means leaving your self-despisings behind and learning to love and forgive yourself. If you receive this gift as the result of an inspirational leader or friend, express your gratitude to that person. Then try to pass it along to someone else.

≈ *Tip for the Day* ≈
Are you free of your own feeling of self-hatred? If feeling bad about yourself is hindering your weight-loss efforts, find someone who can help you develop a kinder and more realistic picture of yourself.

"Mid pleasures and palaces though we may roam, / Be it ever so humble, there's no place like home."

JOHN HOWARD PAYNE

Many people who have home-based businesses are discovering what full-time homemakers have long known—that being at home full time makes weight control more difficult. They find that food is always close by and mealtimes or coffee breaks tend to be unscheduled. When the work is piled high, it's easy to skip a meal, then grab a snack later when you're very hungry and too busy to pay attention to what you're eating. But with a little thought and planning, you can minimize these problems.

Keep tempting treats out of sight. It's best not to purchase them in the first place, but if they are in your house, store them out of sight, perhaps in a jar on a high shelf behind closed cabinet doors. Recognize the importance of a regular routine. Start your day at a specific time each morning and schedule a regular lunch break for yourself. Parents at home with young children know that the day is easier when the children are on a regular sleeping and eating schedule. An established routine makes it easier to plan meals and exercise periods. And pay attention to the clock so that you don't end up working too many hours at a time without a break.

Remember that working at home has some big pluses, too. You can schedule your day around your body clock, an advantage for night owls. It's easier to exercise—just tie on those walking shoes and head for the front door. And if your children are still at home, you have the satisfaction of watching them grow and learn every day.

Tip for the Day
*Plan a snack time for yourself today. Keep a piece of fruit on hand,
then stop working long enough to enjoy the taste
and recharge your body and mind.*

"The strongest principle of growth lies in human choice."
GEORGE ELIOT

When you decide to apply your energy toward losing weight and exercising, you have made a choice to live healthfully. But there are many other choices remaining: What will you eat? How much will you exercise? And how much energy will you apply toward changing your lifestyle? Use this power of choice wisely. Making well-informed decisions gives you self-confidence and serves as a reminder that you are responsible for reaching your goals.

Having the freedom of choice in Weight Watchers meal plans means that you are the one in charge of your success. Making smart choices isn't always easy though. For example, if you are at a buffet or an all-you-can-eat restaurant, it will take some inner resolve to resist food you'd like to eat but that doesn't fit into your meal plan. It can be hard to choose to exercise when you're tired or the weather is dreary. But successfully dealing with situations like these will make you grow and give you the knowledge that you can succeed.

Be aware of the many choices you can make today to lose weight and be healthy. Start with preparing a nutritious breakfast. When you take this action, are you becoming accustomed to making these types of smart choices? Congratulate yourself every time you do something that will help you lose weight and be fit. Remember, the more you choose to live a healthy lifestyle, the more empowered and self-confident you will be.

∽ *Tip for the Day* ∽
Be conscious of the choices facing you today. Congratulate yourself whenever you make one that is difficult but correct for you.

"Temptation rarely comes in working hours. It is in their leisure time that men are made or marred."

W. N. TAYLOR

Many of you have no problems remaining goal-oriented and focused during working hours, particularly if you are trying to impress your colleagues or superiors. Adhering to a sensible meal plan at lunch may present no difficulty. Yet many people get into trouble when the working day is over and unstructured time lies ahead.

One of the most unstructured "leisure" times you have is in the car. You may face a long daily commute, hours of carpooling or waiting in seemingly endless traffic jams. If you're not careful, boredom or frustration can tempt you to snack or stop at fast-food places. This is perilous behavior if you are trying to lose weight.

If traveling in your car tempts you to snack, resolve not to bring along fattening foods or stop at fast-food restaurants. Schedule healthy snacks during the day to prevent late afternoon hunger and carpool with someone who is supportive of your weight-loss goals. The more precautions you take to keep your idle hours from marring your self-improvement efforts, the less likely you'll be to succumb to temptation when it suddenly presents itself during your "leisure time."

⇌ *Tip for the Day* ⇌
Think of some snacks you can have with you if you frequently are beset with hunger pangs in the car, such as carrots, popcorn cakes or noncaloric drinks.

*"Brush them and floss them and take them to the dentist, and they
will stay with you. Ignore them and they'll go away."*
ADVERTISEMENT BY THE AMERICAN DENTAL ASSOCIATION

There are some gifts everyone is born with, and one of them is
a set of teeth. Unfortunately, years of eating sugary foods or
drinking sodas can leave them decayed and in poor shape.
Neglect can also occur if you're overweight because you may
not care enough about yourself or your appearance to make
regular visits to the dentist.

Remember today that your teeth are precious. Everything
you can do to protect them will ensure that you have them as
long as possible to help you enjoy your meals.
Dentists advise brushing and flossing regularly after meals,
avoiding sugary drinks that hasten the decaying process and
being careful about what foods you eat. Foods like oranges,
cherries, raisins and dates with naturally occurring sugar are
always better than foods with refined sugar. But because all
foods will stick to your teeth to some degree, brush after every
meal if possible and floss daily.

Just as you eat your meals regularly, plan to follow them
with regular and proper dental care. Make sure that you schedule appointments for routine cleaning to help you maintain
their health and sparkle. One added benefit to all this preventive work: The smile you flash to celebrate your weight loss
will complement your new figure.

Tip for the Day
*Buy some mint-flavored dental floss to motivate you to floss your teeth.
Leave it out where you're sure to see and use it.*

"An optimist is the human personification of spring."
SUSAN J. BISSONETTE

Most people find that springtime ushers in a period of optimism, energy and happiness. Longer days and milder weather enable you to be outside more. It's easy to be active and feel energized when nature changes from dreary gray to bright and vibrant colors. People who have found it hard to be motivated during the winter months often decide that spring, a time of change and vitality, is the perfect season to begin a weight-loss program.

If springtime makes you eager for a fresh start, remember that the same enthusiasm can be generated throughout the year. Surround yourself with people who are the human personification of this season. If your circle of family and friends are "can do" people who are always trying to improve themselves, it's likely that you will adopt the same attitude. If you are surrounded by negative thinkers, however, you're likely to be easily discouraged by setbacks like weight plateauing or physical injuries.

Are the people around you optimists or pessimists? When you are down, will your friends be more likely to reinforce your sadness or encourage you to look on the bright side? Create a feeling of eternal spring in your life by surrounding yourself with vivacious and spirited thinkers. With their influence and inspiration, you'll find that you've become that way too.

 Tip for the Day
Infuse yourself with springtime enthusiasm by being around people who evoke that feeling in you.

"People fail forward to success."

MARY KAY ASH

Kerry began a small business several years ago that had a promising start. She grew steadily, gradually adding staff and expanding the products she sold. But just as the business entered its fourth year, a chain store opened nearby, undercutting Kerry's prices and pulling her customers away. Business dwindled and Kerry eventually had to declare bankruptcy. Now she is bitter and cynical. She sees the experience negatively and herself as a failure.

Failure is not necessarily a bad thing. Many have failed at something on their way to success. Thomas Edison made numerous mistakes on his way to inventing the lightbulb. If he'd chosen to give up along the way, he'd never have revolutionized the world. Similarly, if you have "failed" at something like stopping smoking, dieting or changing a negative behavior, remember that you were building toward success. Calling yourself a failure only ensures that you remain further away from achieving your goals.

If you stumble today, remind yourself that you are failing forward. Don't let a past failure prevent you from taking action toward a positive future. Try to recast your experience in your mind. No one enjoys being unsuccessful, but those who can learn from those experiences and move forward are the ones who ultimately achieve success.

⚬⟐⟐ *Tip for the Day* ⟐⟐⚬
*Think about all the positive things that have occurred
as a result of a "failure" in your life.*

"To say something nice about yourself, this is the hardest thing in the world for people to do. They'd rather take their clothes off."

NANCY FRIDAY

If you've struggled with weight all your life, you may have begun to think of yourself as a dieting failure who can't do anything right. One well-known talk-show hostess says that her twenty-year battle of the bulge completely overshadowed her other achievements to the point where she felt that nothing mattered except whether or not she was able to fit into her size 6 jeans.

As you work toward your weight goal, it's important that you remember to compliment yourself on other achievements or features about yourself that you like. Look in the mirror and say, "You have a beautiful smile," or "You were honest and thoughtful today." Perhaps you prefer affirmations like "I am creative" or "I am a good mother." Complimenting yourself aloud gives the words added force and more power than if you simply think them to yourself or write them in a journal.

Remember to compliment yourself today. Pick something you do well, such as the way you prepare a certain dish, the times you visit sick friends or how often you volunteer to help various groups. The more you can learn to recognize and affirm to yourself that you are a wonderful person in many different areas of your life, the less likely you'll be to define yourself only by your weight.

Tip for the Day
Think of one thing you did in an unselfish and loving way.
Remind yourself of that act whenever you are tempted
to put yourself down because of your weight.

"When you make a world tolerable for yourself, you make a world tolerable for others."

ANAÏS NIN

Although you are the greatest beneficiary when you decide to commit yourself to a healthy way of life, the other people in your life will be positively affected as well. If you are a parent, modeling sensible eating and exercise practices for your children is one of the best ways you can ensure that they won't grow up to be overweight and sedentary. When you successfully reach the goals you set for yourself, you show them how to work toward their dreams and take responsibility for their own actions.

There are many other compelling reasons for helping your children adopt a healthy lifestyle. Overweight boys and girls tend to become overweight adults. Studies have shown that sedentary children who watch two or more hours of television each day run a high risk of developing high cholesterol and weight-related problems. Involving them in food preparation and exercise routines will help them physically as well as provide opportunities to bring the family closer together.

Take stock of the positive effects you've had on others, particularly family members, since beginning a weight-loss program. Have rich desserts become a thing of the past? Is exercise a daily priority? Do you and the family watch less television and spend more time outdoors? You'll find that as you continue to make your life healthy, everyone around you will reap the fruits of your labor.

⟶ *Tip for the Day* ⟵
Include your children or other family members in grocery shopping and nutritious meal preparation today.

"Walking is also an ambulation of mind."

GRETEL EHRLICH

Sensible weight-loss programs encourage members to exercise every day. Walking is a popular choice because it burns calories, raises the heart rate and is convenient. Unlike some sports, walking doesn't require start-up costs for special clothes, equipment or space. The one expense to consider is a pair of walking shoes that will provide you with maximum support and flexibility.

Some people use walking as a social activity. Walking with friends keeps their minds occupied and makes the time pass faster. Others like to walk with headphones so that they can listen to music, books on tape or radio news. Many, however, like to walk without distraction because of the feelings of peace and solitude that come with rhythmic exercise. One woman walks through her neighborhood for an hour five times a week. She says that walking helped speed up her weight loss and tone her body. And it also brought her the psychological benefits of just letting her mind wander.

If you haven't yet started walking as part of your weight-loss program, check with your physician to make sure that you are ready for exercise. Then set aside a regular time to walk, either with a friend or by yourself. The more ways you can find to move your body and free up your mind, the healthier you'll be in all respects.

∞ Tip for the Day ∞
If you usually walk with headphones or friends,
plan at least one walk each week in silence.

"Before he sets out, the traveler must possess fixed interests and facilities to be served by travel."

GEORGE SANTAYANA

Mary wasn't making much progress on her own in changing to a healthy way of eating or regular exercise. She decided to go to a fitness spa for a week to see if she could become motivated. There she discovered that low-fat food can be tasty and interesting and that the right type of exercise can be fun. As a result of that one week, Mary now has established a healthy lifestyle for herself and returns to the spa once a year to keep her enthusiasm high.

Vacations are often times when we relax and revel in self-indulgence. Now, however, the fitness vacation market is booming as people combine leisure time with self-improvement. Many spas are well-known for their fitness and relaxation programs. It's also possible to go on bike tours, hike through national parks and go whitewater rafting in a group. It doesn't have to break your budget, either; costs can be quite reasonable if you have moderate sleeping arrangements or plan your stay for the off season.

If you plan a vacation this year, consider one that will enlarge your fitness and nutrition horizons. Pick from a wide range of activities and sports, including yoga, swimming, skiing, backpacking, running, rock climbing, kayaking, windsurfing and mountain biking. Then match your expertise to the right trip. If you are prepared to learn new ways of incorporating fun and fitness into your life, you'll be making a wonderful investment in a healthy future.

⟫ *Tip for the Day* ⟪
*Plan a vacation that will bring you health-related benefits,
even if it's just a weekend getaway.*

"To eat is human / To digest divine."

MARK TWAIN

A foreigner commented to an American friend one day that Americans rushed through their meals, rarely pausing to talk to others or savor the taste of their food. She contrasted that with the custom in her country where families routinely come home from work and gather together, cooking and eating a leisurely meal, exchanging stories about their day. In other countries, lunchtime is the big event of the day and stores even close for several hours in the afternoon to accommodate this ritual event.

Although the pace of life in America isn't always conducive to spending several hours cooking and eating each day, you can try to find ways to make your meals more relaxed, thereby improving your digestion. One man has a pact with himself not to eat any meals standing up or in a car. Another person won't dine unless she has a placemat and nice utensils. And some families insist on gathering at a regular time for dinner, even if a family member has to go out again afterwards. Guidelines like these may not guarantee an elaborate meal, but they do ensure that you'll have a greater chance of "divine" digestion.

Pay attention today to how much time you allow for proper digestion after meals. Instead of jumping up after a quick dinner to start doing a load of laundry, try to linger and share events of the day with a family member. Or if you are accustomed to interrupting your breakfast to wait on everyone else, try getting up ten minutes earlier and having some quiet time before you eat. Remember that what you eat is a big part of your satisfaction, but giving yourself time to enjoy it is what will bring you the most fulfillment.

≈ *Tip for the Day* ≈

Even if you want to jump up and do something immediately after finishing a meal, commit yourself to take a few deep breaths and remain seated for at least five minutes.

"Nothing stimulates the practiced cook's imagination like an egg."
IRMA S. ROMBAUER AND MARION ROMBAUER BECKER

In recent years, eggs have gotten a bad rap because they've been accused of raising cholesterol and increasing fat in the diet. As a result, many have shunned eating this important source of protein and perhaps unwittingly turned to other higher-fat sources of protein such as cheese and meat. The truth is that for most people eggs are a valuable part of a balanced diet, supplying vitamins, protein and some fat in a compact and tasty way.

Eggs can still be part of a balanced meal plan as long as you partake with moderation. Eggs contain 215 milligrams of cholesterol per egg, less than once thought. Guidelines published by the U.S. Department of Health allow up to four eggs per week. The real culprit, saturated fat, is more abundant in other things like meat and cheese. You can take advantage of nonfat egg substitute for some of your recipes. Take care in preparing eggs so as not to add additional fat. Try poaching your eggs or frying them in a nonstick pan that has been sprayed with cooking oil.

Eating is meant to be enjoyable, so if the occasional egg dish—scrambled eggs, egg salad sandwich or an elegant omelet—will make weight loss more pleasurable, indulge yourself in moderation.

Tip for the Day
Understand the nutritional benefits and side effects of the foods you eat and tailor your meals to your specific desires and needs.

"There are few nudities so objectionable as the naked truth."
AGNES REPPLIER

At one time or another, nearly all of us have been dishonest with ourselves in order to avoid the truth of a situation. For example, if you want to go to an all-you-can-eat restaurant to eat with abandon, you might try to convince yourself that you're going because it's a nice place to have brunch with your friends. Or if you wear big clothes to hide your girth, you might tell yourself that you're only wearing them because you want to feel unconstricted when you move. Either way, these types of little white lies prevent you from facing the truth about your condition and keep you stuck in a rut of overeating and denial.

Once you've faced your weight problem and you're trying to make positive changes in your life, however, telling white lies may save you from overeating at times. For example, if someone is pushing you to eat something that's not on your meal plan, it might be easier to say you don't like that food or have a stomach virus or food allergy. Or if someone disapproves of your efforts to lose weight and tries to sabotage your progress, you might consider telling him or her you're going to run errands rather than explain you're on the way to a weight-loss meeting. Half-truths such as these can protect you and keep you moving toward success.

Be aware of the difference between being dishonest to keep yourself from facing something unpleasant and misleading others in order to protect yourself. The naked truth is sometimes objectionable, but knowing when to face that unpleasantness may spell the difference between success and failure.

Tip for the Day
Keep track of the times you're not truthful today and take note of whether they help you or hurt you in achieving your goals.

*"Just as you began to feel that you could make good use of time,
there was no time left to you."*

LISA ALTHER

Successful people will tell you that one of the main reasons they have achieved their goals is because they are disciplined and organized. These men and women prioritize their tasks and tackle them immediately. They also don't get sidetracked by distractions that take them away from their schedules. They balance their lives carefully so that they don't become burned out by spending too much time in one particular area.

If you frequently find yourself running out of time, here are some tips that will help you streamline your day while giving you enough time to eat and exercise sensibly. Have a list of things you'd like to accomplish and put the most important at the top. Create a schedule and stick to it. For example, if you have set aside an hour after work to exercise, turn down a colleague's request to go out for a drink. As for a workout, keep in mind that you can do a good resistance-training workout in as little as ten minutes. So even if you're squeezed for time there's always something you can do to tone your body.

Time has a tendency to get away from you when you aren't paying attention. Treat time as a precious commodity and parcel it out carefully. Try to start each day with a clear idea of what you want to achieve, then diligently create periods when you can carry out your tasks. Do these things and success in weight loss and physical fitness can come to even the busiest person.

⟿ *Tip for the Day* ⟾
*If you seem to have no time to plan balanced meals,
exercise or accomplish important tasks, think of at least one way
you can be more efficient.*

> *"Golf is the most fun you can have without taking
> your clothes off."*
>
> CHI CHI RODRIGUEZ

When Roger was 60 pounds overweight he found pursuing his favorite sport, golf, to be very difficult. A good swing was hard because of his large stomach, and he frequently became winded just walking down the fairway to reach his ball. After losing weight at Weight Watchers he discovered a renewed zest for the sport. He now brags that he can walk the full 18 holes without getting into a cart once!

Golf is a popular sport. With the proliferation of public courses, the number of players is growing. For those who haven't yet tried it, it can be a wonderful complement to your exercise and stretching program. Not only will you get in several miles of walking if you pull a bag cart, but you can make it a social outing by going with friends.

If you haven't tried golf, consider taking it up. Golf can be learned at any age, and there are many instructional videos and television programs. It's easier to get regular aerobic movement into your day if you enjoy what you're doing. Make sure that you keep your exercise options—such as golf—open so that you can have as many choices as possible.

Tip for the Day
*Locate the closest public course or indoor practice range
and go hit a bucket of balls this week.*

"Our remedies oft in ourselves do lie."
WILLIAM SHAKESPEARE

In our media-driven society, women may become easily dissatisfied with their bodies because they are surrounded by images of impossibly sleek and toned young models. Even though this ideal is unrealistic, many women fixate on their appearance and berate themselves because they don't measure up.

One therapist who works with weight-obsessed clients says that some people will focus on a specific body part, such as their hips. She helps them see that they are a whole person, not just a single body part. She also reminds her clients that the brain is like a computer and can be programmed just as easily with positive messages as negative ones. Counterprogram *yourself* with positive messages. If you exercise regularly each week, think of yourself as an athlete. If you are following a sensible eating plan, tell yourself that you are a person in control of your choices.

As you lose weight and become more fit, remember that your self-esteem can be strong even before you achieve your desired weight goal. So instead of defining yourself only by your weight or your physical appearance, put other attributes about yourself into perspective. Be proud of your strong moral and ethical behavior, your nurturing abilities and your intelligence. When you think of yourself in a flattering light, it will be easier to stop weighing your self-esteem.

∽ *Tip for the Day* ∽
Name three things you like about yourself and that give you feelings of self-esteem.

"An occasional sweet is sometimes good for the soul."
NANCY GAGLIARDI

Many people justify their habit for sweets by saying that their body "craves" candy and that indulging the craving satisfies a deep, primal need. It's true that our bodies need a certain amount of sugar to function properly but there's no biological or nutritional need for sugar doughnuts, for example. Fortunately, it *is* possible to become hooked on the right kind of sweets to nourish your body and help you lose weight at the same time. Fruits and complex carbohydrates such as oranges, cherries or sweet potatoes can perform the same metabolic function as a candy bar. The main difference between natural sources of sugar and processed candy is that the candy produces a blood sugar "crash" that leaves you feeling lethargic, irritable and moody. Complex carbohydrates, on the other hand, keep blood sugar levels on an even keel.

If you include naturally sweet foods in your meal planning yet still desire an occasional treat, indulge yourself wisely. Budget your calories so that you can eat without guilt and try to substitute low-calorie alternatives whenever possible. If you crave cheesecake or ice cream, check the dessert section of the supermarket for low-calorie versions that won't undo your day's planning. Take the time to savor the food so that the experience will last you for a long time. Instead of standing at the kitchen counter eating furtively, sit down with a plate and utensils and enjoy every bite of your treat.

Don't berate yourself if you want to have a little sweetness at your meals, but be smart about your choices. With some planning and an openness to letting your body get used to naturally occurring sugars, it's possible to nourish yourself well and include the treats that prevent you from feeling deprived.

Tip for the Day
Before you give yourself permission to have a high-calorie treat, first try to satisfy your cravings with a new variety of fruit.

"Nothing is more pleasing and engaging than the sense of having conferred benefits. Not even the gratification of receiving them."

ELLIS PETERS

When you join a weight-loss program, you realize that you have to find incentives other than food to reward yourself for achievements. For example, whenever you lose five pounds or celebrate a milestone in your life, instead of a food reward, you can give yourself new lingerie, an unhurried long-distance phone call or a best-selling book you've been wanting.

It's a good idea to buy nonfood gifts for others, too. A recent Gallup Poll found that most people who are celebrating a change or fresh start prefer gifts like plants, flowers, clothing or tickets to a sporting or entertainment event.

When giving gifts, remember to be as considerate of others as you are of yourself. If a friend has earned a degree or promotion, think of something special to mark the occasion besides a celebratory meal or a pan of homemade brownies. If a colleague has a baby, consider giving her an appointment for a professional massage instead of making her a casserole. Thinking of new and creative ways to honor other people won't just make you feel good, it will provide you with more ideas of nonfood ways to take care of yourself, too.

Tip for the Day
List three nonfood ways you'll help a friend celebrate
her birthday this year.

"What worries you masters you."
HADDON W. ROBINSON

No matter how carefully you try to manage your affairs, some days you're going to encounter stress and frustration. Whether it stems from not allowing enough time to read the newspaper in the morning, having a bad day at work or getting stuck in a traffic jam, stress is something everyone has to cope with. And how you deal with large and small problems may have something to do with whether or not you are successful in losing weight.

Research has shown that men and women respond very differently to stress. When shown upsetting movies, men tend to lose their appetite and shut down their digestive process. Women, however, tend to use food as an emotional crutch, so stress tends to lead them to ignore hunger signals and overeat. When stress and overeating become a common pattern, food takes on the role of comforter and friend instead of nourishment.

If you're prone to overeating when upset, monitor yourself when an unexpected bump appears in your day. Instead of absentmindedly turning to food, listen to the signals your body is sending you. Think of a different way to soothe yourself. Above all, remember that much of what happens to you is unavoidable anyway, and that keeping your troubles in perspective can be an effective way of breaking the habit of eating under stress.

᠅ *Tip for the Day* ᠅
*Resolve today to soothe yourself with a long walk
followed by a luxurious bath.*

"First cobwebs, then chains."

SPANISH PROVERB

When Roz gained 17 pounds, it went straight to her stomach, causing her to limit her clothing choices to bulky sweaters and elastic-waist slacks. When she lost weight, she still clung to this clothing combination, unable to perceive her shape as thinner or more attractive. Finally a friend asked, "What was the point of losing weight if you're still wearing the same old things?" Spurred by this comment, Roz decided to try knit sweaters and dresses that showed off her new figure.

Sometimes your habits—like wearing bulky sweaters or dark colors—start as innocent "cobwebs," but you don't see that they've become "chains" until someone jolts you into that realization. One woman in her thirties was hurt when a colleague gently told her that wearing bright blue eye shadow was more appropriate for a teenager. But inside she was grateful and soon updated her makeup to a more mature look. Similarly, another woman ran across some college pictures of herself. She realized with a start that she had the same hairstyle she'd worn 20 years earlier. Since she had changed emotionally and physically since she was 20, why shouldn't her hair change too?

Have you unknowingly bound yourself with some chains that started as cobwebs? Whether you are stuck in a clothing time warp, an attitude that isn't appropriate any longer or a behavior that is restricting you, you owe it to yourself to break free of unhealthy restrictions and create a life that reflects who you are today.

≈ *Tip for the Day* ≈
Think of at least one habit you've acquired as a result of being overweight—like avoiding belts—and resolve to try a new solution today.

"[Digestion is] the great secret of life."

SYDNEY SMITH

One of the most unpleasant side effects of eating a large meal is heartburn. In fact, about 10 percent of all United States adults get heartburn daily, and lying down after eating raises the risk of developing heartburn. The condition occurs when stomach acid backs up and irritates the esophagus. A fatty meal can trigger an episode by relaxing the sphincter and allowing the acid generated by digestion to back up the esophagus more easily.

There are several ways to lessen the chance of suffering from heartburn. One of the best ways is to lose weight because that will relieve abdominal pressure. It's also advisable to wait at least three hours after eating before lying down, then lie on your left side instead of your right. Avoid fatty foods, chocolate, alcoholic beverages and cigarettes. If heartburn persists, prop up your head or the head of your bed by about six inches. If the problem recurs on a regular basis, see a physician for a prescription drug that will suppress the production of stomach acid.

Eating a low-fat diet and keeping yourself active is a prescription for weight loss and a fit body. And fitness will also be enormously beneficial in preventing you from suffering from other discomforts as well.

≈ *Tip for the Day* ≈
Review your lifestyle. What can you change to prevent heartburn?

"Certainly, travel is more than the seeing of sights; it is a change that goes on, deep and permanent, in the ideas of living."

MIRIAM BEARD

One of the things many people comment on after visiting Europe is that people are trimmer, but seem to eat more—and richer—food than their American counterparts. The solution to this puzzle is that the Mediterranean lifestyle and cuisine are actually quite different from ours.

There is a larger emphasis on grains such as polenta, couscous and tabbouleh in Greek, Italian and southern French diets, so people there naturally eat a lot of fiber. They eat more poultry and fish than red meat, and there is an emphasis on using herbs such as oregano, tarragon, rosemary and thyme. Also, although people in the Mediterranean region eat high-fat cheeses, they eat far smaller portions than Americans; the flavors are so intense that a little bit goes a long way. Meatless protein sources such as hummus on pita bread are popular, and snacking is less common. One nutritional adviser to the World Health Organization says that the "appetizing, cheap, sweet and fat" snacks in America are the biggest downfall of American eaters. Finally, people in the Mediterranean are accustomed to walking and bicycling and being more active than those who live in our own automobile-driven culture.

Tip for the Day
Create a classic Mediterranean meal this week that contains many of the elements of this sound diet.

*"It is in his pleasure that a man really lives; it is from his leisure
that he constructs the true fabric of self."*
AGNES REPPLIER

Living means learning how to live a balanced life. It's
unhealthy to spend so much time at work that your leisure
time is either rushed or nonexistent. It's also unwise to spend
so much time caring for others that when it comes to
taking care of yourself you feel depleted of both time and energy.

It's not uncommon for people who live unbalanced lives to
feel deprived and then to indulge themselves with
a treat—usually food. To succeed at weight loss, it's
important to set up a schedule that includes enough time for
work and for pleasure, because the balance helps to
prevent turning to food for an emotional boost. One woman
who recognized this tendency in herself found that scheduling
a biweekly massage and taking a ceramics course helped her
feel happier and more in control of her life. This in turn less-
ened her desire to overeat whenever she felt under a great deal
of stress.

If your schedule is routinely filled with work obligations or
commitments to others, make sure you plan some nonfood
treats for yourself that will bring more balance into your life.
Think about joining a book club or investment club, or set
aside time each week to pamper yourself with an at-home manicure and some uninterrupted time with your favorite reading
material. From this important leisure time you'll ensure that
feelings of deprivation don't lead you to overeat and you'll get
back the sense of balance you may have lost.

↫ *Tip for the Day* ↬
*Make a list of activities that create feelings of warmth and satisfaction
and then make sure you include them in your schedule
at least once this week.*

"Truth is the only safe ground to stand on."

ELIZABETH CADY STANTON

When you are looking for solutions to weight problems, it's tempting to believe that there is a fast and painless way to success. As a result, many people buy questionable products to help them lose weight and tone their bodies but are usually disappointed by the lack of results. The sad reality is that permanent or beneficial change usually comes with hard work and perseverance.

Peggy says that before joining a balanced weight-loss program she bought lots of pills, candies and creams that were supposed to help her speed up her metabolism and lose weight. Few of them worked for long, if they worked at all. She found that rubbing lotions on areas with cellulite never made the problem go away, nor did sleeping with rubber bands around her body ever tone up her figure. What these experiences taught her, she says, is that eating right and exercising are the only ways to achieve long-term change.

Don't be seduced by the claims of companies that try to make you buy their products to help you lose weight, change your body's physique or erase the signs of aging. A weight-loss program that incorporates moderate meal planning with regular exercise is the most reliable way you'll be able to lose weight and keep it off. Although this truth may be more difficult to accept than some of the miracle cures you hear about, it is the only "safe ground" there is if you want to succeed.

Tip for the Day

Have realistic expectations about how long it will take to achieve your weight-loss and fitness goals.

"We can now prove that large numbers of Americans are dying from sitting on their behinds."

BRUCE B. DAN, M.D.

One of the first things you learn in Weight Watchers is that watching your diet carefully is not enough if you want to attain a healthy body and maintain your weight goal. Exercise is a key component in losing weight and regaining muscle tone. With exercise, you replace time once spent eating with an activity that benefits both your body and your mind.

Weight Watchers encourages members to exercise regularly for several reasons. First, exercise burns calories and promotes physical fitness. Second, exercise helps you create healthier behaviors that will enable you to reach and maintain your weight goal faster. Third, exercise is a well-known stress reliever and depression buster. Researchers have said that regular exercise can reduce anxiety, mild to moderate depression, tension and stress.

Be sure that your daily routine today involves a period of exercise. Find ways to incorporate aerobic movement into your normal activities. For example, park in the farthest spot at the grocery store, take the stairs instead of the elevator and walk to neighbors' houses instead of driving. You'll find that the more you make exercise a regular feature of your life, the easier it will be to have the body you've always wanted.

⋙ *Tip for the Day* ⋘
Set aside at least ten minutes today for a brisk walk.

"Television has proved that people will look at anything rather than each other."

ANN LANDERS

If you are overweight there's a good chance that you spend a lot of time sitting during the day. Some of that time may be devoted to television watching.

Anne, a fiftysomething weight-loss program member, says that she once fit this profile. She remembers feeling depressed about her size and too embarrassed to exercise, so television became her only friend. After joining a weight-loss program, she discovered new ways to fill her leisure time and now she has a new world of friends, activities and pleasures that have replaced the television. Instead of watching television and eating, she gardens, goes for walks, visits friends and tries to sit as little as possible.

Challenge yourself to watch as little television as possible today. Use those hours to do worthwhile activities such as exercising, volunteering and improving yourself in some way. You'll discover that the less you can sit passively and watch other people living life, the more you'll become vigorous, healthy and optimistic.

✎ *Tip for the Day* ✎
Limit your television viewing to just one program today.

*"I had to face facts, I was pear-shaped. I was a bit depressed
because I hate pears."*

CHARLOTTE BINGHAM

When Kyla joined a weight-loss program, she envisioned having long, lean legs when she reached her weight goal. She was disappointed to find, however, that becoming slender didn't change her basic shape, and that even at a low weight she was still bottom-heavy. She says she had unrealistic ideas about how she'd look when she lost weight and that she'd had to come to terms with the fact that she had a pear-shaped figure.

All of us probably think we have figure flaws—perhaps a round face, thick waist or very large breasts—that will magically disappear when we are thin. Many of your trouble spots *will* improve with weight loss and exercise, especially flabby arms and a sagging stomach, but some of them will not. For example, if the women in your family are short or the men are long-waisted and short-legged, you may simply take after them, and these characteristics will remain no matter how much weight you lose.

Examine your ideas about weight loss today. Do you retain the hope that you'll be transformed into something you can never be, or do you accept your genetic makeup? Work on loving yourself today, no matter what flaws you see. Be realistic about what your success will bring you. The more you can accept your body just as it is and banish any envy of others' bodies, the greater will be your self-esteem. You'll bring more confidence to every area of your life.

Tip for the Day
Focus on the areas of your life you can change,
not on the ones over which you have no control.

"Eat breakfast like a king, lunch like a prince,
and dinner like a pauper."

ADELLE DAVIS

One of the biggest misconceptions of people who want to lose weight is that skipping breakfast gives them a head start on losing weight that day. Unfortunately, as many know too well, skipping breakfast only leads to late-morning hunger and feelings of deprivation, resulting in snacking and large dinners later in the day. These two factors are usually cited as causes for excess weight. In fact, a study comparing people who were successful at maintaining weight loss with people who were prone to relapse found that the latter group skipped breakfast more often than the more successful group.

If you are trying to lose weight but still cling to the idea that breakfast is a meal to which you can give short shrift, remember that you are lessening your chances of success every time you skimp on your morning meal. Work on shifting more of your calories to the early part of the day so that you will have more energy to fuel your activities as well as time to burn those calories off. If you can successfully rearrange your meals so that you eliminate any desire to eat late in the day, you will have removed another temptation common to those who battle their weight.

➤ *Tip for the Day* ➤
Review your eating patterns. Resolve to eat a reasonable breakfast
every day this week.

"I cannot pretend to feel impartial about colours. I rejoice with the brilliant ones and am genuinely sorry for the poor browns."

WINSTON CHURCHILL

As you lose weight, the shape and dimensions of your body will change. You may be surprised to discover that you like parts of your body that you may have once disdained. One woman who lost 40 pounds says she was taken aback when she was dressing one morning. She discovered that for the first time in years she had definition in her collar bones. She had hidden behind long-sleeved turtlenecks for so many years that she had forgotten that part of her body could look sexy and pretty.

This woman's experience is not uncommon. People who have invested little energy on their appearance find that weight loss leaves them ill equipped to show off their new bodies. They suddenly need to replace their drab wardrobe with colorful clothes and accessories. Instead of working out in gray sweatpants, why not perspire in bright red or blue? If you want to call attention to your new waistline, wrap a bold scarf around your waist instead of that old brown belt.

Being more colorful means you will probably draw attention to yourself, something you may have avoided before if you were uncomfortable with your appearance. If this is the case, spend some time in the accessories department of a local store. Experiment with hats, scarves, belts and gloves in colors you may not have considered before and become comfortable with the new you. As you become more self-confident and your hard work begins to show, let your wardrobe reflect your new life in a rainbow of pretty hues.

≈ Tip for the Day ≈

Look at the colors of clothes in your closet today. Are they drab and designed to disguise instead of flatter? If so, make a commitment to yourself to add one colorful accessory to your wardrobe this week.

*"People who are always making allowances for themselves
soon go bankrupt."*

MARY PETTIBONE POOLE

For years Shelly made excuses about why she was overweight:
Her family had a weight problem, being a writer kept her near
the refrigerator all day and her husband enjoyed eating gourmet meals. It wasn't until Shelly saw a picture of herself next
to a Christmas tree ("Which one is the tree?" she remembers
thinking), that she realized she had no one to blame but herself for being overweight. After trying to lose weight on her
own and hitting a plateau, she joined a weight-loss program
and began to steadily lose weight for the first time in her life.

One of the best lessons Shelly learned while losing weight
was that her achievements could be realized if she worked toward them diligently. Using her weight-loss
experiences for motivation, Shelly decided to push herself
harder toward reaching a professional milestone. After
letting a novel languish on a shelf for years, she realized she
had to apply "the seat of [her] pants to the chair" and get back
to work. Shelly's efforts paid off. Just as she reached her weight
goal, she finished her novel and got it accepted for publica-
tion.

If you are still making excuses for yourself as to why you
can't achieve a certain goal, remember that this type of behavior will only leave you bankrupt eventually. Instead of looking
for reasons why you can't succeed, think of ways you can change
your circumstances to your advantage. The more you can
choose to see everything as a possibility, the closer you'll be to
your goals.

∞ *Tip for the Day* ∞

*If you catch yourself making excuses today, change them to affirmations
that you can achieve what you desire with perseverance and hard work.*

"I can resist anything but temptation."

OSCAR WILDE

For the person who is trying to lose weight, temptation is always just around the corner. You will be confronted with wedding cake at receptions, for example, or unexpected treats and snack foods at the office. Sometimes you may give in to temptation because it can silence a craving and prevent feelings of deprivation. But it's also smart to plan strategies to help you deal with these kinds of temptations. The more you can learn how to stick to your planned routine, the easier it becomes to handle trigger situations.

One way to deal with temptation is to postpone it. Tell yourself that you can eat what you desire, but only after you complete an onerous task. You might sweep out the garage, write to your congressperson, clean a closet, balance your checkbook or polish the silverware. By the time you finish, the urge to eat will be gone and you will have accomplished something you've been putting off.

Think of ways you can put aside temptation today. When you delay your gratification, you prevent spur-of-the-moment eating, which is a good lesson. And the more you can practice resisting temptation, the more strength you'll have to apply to other challenging situations.

 Tip for the Day
*Think of two ways you will distract yourself
when tempted by an unwanted snack.*

"Total absence of humor renders life impossible."
COLETTE

If you have been struggling with your weight for a very long time, you may have developed a cynical, antagonistic outlook on life. You may believe that you can never look the way you want. Or it's possible that you have played the role of the class clown for many years because you were embarrassed about your appearance. You may have felt that being jolly was a way to be acceptable to others.

Being overweight can be a very painful and shameful condition, giving us little to be happy about. But living without genuine laughter robs you of the opportunity to see the bright side of your challenges. One best-selling author who battled breast cancer has said that finding the funny side of losing her hair and a breast helped her cope with her fears and depression. Another well-known writer has written a book about how laughter helped him overcome a potentially fatal disease.

Instead of looking at what's upsetting and sad in your life today, look on the lighter side. For example, find the humor in how you handled a recent argument. Retell the story so that it is amusing. The more you can learn to see joy where you once saw only sadness or anger, the stronger and more resilient you'll become in every area of your life.

Tip for the Day
Find something funny today and have a genuine belly laugh over it. Share your laughter with a friend.

*"We are always in search of the redeeming formula,
the crystallizing thought."*

ETTY HILLESUM

If you have developed a healthy lifestyle that now includes
low-fat, nutritious foods rather than high-fat and highly processed ones, you have probably noticed a wide range of
benefits, including sounder sleep, weight loss, clearer skin
and improved digestion. One other effect that may not be as
noticeable, but that is equally beneficial, is clearer thinking.
Studies have shown that concentration peaks 15 minutes after
eating a nutritious, low-fat meal.

Experiment today to see if this is the case with you.
After eating a balanced, low-fat meal, assign yourself a
task that requires you to be attentive, such as balancing your
checkbook or reading a complicated newspaper story.
Analyze your cognitive abilities an hour or two later to see if
you feel as sharp as you did right after the meal. If it's true that
a healthy meal gives you a mental edge, arrange your day so
that you will tackle a difficult project after a meal, when your
mental abilities are at their peak. Whether you ponder a di-
lemma or write a memo, improved mental ability will help you
do a better job.

Tip for the Day
Observe the effects of a healthy, low-fat meal on your mental processes.

"Vegetarianism is harmless enough, though it is apt to fill a man with wind and self-righteousness."

SIR ROBERT HUTCHINSON

One of the most joked-about foods is beans because of the indigestion and discomfort they can induce. Because of past unpleasant experiences, some people steer away from bean dishes because they fear intestinal gas or they think they'll be dissatisfied with the meal. This problem has been solved with food enzymes that can be sprinkled on the bean dish and cooking techniques now make vegetarian meals tastier than they've ever been.

Beans and legumes are an important part of any sensible food plan because they provide fiber and essential nutrients without much fat. If you're unaccustomed to eating beans, spend some time learning about their healthful properties and the ways you can work them into your regular meals. Beans can take the place of meat in some dishes and bean derivatives, such as tofu, can be added to almost any dish because it takes on flavors easily and adds a lot of protein without saturated fat.

If you want to incorporate more vegetarian dishes into your meal plan, look for interesting recipes in the cooking section of your local newspaper or check out a vegetarian cookbook from the library. Many grocery stores have free recipes and recommendations for cooking in the produce section too. With the right combinations and cooking techniques, you can get all your daily nutritional needs met and still feel comfortable after your meals.

⋙ *Tip for the Day* ⋘
Try at least one new bean or legume dish this week.

"The self is not something ready-made, but something in continuous formation through choice of action."

JOHN DEWEY

For some people, it's hard even to imagine being slender or fit, or being able to shop for clothes without embarrassment, cross their legs without difficulty or pass a mirror without grimacing at their reflection. For them, starting or staying committed to a weight-loss and fitness program is difficult because the desired result seems so distant and unlikely.

If this is your tendency, one way to remain motivated is to streamline your goals and keep them simple. Instead of telling yourself that you have to do a number of things every day to be successful, pick just one thing to concentrate on, such as exercising more or avoiding fat or eating fiber or not snacking. This could also include exercising for just 15 minutes every day for a month or eating one-third less than normal for the same period of time. The trick is to get into the habit of doing one thing that will get you on the path to better fitness and well-being. This will help you build your self-confidence enough to believe that you can achieve your weight-loss goals.

Remember today that you can become the person you want to be, but that this involves taking one small step at a time. Trust that you will gradually start to believe that you will be successful. Start by choosing an action that doesn't overwhelm you and then stick to it for a reasonable period of time. You might be surprised to find that the more you can take little steps that carry you gradually toward your goal, the sooner you will become the person you desire.

≈ *Tip for the Day* ≈

Choose one small action today that can start to carry you toward having a behavior or characteristic you desire.

"Sport is imposing order on what was chaos."
ANTHONY STARR

One of the most important and necessary components of losing weight is including regular, aerobic exercise into your day. For many people this can be a challenge, especially in the beginning. But after awhile, exercise often becomes enjoyable, an activity that most look forward to doing.

Exercise has many side benefits apart from improving your physical well-being. First, setting aside regular time to exercise, especially when you are busy, imposes order on the day and helps to assign priorities to your tasks. Second, exercise boosts levels of endorphins, so-called feel good chemicals, making you feel happier afterward. Third, it imbues the exerciser with self-confidence. In one study 98 percent of the subjects who exercised reported improved self-esteem. Finally, exercise can revive a flagging sex life: It improves stamina and increases arousal, and the resultant weight loss makes you feel more attractive to your partner.

Keep in mind today that getting enough exercise will improve many other areas of your life besides your physical fitness. Instead of viewing exercise as a dreaded "must," remember that it will streamline your day, boost your energy and makes weight loss a much easier task.

Tip for the Day
Whenever your life feels chaotic, add some exercise.
It will give you the self-confidence to take charge.

"A schedule defends from chaos and whim."
ANNIE DILLARD

Some people who join Weight Watchers find the idea of writing down their meal plans too restrictive. "I can't remember what the right portion size is!" they protest, or "I don't have time to do all that!" But part of being successful with any weight-loss plan is becoming aware of exactly how much you are eating, what types of food you are eating and which food combinations make you feel best. To guess or be casual about meals invites chaos and unplanned eating.

When Sherry plans her week's meals every Sunday she finds that it takes a burden off her shoulders during the rest of the week. Instead of worrying each day about how to meet the program's requirements, she has a preplanned schedule that saves time and energy. Because she has a specific list when shopping for groceries, she finds that she is less prone to impulse purchases.

Make sure that you use meal planning to your advantage today. Take a few minutes to design some creative menus that will increase your satisfaction and reduce boredom. As you become accustomed to planning ahead and creating an environment for success, you'll find that the old adage, If you fail to plan, you plan to fail, is no longer true for you.

Tip for the Day
Make sure that your weekly meal plan is completed today.

*"For you to be successful, sacrifices must be made.
It's better that they are made by others but failing that,
you'll have to make them yourself."*

RITA MAE BROWN

When you begin a weight-loss program, be honest with yourself and make no promises that weight loss is going to be a snap. Although a good program is flexible and offers a variety of choices so you can make it work best for you, you still will have to make sacrifices and alterations in your life if you are to achieve your goals. While some of these changes won't be difficult, others will require a major readjustment of your behavior and activities.

One of the most important adjustments is learning not to turn to food for comfort when you are upset or anxious. Another sacrifice is varying your behavior so that you exercise regularly instead of sitting or sleeping. You may have to spend less time with friends who encourage you to overeat, or better, you may decide to make new friends with supportive people who don't try to sabotage your progress. Visits to favorite restaurants or fast-food places may also have to be forfeited and replaced with more healthful outings.

As you go about making changes in your life that will help you be more successful in the long run, try not to think of them as sacrifices. Assure yourself that new habits will eventually feel comfortable to you. Remember, too, that one of the most effective deterrents to regaining lost weight is behavior modification. This may not be easy at first, but the long-term benefits will prove to you that your efforts are worthwhile.

᠁ *Tip for the Day* ᠁
*Ask yourself if you're still holding on to behavior that is impeding your
progress and if you are truly willing to make necessary sacrifices
to achieve your goals.*

*"Change has considerable psychological impact on the human
mind. To the fearful it is threatening because it means that things
may get worse. To the hopeful it is encouraging because things
may get better. To the confident it is inspiring because the
challenge exists to make things better."*

KING WHITNEY, JR.

One woman discovered after reaching her weight goal and rejoining the work force that temptation on the job was difficult
to resist. At home she'd been able to create an environment of
nutrition, but at work she was constantly presented with pit-
falls like candy on colleagues' desks, fat-rich muffins in the
cafeteria and the midmorning pastry cart. After going up a
dress size, she decided to take action to make her office
healthier: She organized a thrice-weekly walking group, which
earned her boss's praise of her leadership skills. Another woman
found that the pastries and candy at her sobriety support group
were threatening her progress in weight loss, so she started a
popular meeting that didn't have food as a distraction.

You'll inevitably have to introduce change into your life if
you want to maintain progress in weight loss. If there is a situation at work or elsewhere that has a negative effect on your
efforts, confront it by suggesting cafeteria changes, an on-the-
job weight-loss support meeting or a midday exercise group.
Although it's always risky to be the one that stands out, it's
only by facing your challenges that you make progress toward
your goals.

᪣ *Tip for the Day* ᪣
*Be assertive about making changes in situations where your
health is threatened, such as being served unhealthful foods
or inhaling secondhand smoke.*

*"Working in the garden…gives me a profound feeling
of inner peace."*

RUTH STOUT

One of the ways therapists often encourage people to cope with
stress or anxiety is to spend time outdoors, especially gardening. Immersing yourself in an activity that occupies your mind
and keeps your hands busy can keep a negative mood away.
And if you are contemplating overeating, gardening removes
you from indoor temptations and places you in a sunny and
nurturing environment.

One way to make gardening an integral part of your weight-
loss efforts is to plant a vegetable garden that will supply you
with healthy foods. It's always more satisfying to eat something
you have planted and nourished. If you don't have space for a
garden you can always set aside some pots in the windowsill
for herbs, which can be grown indoors and will enliven any
meal.

Make a commitment to spend some time outdoors
today, particularly in a garden, if possible. Channel the
energy you once spent on overeating into growing things that
can nourish you and provide feelings of accomplishment. By
so doing, you will help your diet and you'll grow as a person,
too.

≈ Tip for the Day ≈
*Even if you don't have a green thumb, buy a plant that is easy to care
for, such as a pot of ivy. Every time you water or feed it, affirm to
yourself that you are nourishing yourself, too.*

"Although the world is full of suffering, it is full also
of the overcoming of it."

HELEN KELLER

Over the course of a lifetime many of us will face times of pro-found sadness, also known as "the blues." Studies have shown that current generations are far more likely to suffer from de-pression than previous generations and that women are twice as likely to be affected than men, particularly between the ages of 18 and 60. Chief among the symptoms are weight gain or weight loss and feelings of hopelessness and lethargy.

Susan found that despite reaching her weight goal, she still grappled with anxiety and sadness. During these periods, she wanted to pull down the shades and stay home all day. When these times hit, she'd also fight a desire to overeat, which scared her. After consulting with her physician, Susan started therapy. Within several months she not only felt relief from depression but she had more energy and her cravings dis-appeared. Susan's case isn't unusual; depression is a very treat-able illness and relief often comes in a relatively short period of time.

If you've been successful at weight loss yet are still plagued with feelings of sadness, anxiety or self-doubt, consult a pro-fessional. Sometimes you aren't always aware of forces that af-fect you and your feelings about food. But with the help of skilled professionals, you will understand yourself better. And you'll have more tools at your disposal to help you live a re-warding and healthy life.

Tip for the Day

Ask yourself if your down times are occurring too often or otherwise
interfering with your life. If so, ask your physician today to recommend a
mental health professional for you to see.

"One chops the wood. The other does the grunting."

YIDDISH PROVERB

Maria and Jonathan used to eat rich meals and complain about their weight together. After becoming increasingly unhappy with her appearance, Maria decided to join Weight Watchers and lose weight in a sensible way. Knowing how unhappy her husband was with his weight, Maria encouraged him to join with her. He refused, saying he didn't have the time to devote to it. Now, although Maria is trim again, Jonathan is still eating—and still complaining about being too heavy.

There are two distinct groups of people: those who take action and those who don't. Maria is one who "chops wood": She has done the hard work of confronting her weight problem and making the appropriate changes to be successful. Jonathan is the one who "grunts": He makes noises about his weight but never does anything about it. Experts say that people who prefer to complain more than attack their problems can't be forced into changing their habits. Until they decide for themselves to lose weight, nothing anyone else says or does will ever convince them to change.

If you're frustrated by grunters in your life, avoid lecturing them on what you think they should do. Instead, focus on being an example by silently continuing to do your own work in this area. Remind yourself that you won't get anywhere through confrontation or nagging. But if you remain positive, supportive and willing to help, you can be a positive influence.

⇜ *Tip for the Day* ⇝
Remember today to be a "chopper" and not a "grunter"
in everything you undertake.

"We think of vinegar as a very practical natural product."

JULEE ROSSO AND SHEILA LUKINS

To the uninitiated, vinegar is just an ingredient in salad dressing and a not very tasty one at that. But vinegar can be part of a healthful meal plan and even a versatile household helper. This is now especially true since the advent of "light cooking" has made vinegar such a desirable ingredient.

Here are some ways vinegar can help you, both in weight loss and around the house:

- Flavor vinegar with herbs such as rosemary, thyme, tarragon, oregano, dill or other pungent flavorings. This can add zip to any recipe that calls for vinegar.
- Make soured milk by adding 1 tablespoon white vinegar to a cup of milk.
- Make rice fluffier by adding a teaspoon of white vinegar to the boiling water just before stirring in the rice.
- Gently mix a pint of sliced fruit, such as strawberries, with two tablespoons of sugar and one tablespoon of balsamic vinegar for mouth-watering tang.
- Before serving bean or vegetable soups, splash in a teaspoon or two of red wine vinegar for tartness.
- Marinate and tenderize meats with vinegar.
- Add a tablespoon of vinegar to the water when poaching eggs to help the whites retain their shapes.
- Add vinegar to the cooking water of artichokes and red vegetables to prevent discoloring.

Tip for the Day
Instead of just thinking of vinegar as an adjunct to salad, explore ways to make it work elsewhere for you in the kitchen.

"Peanut butter is the pâté of childhood."
FLORENCE FABRICANT

Many overweight adults learned poor eating habits as children and may well have started grappling with weight problems at a very early age. In fact, studies have shown that girls who are overweight at three years of age have a 50 percent chance of being overweight adults. The same is true of boys who are overweight at the age of six.

If you have children, it's very important that you begin to instill good eating habits early. If their favorite food is peanut butter, it's a good idea to introduce them when they're young to less fatty sources of protein, such as cottage cheese or lean meats. If they spend much of their free time in sedentary pastimes like playing video games or watching television, insist that they join you in some fun, child-friendly fitness activities like raking leaves or a game of tag. Have healthy snacks available, such as fruit or popcorn. Make sure that chips or fast-food fare is a less convenient alternative.

Start today to set your children on the right road to good health. Begin by improving your own habits and model the kind of behavior that will give them the greatest chance of succeeding. Also, make information about nutrition available and talk about sensible choices they can make. Good health is probably the best gift you can ever give to yourself and your children. And when you share the essentials of creating this physical well-being with your children, you'll be giving them something that money can't buy.

❧ *Tip for the Day* ❧
Play with your children outdoors for at least an hour today. Ride bicycles or go for a hike. Or invite a niece or nephew to join you.

"It has long been my belief that in times of great stress, such as a four-day vacation, the thin veneer of family unity wears off almost at once, and you are revealed in your true personalities."

SHIRLEY JACKSON

Although vacations are meant to be fun experiences, they can be upsetting when you don't enjoy yourself or the experience doesn't match your expectations. When this happens, you might be inclined to revert to old eating habits, partly to soothe yourself and partly because you believe that being on vacation means you can be on vacation from your weight-loss program as well.

Peggy once thought that she deserved to overeat whenever she went on vacation. As a result, she'd lose weight before she went and then she'd have to buy bigger clothes to come home in. Gwen also suffered from what she called "vacation brain." If she started to snack on the plane or in the car, she'd give herself license to overeat during the rest of the vacation because she figured she'd already blown it.

Remember today that going on vacation means you have to prepare yourself emotionally ahead of time to stay committed to your program. Explain to others that you need their support now more than ever. Carry pictures of yourself at a high weight to remind yourself of your goals. Or see if you can attend a support group meeting wherever you go. The more realistic you can be about the temptations and distractions of being on vacation, the better you can arm yourself to return in a positive and successful frame of mind.

Tip for the Day

Think about previous vacations you've taken when you overindulged. What will you do differently to make your next vacation successful?

"When I am attacked by gloomy thoughts, nothing helps me so much as running to my books. They quickly absorb me and banish the clouds from my mind."

MICHEL EYQUEM DE MONTAIGNE

A wonderful antidote to feeling down or being preoccupied with personal concerns is to immerse yourself in a good book. When you read, you can accomplish many things: You can transport yourself to a fictional world, pick up new self-help tips from an expert in the field, discover a new recipe to try later and learn about a part of the world you've never seen. There are also many magazines to choose from, so you can always find a periodical that satisfies your urge to read, whether it's about celebrities, entertaining, decorating, fashion, food, literature or computers.

If you feel blue or unsettled today and find yourself rummaging around the kitchen for cookies, grab a book or magazine instead and take a respite. By doing this you will give yourself a much-needed break, and you may learn a new technique for bench-pressing or read an inspiring story of someone's motivation to reach a goal or get ideas for a family getaway. You always are learning when you're reading, so set aside time today to leave your cares behind and broaden your horizons.

Tip for the Day

Is there a certain magazine or periodical that you buy every month?
If so, treat yourself to a subscription today
for 12 months of pleasure to come.

*"I think wholeness comes from living your life consciously
during the day and then exploring your inner life
or unconscious at night."*

MARGERY CUYLER

Before Marge joined a weight-loss program she had a persistent dream of going up to the front door of a large house and
being unable to get in. She recalled that she would knock and
knock, but no one would let her in. After successfully changing her eating and exercise habits, the dream changed significantly. She was now able to get into the house, she says, which
to her meant that before she lost weight she felt shut out of
life.

As you lose weight and develop healthier behaviors, you'll
become more aware of your true emotions and feelings and
not mask your needs with food. Instead of turning to food,
learn to sit quietly and try to decipher why you are feeling a
certain way and what you can do if you need to make a change.
A key time when many people are given clues about their internal state is in the dream state, when the subconscious can
communicate without restrictions. Through dreams you can
often face areas of your life that need attention or behaviors
that are holding you back.

Before you go to bed tonight, think about your plans for
weight loss and allow yourself to receive useful information
from your subconscious. Quite frequently you will awaken with
an image or word in your head that may be significant, like
seeing yourself being "shut out" of life. If you can learn to tap
into the power of your mind at night as well as during the day,
you'll have access to some of the best guidance available.

⟐ *Tip for the Day* ⟐
*Keep a notebook and pencil by your bedside tonight and jot down any dream or
image that may have to do with weight loss.*

"The most dangerous food is wedding cake."

AMERICAN PROVERB

Lily is successful in withstanding the temptations of fattening foods and sweets when she is eating or at a party, but the one social gathering that always presents a problem is a wedding. She says she feels guilty if she doesn't eat the wedding cake because she wants to enter into the celebration with everyone else. But when she does succumb to this temptation, she tell herself that she has "blown" her week and there is no need to continue to eat properly.

People pleasing is a tendency that many overweight people have. Because you don't feel good about yourself, you often cater to others in the mistaken notion that it will make you happy. Eating cake at a wedding, sampling the homemade pies Mom has baked especially for you or going back for seconds at a dinner party are just some of the ways you act this out. The problem with this—other than it derails your meal plan—is that it keeps you from being in control of your own life.

Practice looking in the mirror and saying a polite "no thank you" for the times you are plied with unwanted food at a wedding or other social gathering. When you actually get a chance to say no, you might be pleasantly surprised to discover that most people aren't as concerned about your intake as you are.

❧ *Tip for the Day* ❧
Think about various parties and weddings you've attended and how you handled the food that was offered. Can you think of ways to behave differently next time?

"There is a great difference between a good physician and a bad one."

ARTHUR YOUNG

A study of overweight women showed that most put off even routine visits to the doctor, citing a fear of the scales or embarrassment about ill-fitting paper gowns. The main reason most avoided going to the doctor, however, was because the doctor made them feel ashamed of their weight. When asked about birth control, one physician replied to an overweight woman, "What would *you* need it for?" The study also found that the doctors also frequently cited the excess weight as the cause of a medical problem, neglecting to do a thorough exam to rule out other possibilities.

If you have been the victim of bias or rudeness because of your weight, it's important that you find someone with whom you are comfortable and who will treat you with dignity. Putting off checkups that are potentially life saving because of one doctor's attitude will only hurt you. You deserve the right to the same medical care as anyone else—whether overweight or thin—and avoiding medical care because of embarrassment will only potentially endanger your health.

Ask friends for recommendations and be up front about your feelings at your first appointment. Finding a doctor who will take time to listen to your concerns, support you in your weight-loss efforts and help you develop a healthy lifestyle is one of the best investments of time you can make in yourself and your future.

Tip for the Day

Persevere in your search for a physician who can address your concerns with understanding and dignity.

"The cherry tomato is a marvelous invention, producing as it does a satisfactorily explosive squish when bitten."
JUDITH MARTIN

Most people, whether their weight is an issue or not, are conscious of the texture of the foods they eat. Food texture refers to the feel of the food when it is being eaten, such as soft, hard, crunchy, creamy, chewy and so on. Texture is one of the qualities that makes food interesting and enjoyable to eat. But be careful not to confuse texture with taste. Elinor, for example, says she was once quick to associate chewy with sweet (caramels) and crunchy with salt (potato chips). But now she turns to a good steak or the skin of a baked potato when she desires chewy foods. Her favorite crunchy food is fresh sugar-snap peas in the spring from her sister's garden. And most important, she points out that all these foods are easily part of a nutritious food plan.

Perhaps there are some foods that you don't like simply because of their textures. Louis likes the flavor that mushrooms add to various dishes, but he'll always pass up a real mushroom. It's too rubbery, he says, adding that shrimp has a similar texture as far as he is concerned.

If you are trying to lose weight, pay attention to the way food feels in your mouth. When you eat fast and bolt your food, you're not giving yourself a chance to enjoy the texture of what you're eating. When you appreciate all the qualities of food—not just the salt or sugar content—you derive more satisfaction than merely the fullness in your stomach or the taste on your tongue.

Tip for the Day
Be aware today of the texture of the foods you are eating. Resolve to add five minutes to each meal so that you take the time to pay attention to what's in your mouth.

"If people only knew how hard I work to gain my mastery, it wouldn't seem so wonderful at all."

MICHELANGELO BUONARROTI

All of us want wonderful things to come in our lives such as fulfilling relationships, good health, becoming widely respected for something we do well and financial freedom. But these things don't just happen; you have to prepare the way for good to come to you. One way to begin is by doing for others. Here are some simple steps:

- If you want to receive, give. Before buying a whole new wardrobe, give away some ill-fitting clothes to a worthy charity, like a shelter for homeless men or battered women. By thinking of those who have less, you may feel that you need less than you once thought.
- Make choices. No one has everything at once, so narrow your goals. One woman decided that she couldn't manage being both full-time mother *and* a law-firm partner. She decided to stay home while her children were small and return to work at a later date. She fulfilled her professional desires by volunteering her legal services to her children's preschool.
- Work toward your goal every day. If you want a beautifully decorated house but you're low on funds, browse in stores for ideas. A clever way of arranging the furniture might inspire a no-cost renovation.
- Be thankful for what you *do* have. The more attention you give to your blessings, the likelier they are to increase. When you nourish the good things in your life, they will gain strength and multiply.

Tip for the Day

Remind yourself that most lucky breaks are the result of patience and hard work. Do two things today to improve your luck.

"Progress is based on perfect technology."

JEAN RENOIR

An invention that has had a huge impact on the way Americans do both business and personal work is the computer. While the personal computer is often used for a variety of personal functions, it can also be used for health and fitness purposes.

If you have a computer or access to one, look into programs that might be useful in your weight-loss efforts. Some, for example, will simplify your week by planning your menus with the ingredients you specify. They can also analyze your nutritional intake, letting you know whether you achieved recommended levels of nutrients and vitamins. There are also programs that will organize your recipes, modify them according to your specifications and print them out on demand.

Many health clubs and YMCAs also use computers to provide a general assessment of your fitness. After a series of easy tests and measurements, computer programs can analyze your aerobic fitness, body composition, flexibility, muscular strength and endurance. This type of information is useful in helping to set up dietary and exercise guidelines specifically for you.

Computers are now within financial reach of most people, especially considering how quickly models are discounted when technology moves ahead. If you haven't yet explored ways you can use the computer to assist you in creating a healthy lifestyle, do so today. Go to a computer store and browse, see if your local library has a computer for use and ask friends who have computers for ideas about networks you can join where you can interact with supportive people. Using a computer can always make life more efficient, but with the right software it can also give you a healthier lifestyle.

～ *Tip for the Day* ～
*Try using a computer to help you track your nutrition
and exercise activity.*

"People who make some other person their job are dangerous."
DOROTHY L. SAYERS

If you have made changes in your lifestyle that have resulted in weight loss and more vitality, you probably are eager to share your joy with others. If you decide that you are going to use your experiences to change another person, you're probably in for disappointment because it's impossible to control others or make them do as you want. You may even have the opposite effect on them, causing them to dig in their heels and persist in their self-defeating behavior.

One woman who successfully lost weight decided to focus next on her overweight son. She offered him a new stationary bicycle and a health club membership. She even took bags of fresh vegetables to his house to try to encourage him to adopt a healthier lifestyle. His reaction was simply to become more defensive about his eating and exercise habits.

However tempting it might be, don't make anyone else your job today. If you continue to follow your new lifestyle and the results invite queries or compliments, that is the time to share your point of view. Foisting yourself on others is likely to make them feel inadequate and angry, and it may end your relationship with them.

Tip for the Day
Focus on improving only yourself. Allow others to make choices different from yours, even if you feel their choices are unwise.

"I never saw an ugly thing in my life: for let the form of an object be what it may, —light, shade, and perspective will always make it beautiful."

JOHN CONSTABLE

Quite often when people are overweight they develop the conviction that they are unattractive and sexless. Monica was breathtaking on her wedding day but 100 pounds overweight several years later. She felt that when she walked into a grocery store, men avoided eye contact and no one flirted with her anymore. It was difficult to find clothes that were stylish and flattering. She felt ugly.

The fact is, however, that Monica is still very pretty. She has begun to take charge of her life by joining Weight Watchers and she is slowly losing weight now. But because she still has periods of feeling unattractive, she doesn't always take the time to enhance her best features. It's important that you not neglect your self-care rituals just because you're overweight. Study the makeovers in women's magazines, and watch television shows that feature the latest styles. Sometimes a new haircut or color, a different shade of lipstick or carefully tweezed brows can provide a lift and give you the self-esteem you need to feel pretty, positive and self-confident.

Make grooming an essential part of every day. Invest in items that will make your makeup ritual more enjoyable, such as good hair-styling aids, high quality cosmetic brushes and sponges and makeup that matches your skin tone and features. Everyone can enhance her best features with some careful attention. Decide that you are worthy of the effort and then make sure to follow through.

Tip for the Day
Analyze the makeup items you have, then schedule a free makeover at the cosmetic counter of a nearby department store.

"Variety is the soul of pleasure."
APHRA BEHN

One night when Kristine was doing her grocery shopping she lingered in the produce section. She looked longingly at some of the vegetables and fruits she wanted to include in her meal planning, but she felt she couldn't afford them. She wound up purchasing the usual items on her list, but then on the way home stopped at a doughnut store where she bought and ate a half-dozen doughnuts. She realized as she drove home that she'd spent more on her overeating than she would have spent on imported red peppers. As a result she now buys healthful foods, even if they seem expensive, because she knows she's investing in herself and staying committed to her weight-loss goals.

Are you excluding certain types of foods from your meals because they appear to be too expensive? Has this resulted in a lack of variety in your meals? If so, consider treating yourself regularly to some of the items you long for—like out-of-season fruits, imported vegetables or impeccably fresh fish. Weigh their costs against what previous episodes of overeating have cost. Use splurging on good food as a form of insurance to keep you from feeling deprived and bored with your meals. It could be the best purchase you'll ever make.

⋙ *Tip for the Day* ⋘
Spend some time at the supermarket identifying foods that would make your meals feel more special, like fresh shrimp or kiwi fruit.

"A ship in port is safe, but that's not what ships are built for."
GRACE MURRAY HOPPER

Entering a weight-loss program is a very brave step for a person to take. It's not easy to admit to a group of strangers that you need help structuring a lifestyle that includes balanced eating and exercise habits. It's also hard to develop the discipline that enables you to succeed at weight loss.

But once you've seen that you are capable of setting weight-loss goals for yourself and reaching them, it's important to broaden your horizons in other areas. If self-consciousness and excess weight have caused you in the past to avoid social gatherings and reaching out to meet others, this is the time to try those things. While it may be scary to attempt something new, to risk being disappointed and appear vulnerable to others, being uncomfortable indicates that you are making an effort to experience as much of life as possible. And the more you attempt to spread your wings and fly, the further and higher you are bound to take yourself.

Think of ways you can challenge yourself to learn and ex-perience new activities. You'll find that the more you can do this, the more likely you'll be to create an exciting lifestyle that matches the new body you're working so hard to create.

꿍 *Tip for the Day* 꿍
Analyze ways you make yourself feel safe and decide to try at least one new endeavor that challenges that feeling, such as offering to head a committee for a group to which you belong.

*"Take away the miseries and you take away some folks'
reason for living."*

TONI CADE BAMBARA

Cassie was certain that no one would ever love her because
she was so heavy. She built a wall around herself, assuming
that everything that was a problem in her life pertained to
being overweight. Eventually she dropped 75 pounds but was
surprised to discover that she was still plagued with insecuri-
ties and unresolved anger. With the help of a therapist Cassie
learned that for years she had used her weight to mask other
unrelated problems.

For some people, excess weight is an easy rationale to explain away problems. But it's not always the real cause. When
you set out to lose weight, ask yourself if you have used your
weight in the past as an excuse for not trying something new
or to explain why you didn't get hired for a job you wanted. If
so, you need to look within and find other reasons for what
happens in your life. Part of your weight-loss program should
include learning how to improve your behavior or attitude.
Otherwise, you'll be vulnerable to going back to overeating so
that you can hide behind a weight problem again.

When you no longer have extra weight on your body, will
you feel secure about yourself? If not, it's a good idea to look at
how big a role talking about your weight and your efforts to
shed it plays in defining who you are and what you want out of
life. To be successful at weight loss and in life, you need to
have motivations in your life that are positive and beneficial.

∽ *Tip for the Day* ∽
*Do you spend a lot of time complaining about your weight? Will you have
something else to talk about when you are slender?*

"He wants the natural touch."

WILLIAM SHAKESPEARE

When you're tired or your muscles ache and you want to comfort yourself without turning to food, try acupressure. Acupressure is an ancient Asian healing art of pressing key areas on the body that are thought to stimulate natural healing.

One quick way to relieve shoulder tension is to hook one arm behind your neck and reaching over to the opposite shoulder. Press hard into the shoulder muscle for 15 seconds. To relieve mental tension and anxiety, use your thumbs to press upward at the base of your skull. Strained eyes will benefit from using your three middle fingers to press on the eye socket area just under your eyebrows. To eliminate sinus and arthritis pain, squeeze the fleshy area between the thumb and forefinger. Be careful, however, of working on skin that is ulcerated or infected.

Consider an alternative health technique to supplement your health care today. The next time you are feeling irritable, confused, sad or tired, use acupressure as a free and effective resource. Learning how to undo some of the damage that stress, worry and tension can have on your body will bring more physical balance in your life.

⟡ *Tip for the Day* ⟡
Use acupressure today whenever you are feeling
tired, anxious or achey.

"Gluttony is an emotional escape, a sign something is eating us."
PETER DE VRIES

Stress is an unavoidable part of everyone's life, but, if constant, uncontrolled stress can affect your health and your relationships with others. Stress can also trigger a ruinous cycle of eating to calm yourself, which adds extra pounds, which means more stress. A clinical psychologist who is an expert on stress states that stress makes you feel like you're chronically in over your head, and when you're continually in a situation you can't master your self-esteem will begin to suffer. Although the tensions and obligations of everyday life are unavoidable, there are some things you can do to manage stress better.

First, accept the fact that you can't do it all. Hire outside services to help with house and yard cleaning. Teach family members how to pitch in; your spouse and children can help with picking up toys and newspapers and loading the dishwasher. They may not do it as perfectly as you'd like, but it's better than trying to do it all yourself. Next, create a routine so that you can keep up with ongoing tasks like paying bills or doing laundry. Attending to chores regularly is less stressful than falling behind. Finally, practice patience. You might as well learn to be more tolerant of delays because they're probably not going to go away. That traffic jam on the thruway is going to be there every morning, so expect it instead of letting it anger you.

There is no magic formula to remove the stress from your life. But you can become aware of the kinds of stress that are hardest on you. Self-knowledge is an important step toward taking care of yourself. And when you begin to make choices that benefit you, you're well on your way to managing stress effectively.

Tip for the Day
Ask yourself what kinds of stress are likely to send you to the refrigerator.
Decide what you will do to provide relief besides eating.

"They were so strong in their beliefs that there came a time when it hardly mattered what exactly those beliefs were; they all fused into a single stubbornness."

LOUISE ERDRICH

Many people have rigid ideas about food and eating because of what they've heard about certain foods. Although these ideas have been around for a long time and some will withstand scrutiny, others are simply not true. For example, you may worry that cooking vegetables kills all vitamins, but this is not true. If cooked properly, vegetables will retain most nutrients, color and flavor. Use a minimum amount of water or oil and cook only until vegetables are tender yet crisp. Steaming and stir-frying will give you nutritious veggies every time.

It is commonly thought that only children need milk and other dairy products. In fact, adults need milk too. Foods that are high in calcium keep bones strong and help prevent the effects of aging and osteoporosis. Another assumption is that a glass or two of water daily is sufficient. But the human body requires 6 to 8 cups of water each day to keep your internal organs running smoothly and your electrolytes in balance. Protein is necessary to build and repair muscles, but most Americans already consume plenty. Extra protein does not increase strength; carbohydrates and fats are what supply energy to muscles.

To be successful at weight loss you must understand various foods' properties and their effects on you because they can help or hinder your efforts. If you find yourself avoiding certain foods because of something you've been told, investigate whether this is based in fact. Sorting fact from fiction can underscore the importance of including some foods in your regimen and eliminate notions that may be preventing you from enjoying a pleasurable dish.

꘎ Tip for the Day ꘎
Instead of believing everything you've heard about certain foods or substances, experiment on yourself to see if the theory holds up.

"[Time is] the most valuable thing a man can spend."

THEOPHRASTUS

The next time you are faced with 10 or 15 spare minutes, turn it to your advantage by getting a quick, efficient workout. Here is what trainers suggest for people who are pressed for time but still want to be in shape.

First, have a pair of hand weights available. Start with two minutes of marching in place with vigorous arm-swinging to warm up the muscles. Then do a minute of stretching the major muscle groups—back, chest, arms and legs. Perform as many pushups as you comfortably can in 60 seconds. If regular pushups are too difficult, push up from your knees instead of your feet. Next, use the hand weights to firm up your triceps. Grasping the weight with an overhand grip, flex your arm and extend your elbow up over your head. Extend your arm fully overhead, then slowly and carefully lower the weight to the starting position. Repeat with the other arm. Another easy exercise is to hold the weights at chest height and flex and extend your elbows by moving the weights in and out for one minute. Follow this with several minutes of sit-ups and crunches for your abdomen. Now do some squats while holding the weights and then finish with some gentle stretches.

To ensure that you do the exercises properly, buy a fitness magazine, rent a video or ask a trainer to show you the right movements. If this workout gets boring, create one with your own favorite movements. By using a spare bit of your time to improve yourself, you'll find that even the busiest person can have a toned body.

⟡ *Tip for the Day* ⟡
Design a ten-minute workout for yourself. Be sure to include some stretching, light weight work and abdominal exercises.

"Art is the desire of a man to express himself, to record the reactions of his personality to the world he lives in."

AMY LOWELL

Art therapy is often used to help people with food or behavior obsessions. Through drawing, sculpting a clay figurine or working with other decorative techniques, a person can use self-expression to help the therapist identify the areas that need the most healing. One woman who often turned to food when angry drew herself as a person without a mouth; this helped her realize she couldn't speak up for herself. As a result, part of her therapy included assertiveness training so that she could learn how to state her needs without using food to express her anger.

Try your hand at artwork depicting how you feel about yourself. Select some paper and writing utensils and then draw yourself. Analyze the type of emotion that emanates from your picture. Do you use bright colors and bold strokes? Or are you small and defenseless without much definition? Although you may think you know why food is a problem in your life, it can be helpful to allow your subconscious to express itself and you will undoubtedly learn something valuable about yourself.

Art can also become a wonderful hobby that creates feelings of fulfillment as well. Check a local art studio or community college for art appreciation courses. If you want to learn how to draw, sign up for a drawing course for "nonartists." Use the world of art, color and design to help you see the world in a new way as well as express your feelings about your place in the world.

Tip for the Day
Explore new ways of self-expression today. You may wish to consider ceramics, landscaping, gardening, weaving or building models.

"Every man shall bear his own burden."

GALATIANS 6:5

Sam was ready to embark on a weight-loss program, but he was annoyed about his wife. Although she was willing to prepare nutritious meals as recommended by his program, she didn't like to exercise with him. If, like Sam, you're waiting for someone else—a close friend, spouse or significant other—to take charge and tell you what to do, committing to a sensible lifestyle and healthy eating habits may be an unsettling experience. Instead of counting on other people to help you achieve your goals, you must take individual responsibility to eat carefully, exercise regularly and change your behavior. Yes, you need positive support and encouragement, but the ultimate responsibility rests on you.

If you haven't been successful at weight loss, examine your ideas about self-responsibility. Are you comfortable making your own decisions and working to reach your goals? Or do you usually count on others to help you? Be honest with yourself as you reflect on these questions. Ask yourself if you're really ready to do what it takes to change your lifestyle. You'll find that as soon as you are determined to be responsible for the steps that will lead you to success, achieving your goals will be easier than you think.

Tip for the Day

Think of areas in your life where you take the initiative to change situations that aren't working for you. Can you come up with a lot of examples, or do you abandon your efforts when the going gets tough?

"You always pass failure on the way to success."

MICKEY ROONEY

Not all people succeed at weight loss on their first try. Some people may not truly be ready within themselves to change their behavior positively. Others may not have the support they need from family and friends to maintain a healthy lifestyle. Whatever the reason, if you are trying once again to lose weight after past "failures," don't be pessimistic about your chances for success this time. Your previous experiences may very well have taught you valuable lessons.

Karyn says her pattern with weight-loss organizations used to be "join and quit, join and quit," until she met someone who fired up her enthusiasm and convinced her that she could be successful. The leader likened the challenges of weight loss to avoiding potholes—even if you hit one, you learn to steer more carefully and keep going. With this new attitude, Karyn proceeded to lose 30 pounds. She says it's a wonderful feeling not to be afraid of what the scale will say when she gets on it now.

If you've lost your confidence because you've failed at weight loss or some other endeavor in the past, remind yourself that you have the choice right now to make your present different. Review what you gained from your past attempts and incorporate those lessons into making your current effort successful. Everyone will fail at something at some point. But the wise ones use the opportunity to create a brighter future.

⟿ *Tip for the Day* ⟿
Remind yourself that the past is over and that your only goal is to make today the best it can be.

"Happiness is that state of consciousness which proceeds from the achievement of one's values."

AYN RAND

Susan Thesenga, the author of *The Undefended Self*, believes that many of our counterproductive habits, like overeating, are repetitive reactions to trying unsuccessfully to get our most important needs met. These simple human requirements—care, nurturance, attention and appreciation of one's uniqueness—can only be met through loving and being loved, but some people turn to food, sex, work and other distractions instead. The result, Thesenga says, is that you become "numb" and your habits intensify. For example, if at first it took only an hour of television and a bag of popcorn to satisfy your inner longings, you will eventually crave and feel you need greater amounts of these things to get the same result.

The solution is to have contact with other people instead of quieting your feelings with momentary gratification. Food doesn't provide internal happiness, but being with others does. So if you are lonely and food is your main friend, it's important to acknowledge that you need more contact with other people. Joining a weight-loss program is one good solution, but there are many other ways to find companionship. Get active in your church or volunteer your time and expertise to a service organization. One retired woman found an innovative way to generate and receive love by volunteering as a "hand holder" during eye surgery.

The next time you find yourself turning to food, ask yourself if your needs can be better satisfied by being with others or by being of service in some way. When you can address your longings in a way that enriches and uplifts you, the healthier and happier you will be.

◆◇ *Tip for the Day* ◇◆
*Call your local hospital today and find out how to join
one of their volunteer groups.*

"['Summer' is] the most beautiful word in the English language."
ANONYMOUS

Many people like to embark on a weight-loss program in the summer months because they realize that they can't camouflage their excess weight under bulky sweaters and coats. One man who joined a weight-loss program during the summer months says his impetus was that his daughters had asked him to go swimming with them and he'd been too embarrassed by his weight to do it. He realized that he was not just upsetting himself by being overweight; he was also disappointing his kids.

There are a number of reasons why summer can be a good time of year to begin a weight-loss plan. There is the obvious motivation of seeing thin people in shorts, sleeveless shirts and bathing suits. It's also normal for the body to desire less food when the weather is warm because your metabolism slows down. The availability of fresh fruit and vegetables at roadside stands and supermarkets also makes preparing light, low-fat meals much easier.

If you are just embarking on a weight-loss program, take advantage of what the summer offers to help make your efforts successful. Enjoy the pleasant weather by getting outdoors and exercising. Load up on farm-fresh produce for nutritious meals. Although weight loss can be successful during any time of the year, these next few months can provide you with a number of benefits that will make your job that much easier.

Tip for the Day
Cooking outdoors is one feature of the summer that can help you to eat more effectively. Ask yourself what other reasons to either eat or exercise more effectively the summer has to offer.

"A man can do all things if he but wills them."

LEON BATTISTA ALBERTI

Two authors set out to study men and women who'd been successful at losing weight and keeping it off for many years. One of the common tendencies they discovered was that these people set realistic and attainable goals. Instead of vowing never to eat chocolate cake again, for example, successful weight losers decided to have it only occasionally. They also looked for gradual improvement instead of perfection. These men and women had "I will do" goals, not "I will be" goals. Instead of vowing to be more athletic, for example, their goal would be to do a specific athletic activity, such as walk three miles three times a week. They avoided using *should* or *have to* when talking to themselves. If they were tempted at a picnic by fried chicken, they'd say, "I choose not to have that food." In this way, they controlled the food, not the other way around.

Think about the way in which you set goals for yourself. Does only flawless behavior satisfy you? If so, try to emulate the outlooks of these successful men and women and be more moderate in your approach.

“ *Tip for the Day* ”
Develop two short-term goals today,
and make them action oriented and achievable.

"I generally avoid temptation unless I can't resist it."
MAE WEST

There are times when following a weight-loss program feels effortless and temptation is a million miles away. These are usually periods in your life when you feel secure and in charge. There are also times when you don't feel so secure, however, and food looms large in your thinking. It is these moments that you must prepare for because this is what can knock you off balance and cause you to abandon your meal plan.

Research has shown that there are several times in your life when you are most at risk for gaining weight. Several of the most difficult times concern employment status. If you're home all day, you're more vulnerable to snacking than people who aren't. One group of stay-at-home mothers solved this problem by forming a co-op and trading afternoons off so they could exercise. Another risky time is reentering the work force. The stress of reentry often throws exercise and eating habits into chaos. Experts suggest scheduling lunchtime walks or exercise classes to ensure continuity in exercising. Make mealtime easier by preparing meals ahead on weekends and freezing them. The Crock-Pot is another friend to the working person who wants a hot, low-fat meal waiting when he or she arrives home at night.

Keep in mind today that everyone has times that make one especially vulnerable to overeating. To cope with them successfully, you must have strategies worked out to help you avoid temptation. Whether your toughest times are vacations, after quitting smoking or during spells of the blues, remembering that you need extra support and preparing for those times is a wonderful way to enhance your chances of success.

∞ *Tip for the Day* ∞
Whenever you have a major change in your life, be careful about becoming distracted or slipshod in preparing meals or getting enough exercise.

"No time like the present."

MARY DELARIVIER MANLEY

A respected doctor, an expert in heart disease, has helped thousands of patients significantly improve their health by radically changing their life and their meals. By reducing the amount of fat in their diet, walking regularly, participating in group discussions and stretching with an activity like yoga, men and women who were once given a short time to live now are thinner and healthier than they've been in years. While they once craved rich, artery-clogging foods, they now say they prefer lower-fat alternatives.

Some people find it easier if their lifestyle changes are immediate rather than gradual. For example, instead of slowly reducing the amount of mayonnaise in their sandwiches over time, they start right out on nonfat alternatives. For many people this is the approach that produces the most beneficial results. Comprehensive changes can make you feel better fast, the doctor explains, and that's a great motivator.

If you are the type of person who thrives on making a clean break with the past, go "all the way" and move quickly toward a goal. Instead of slowly reducing your reliance on fatty meats, try eating only legumes and low-fat proteins. And instead of gradually weaning yourself off caffeine or artificial sweeteners, cut them out completely today. While this radical approach may not work for everyone, if you are motivated by making positive, sweeping changes, you may want to seize today and move boldly toward one of your goals.

⟶ *Tip for the Day* ⟵

Ask yourself if pronounced changes might work better for you than gradual changes. Is there something you could accomplish better by doing it all at once?

"The one way to get thin is to re-establish a purpose in life."
CYRIL CONNELLY

There are times when you may have overeaten because you're bored or don't have a clearly defined purpose. Coming to Weight Watchers helps give you a direction because you select a weight goal and learn how to get there one step at a time. Many people find that when they start on the path to lose weight, they're also motivated to change other areas in their life that are stagnant.

Brenda found that the closer she got to her weight goal, the more she reevaluated how she felt about her office job, which had become unfulfilling. Getting her life together on a personal level gave her self-confidence and strengthened her resolve to go back to school and get a teaching degree. Being slim opened up new avenues, she says, because she didn't feel like she had to hide behind other people or a desk anymore.

Focus on more than your weight goal today. Focus on goals you can set for yourself in other parts of your life too. Is there a person you'd like to meet, a career you'd like to check out or a trip you'd like to take that you put off for weight's sake? Set specific goals for yourself and map out the steps you need to take to get there. If you can transfer your success at weight loss to success in making changes in other areas of your life, you will have more than a new body; you'll have a new life.

Tip for the Day

Begin to make plans for a special goal today. Decide what needs to be done to solve the problem of time or money so that your goal can become a reality.

"And sometimes we are devils to ourselves / When we will tempt the frailty of our powers..."

WILLIAM SHAKESPEARE

Sandra decided to lose the weight that she had gained when she injured her knee and couldn't exercise. Within several months she reached her weight goal and began a maintenance program. She also started to bring some of her former tempting foods into the house to see if she was "strong enough" to have them around. Gradually Sandra started to nibble on the snacks and bake rich desserts, which eventually caused her to regain her weight. Now as she works back to her weight goal, she says she won't make the mistake of tempting herself this time.

If you are trying to reach or maintain your weight goal, it is subtle sabotage to surround yourself with fattening foods or voluntarily put yourself into situations that might provoke overeating. Rather than risk temptation and end up overeating, try to make your environment as conducive to success as possible. You may be able to withstand temptation most of the time, but don't overwhelm yourself with temptation.

There may be a time in the future when you are comfortable having these foods in your house. If you have any doubts about your strength, stock up instead on healthy foods and eliminate temptations.

Tip for the Day

Clean out your cupboards of foods that might sabotage your healthy eating plans.

"The voice of the sea speaks to the soul. The touch of the sea is sensuous, enfolding the body in its soft, close embrace."

KATE CHOPIN

Few places are as universally loved as the seashore. Watching the endlessly flowing waves, walking on the beach, smelling the salt air can calm even the most troubled soul and bring life back into focus. There are many theories as to why the ocean has such a tranquilizing effect on people. Some believe that the even pounding of the surf harmonizes with the rhythms of the body and relaxes the mind into a meditative mood.

As wonderful as the seashore can be, though, a visit can be difficult for people who are trying to lose weight. First, many are concerned about how they look in a bathing suit. There are also many tempting treats available at fast-food stands that encourage people to eat in a rushed, unplanned fashion. Being on vacation also disrupts exercise and scheduled weight-loss meetings. Taking a break from regular routines can foster the attitude that it's okay to take a vacation from living healthfully.

If you are going to visit the seashore this summer, plan ahead to make your trip a success. Shop for a bathing suit that feels comfortable and visualize yourself wearing it and being proud of how you look. Pack or plan to eat appropriate food. If you are going to be out of town for an extended holiday, you might investigate a local support group you can drop in on. Even if you've felt that your weight has prevented you from enjoying previous trips to the beach, with foresight and determination you'll find that the voice of the sea will soothe your soul and become an important part of a successful weight-loss program.

❧ *Tip for the Day* ❧

Try to arrange a vacation or day trip to the seashore where you can absorb the peaceful atmosphere and recharge your soul.

"Some people are addicted to gambling, daytime television,
romance novels. Not me. I am addicted to the bathroom scale.
There is no greater authority."

JUDITH BURMAN

One of the most common mistakes people often make is to
weigh themselves every day, and sometimes several times each
day. Ellen is one such person. She weighs herself the first thing
every day and sometimes after every meal. Even though she
finds it depressing to be checking her weight constantly and
thinking about her weight, she's afraid that if she stops, she'll
lose control and eat everything in sight.

At Weight Watchers you are encouraged to weigh in just
once a week because weight can fluctuate daily. Many women,
for example, retain fluid before their menstrual cycles. And
increasing muscle mass through exercise can keep you at the
same weight despite the fact that you are losing inches. Also,
it is very common to reach plateaus in weight loss. So don't
discourage yourself by hopping on and off the scale. It's better
to set your focus on your behavior and maintain healthy eating habits.

If you have always been a scale addict, release control and
limit your weigh-ins to once a week. And if the scale at home
is too tempting, hide it. Remember that if you keep your mind
focused on exercise and nutritious meals instead of a few numbers on a scale, chances are you'll reach your goal sooner than
you think.

⨳ *Tip for the Day* ⨳
Resolve to avoid the scale on this day. Instead, think about exercising for 30
minutes and eating healthy balanced meals today.

*"One must know oneself. If this does not serve to discover truth,
it at least serves as a rule of life and there is nothing better."*
BLAISE PASCAL

One of the most important tenets of Weight Watchers is that
everyone is unique; therefore each person's approach to weight
loss and exercise is different. Weight Watchers has created a
basic program of healthy eating and activity that will work
whether you are a teenager, young adult, pregnant, retired or
are simply maintaining your weight goal. The way to make
this formula best serve you is to evaluate yourself and then
work the program around your needs.

Serena is a writer who found it difficult to stick to a typical
three-meal-a-day weight-loss plan because of her unusual
lifestyle of rising at four o'clock each morning. Now she eats a
healthy snack upon awakening, writes for three hours until
her children get up, eats a sensible snack with them while they
have breakfast, and then has slightly smaller meals at lunch
and dinner. Serena says it took her years to realize that this
way of eating worked best for her. It gave her the most energy
and helped her maintain her weight, but she resisted it because she thought it seemed a little weird.

Tailor the program to your lifestyle. Finding the solution
that works best for you will make the difference between losing weight and not succeeding. If six snacks a day works for
you, create a meal plan that reflects your preferences. If you're
more comfortable having three established mealtimes, do that.
Remember that you are unique, so honor your differences and
you can create a healthy lifestyle that will give you vitality and
success.

➤ *Tip for the Day* ➤
*Think about ways you can structure a meal plan to meet your own special
needs. Would allotting some selections for a midafternoon break give you a
needed boost?*

"It's not easy being green."
KERMIT THE FROG

For some people, eating vegetables means drowning a lettuce and tomato salad in rich dressing or having a pickle on a greasy hamburger. For others, it may have meant eating vegetables that were overcooked and drenched in butter, effectively eliminating their natural low-fat and low-calorie benefits. Fresh vegetables can provide a tasty, nutritious boost to your weight-loss plan. Learn about the many different kinds of vegetables and nutritious ways to cook them.

In the summer, many vegetables are especially delicious because they are fresh and full of nutrients. Tomatoes, okra, zucchini and corn found at local produce stands are likely to be especially fresh, so prepare them as simply as possible to maximize their flavor. Try experimenting with unusual vegetables if you are looking for ways to add variety to your meals. Instead of just cucumbers, for example, toss pea pods into a salad. Instead of always eating carrots, investigate the unusual tastes of such vegetables as jicama. Don't forget about herbs, either. Fresh herbs will add valuable nutrients as well as flavor to your meals.

To explore the wide world of vegetables, spend some time in the produce section of your supermarket today discovering new ways to add color and flavor to your meals. With minimal preparation and creativity, you might be surprised to find how easy it is to make vegetables an enjoyable part of your day.

 Tip for the Day
If you find yourself always eating the same vegetables, buy one new one and create a main course or side dish around it.

> *"I never cease being dumbfounded by the*
> *unbelievable things people believe."*
>
> LEO ROSTEN

Many people have erroneous beliefs about food that hamper their ability to lose weight and develop a sensible lifestyle. Some of these beliefs arise from being told half-truths in your childhood. Some arise from making assumptions that aren't based on fact. Whatever their origination, however, knowing the difference between fact and myth is the way to lose weight and keep it off.

Here are some popular fitness myths:

- *Don't exercise after eating.* Research indicates that exercising after eating a light snack contributes more to burning the calories contained in the snack than eating the same snack and engaging in a sedentary pursuit. You should, however, avoid eating a big meal right before exercising.
- *Weigh yourself every day.* Getting on a scale every day can be self-defeating because of daily fluctuations due to hormones, fluid retention and other variables.
- *Butter has more calories than margarine.* Not true. They are identical.
- *You should always strive for pain when exercising.* The old adage "No pain, no gain" is inaccurate. If you are in pain while exercising, you should stop. Work a different area of your body until you know whether you have strained, sprained or otherwise hurt yourself.
- *Dinner should be your biggest meal.* In order to feel best and burn off the maximum amount of calories, eat most of your daily calories earlier in the day.
- *If the label says "fat free," it's good for you.* Not necessarily. Many fat-free foods are also high in sugar.

Tip for the Day
Make sure you're up to date on the latest weight-loss findings.
Subscribe to a reputable weight-loss or health magazine today.

> *"One reason I don't drink is that I want to know when I am having a good time."*
>
> NANCY ASTOR

Drinking alcohol and losing weight are usually incompatible activities because alcohol has many calories but no nutritive value. For this reason most people abstain from drinking while losing weight, unless they allot extra calories for an occasional glass of wine or beer. Some regular drinkers find it difficult to limit their consumption, but this can be the perfect opportunity to address a self-defeating habit.

Sheri says that she used to drink heavily at parties because it made her feel less self-conscious about her size. Not drinking while she lost weight opened her eyes to the fact that she'd been using alcohol as a crutch. When she reached her weight goal she chose not to start drinking again. She became more self-assured, she says, when she learned to be herself and not hide behind a glass when she met people.

If you've used alcohol to cope with stress or sadness in the past, it might be a good idea to abstain from it now. Avoiding alcohol will free up more calories for nutritious meals and will force you to learn new and better ways to address uncomfortable emotions. And as you develop a healthier lifestyle that brings you more satisfaction and joy, you'll have the satisfaction of knowing you're having a good time naturally.

Tip for the Day
Can you think of at least one area of your life that would improve if you didn't drink at all?

"I must create a system, or be enslaved by another man's."
WILLIAM BLAKE

Once you've become committed to losing weight, it's a great time to reorganize your kitchen and create a system that complements your efforts. Organizing yourself and your kitchen can be a sign that you're determined to succeed.

Start by throwing away foods that might undermine careful meal planning. Replace them with healthy staples such as tuna, pasta, vegetables, fruit and other foods that are part of a balanced program. Create an interesting spice rack, too. The more flavor you give your food, the more enjoyable your meals will be. Finally, make sure you have all the tools you need to weigh and measure your foods and keep them in a place that's easily accessible.

If you think your kitchen needs an overhaul, make that today's project. Even small changes like cleaning the refrigerator can signal that you're turning over a new leaf and that you want to start each day on the right foot. You'll find that once you create organization and order in your life, you won't be trapped by the mistakes that can arise out of chaos.

⟴ *Tip for the Day* ⟴
Reorganize one area of your kitchen today, an area that you use often when preparing your meals.

"Ritual is the way you carry the presence of the sacred. Ritual is the spark that must not go out."

CHRISTINA BALDWIN

Research has shown that stable, healthy families have regular rituals: visiting the same place on annual vacations, doing shared activities during holidays, eating together at an assigned time each day or just having a familiar bedtime routine. When a family creates this type of "sacred" activity, family members develop a sense of security and there is a predictable rhythm to each day.

Being successful at weight loss means creating certain rituals as well. You may have begun to set aside a certain period of each day for exercise or quiet contemplation. Or maybe you've allotted enough time each morning to have an unhurried breakfast. Take note of behaviors you have started to establish. Foster them so that they become a predictable and comforting part of your day. Try to include your family in some of your new healthy rituals too, such as a nightly stroll around the neighborhood or shopping during the summer at a roadside produce stand for fresh fruits and vegetables.

Examine the structure of your day today. Are there rituals that help your day flow, or are you haphazard in planning times for exercise, leisure, meals and errands? Think of ways to create rituals that will help you reach your goals, such as making and freezing your week's meals on Sundays or attending a lunchtime aerobics class with a friend. The more you can bring this type of regular activity into your everyday life, the more likely you'll be to have a schedule that brings you success.

❧ *Tip for the Day* ❧
Think of activities you can plan on a daily, monthly or yearly basis that will help you feel secure, happy and focused on your goals.

"The great thing in this world is not so much where you stand, as in what direction you are moving."

OLIVER WENDELL HOLMES

Hitting a plateau is one of the most discouraging things that happens when you're trying to lose weight. Countless people can testify to this depressing scenario: Carol lost weight at a steady clip for eight weeks and then suddenly stopped. Margot not only experienced the same problem, but her weight even went up temporarily.

There are many reasons why people reach weight-loss plateaus, so it's important not to take them as signs of personal failure. Keep in mind that women often retain water prior to menstruation. Researchers have found that most people experience a plateau after eight weeks of following a weight-loss plan because the body learns to function well on fewer calories. You may need to reduce food intake or increase exercise to continue to lose weight. Instead of letting this normal occurrence get you down, rev up your motivation by reminding yourself why you wanted to lose weight in the first place. Compare notes with other Weight Watchers members at meetings and ask them how they have survived plateaus. Choose nonfood treats as rewards for yourself.

If you have hit a plateau, don't allow it to undo all your good work. You may feel like you're stalled and standing still, but you are still moving toward a goal. Taking a few days to just celebrate how far you've already come may be the best way to wait out this temporary setback.

⇌ *Tip for the Day* ⇌

Review your daily food intake and exercise log. Look for areas that need tuning up, such as reducing your optional calorie count or increasing your exercise.

"The scouts' motto is founded on my initials, it is: Be Prepared."
LORD BADEN-POWELL

On a long car trip, it's tempting to discard a sensible eating plan and eat fast food, oversized portions and rich entrées. With advance planning and determination to stay committed to weight loss, any road trip can become a healthy journey that benefits everyone in the family.

One mother found that instead of caving into temptation and her children's demands to stop at ice cream stores and burger joints, she preplanned the trip so that the healthy alternatives would be more accessible and appetizing. She filled a cooler with foods such as yogurt, juice boxes, skewers of fruit and vegetables with containers of low-fat dip. She packed goody bags of air-popped popcorn, dried fruit combinations, unsalted pretzels and high-fiber crackers. To cut down on mess she brought along individual packets of low-fat dressings. Plastic utensils and moist towelettes made cleanup easy.

If you will be traveling long distances and you'll need to eat along the way, be prepared. Take the time to pack foods that are both satisfying and store easily. Once you acknowledge that you can succeed on your program despite being away from home, you'll know that nothing can stop you from reaching your goals.

⤞ *Tip for the Day* ⤝
*Make sure you have the items necessary to eat nutritiously while
you travel. Pack a cooler with dried fruit and juice boxes and
put perishables in resealable bags; bring beverages
in insulated vacuum bottles.*

"Truly nothing is to be expected but the unexpected!"
ALICE JAMES

Growing up overweight, Barbara developed the belief that she'd never be slender because she couldn't imagine herself that way. She never had any expectations that she could be slim, she remembers, because everybody expected her to be heavy. Barbara began to change her perception of herself when she lost 50 pounds. And soon her attitude about what she could achieve changed as well because to her surprise she was selected as Weight Watchers World of Success winner.

Whatever your expectations for yourself, remember that the unexpected frequently has a way of popping up and changing your situation. For this reason it's best simply to take one day at a time. Try to let go of erroneous beliefs about what you can or cannot, will or won't do. And don't let your doubts keep you from trying. You might surprise yourself when you least expect to. Like Barbara, you may wind up delighting yourself and showing the rest of the world that their expectations for you have been wrong too!

❧ *Tip for the Day* ❧
Remember that even the most ingrained expectations can be altered.

"An active line on a walk, moving freely without a goal.
A walk for walk's sake."

PAUL KLEE

The top-rated exercise of people who have successfully kept off large amounts of weight is walking. There are many reasons for this. Walking can be done at any time of day; there is no special equipment other than comfortable shoes; it can be done individually or with friends; and it is effective in burning calories and toning the body. As one walking coach points out, "It gives you all the benefits running does, minus the injuries. After all, human beings were born to walk."

For those who are looking to maximize the benefits of their walking time, power walking may be ideal. Power walking is done at a brisk clip, approximately fifteen minutes per mile (or faster). It involves vigorous arm-swinging and a fast stride. To try this, put your hands into a fist and pump them from your hip to up in front of your breastbone as you reach out with your hip, knee and heel. Don't lean forward from the waist. Relax your shoulders and look straight ahead, keeping your head level. Some people opt to walk while listening to music through headphones; music with a driving beat helps them keep up the pace.

Power walking pays excellent dividends. Brisk walkers not only become more fit, but they improve their overall health profile as well. Injury rarely makes them miss workouts because walking doesn't put the same stress on the joints as other, more stressful exercises, such as running. So if you are looking for a low-impact sport with multiple benefits, investigate power walking and hit the road.

❦ *Tip for the Day* ❦
Try power walking in the privacy of your home or around your neighborhood to discover the best technique and pace for you.

"The good or ill of man lies within his own will."
EPICTETUS

There are some common tools used by people who lose weight and keep it off. One is taking swift action if there is a gain of between one and five pounds. Some people monitor this through the fit of their clothes, but the vast majority of people who manage their weight successfully weigh themselves weekly.

If you have already reached your weight goal but it has started to fluctuate, take action immediately so that your problem doesn't become a big one. Many successful weight-loss maintainers cut snacks, sweets or other extras out of their food plan until their weight returns to normal. Others increase their exercise level to burn off extra calories. And some wear their tight clothes as a constant reminder that they need to be careful about what they eat.

Reaching your weight goal and learning how much you can eat to maintain it without fluctuating takes some time. If you're starting to regain weight, take action quickly to get back on the right track. Ignoring warning signs or avoiding the scale when your clothes get tight may mushroom into regaining some or even all your weight. So establish your buffer zone and fight to maintain it.

∾ *Tip for the Day* ∾
Remember that reaching your weight goal also means that you must maintain your vigilance to keep your weight stable.

*"A man may well bring a horse to the water but he
cannot make him drink."*

JOHN HEYWOOD

One of the main strengths of Weight Watchers is the leadership provided at the meetings by men and women who have
reached their weight goals and maintained those losses. Members often say that if it weren't for the enthusiasm, creativity
and inspiration they received from their leaders, they wouldn't
have met their weight goals.

As motivational as leaders are, however, each of us is ultimately responsible for his or her own weight-loss success. Leaders can give you ideas, lift your spirits when you're down and
shore up shaky self-esteem. But they can't guarantee that you
eat properly or exercise regularly. One leader suggests to members that if they're looking for a helping hand, they should
start by looking at the end of their own arms.

Examine your attitude today to see whether you accept responsibility for how well you are doing in your weight-loss activities. Relying exclusively on others to provide you with reasons to stay on your meal or exercise plan will ultimately doom
you to failure. And equally important, it will prevent you from
learning the beauty of being in charge of your own life.

Tip for the Day

*Ask yourself if you are participating to the fullest in your weight-loss
program. If not, what can you do to improve your chances of success?*

> *"To establish oneself in the world, one has to do all
> one can to appear established."*
>
> FRANÇOIS LA ROCHEFOUCAULD

When you're overweight it's easy to lose the motivation to pay attention to your appearance. It's tempting to try to blend into the woodwork and tell yourself that you don't deserve to look pretty because no one will care.

This defeatist attitude will work against you if you are trying to create a healthy and successful lifestyle. A haircut that emphasizes a slimmer face and more prominent bone structure can create the illusion of being younger and more vibrant, as can a change of hair color. Makeup artists can also teach you how to make a good feature more prominent. They can recommend cosmetics that flatter your skin tone and help give you a contemporary look.

Analyze the way you present yourself today. Could you use an updated haircut or color? Is your makeup routine out of date or nonexistent? Look at fashion magazines for ideas about how you might want to alter your approach. Take advantage of free resources at department stores, beauty-supply stores and makeup counters to get professional input. Making steady progress in changing your body and your behavior is important, but don't forget to adjust your image to keep pace with the new you.

≈ Tip for the Day ≈

Ask someone who has a pulled-together look how they have achieved it, and make an appointment to see their hair stylist soon.

"I am never afraid of what I know."
ANNA SEWELL

Many people have only vague ideas about nutrition, healthy portion sizes, the relationship between exercise and diet and the actual content of the foods they eat. Joan was typical of this mentality. She knew all about calorie counts, but not much else, she remembers. Learning about food groups, fat and sodium contents and what an average serving size is demystified the whole process of losing weight and made meal planning much easier for her.

Living a healthy life includes knowing a lot about nutrition so that you can make wise decisions at the grocery store. One way to do this is to become an avid label reader. Most packages now have labels indicating the size of a serving and how many calories the food contains, as well as the fat, fiber and carbohydrate counts. If high blood pressure or heart disease are factors in your life, check with your doctor to learn the correct cholesterol and sodium levels for you.

Be an educated consumer the next time you go food shopping. Set aside enough time to shop slowly, reading labels and checking for ingredients such as additives like MSG that might be unhealthy. Take along some guides to help you do this. Books that count fat grams, fiber grams, calories and the like are available at your local bookstore. You'll find that the more knowledge you can gain about a subject that once baffled or intimidated you, the less likely you'll be to make unwise decisions.

⟴   *Tip for the Day*   ⟴
The next time you go to a fast-food restaurant, ask to see a list of calories, fat grams and nutrients in the foods they serve. Read it before you order.

"Is it so small a thing / To have enjoyed the sun…"
MATTHEW ARNOLD

If you endeavor to live a healthy life, eventually you will be drawn to the outdoors. As you become more active, you will probably make time to play tennis, golf or other sports, as well as walk, jog or work in a garden. Losing weight also confers more self-confidence to be seen in shorts or even a bathing suit, so you are less likely to hide indoors when nice weather beckons.

When you spend more time outdoors, it's important to be aware of the health risks of being in the sun. Although being exposed to direct sunlight is a guaranteed mood booster, the changing atmosphere of the earth has made it essential to protect your skin from damaging rays. Some of the most effective ways to do this include using enough sun screen and reapplying it frequently, wearing hats that shield your scalp and ears and wearing dark, tightly woven fabrics that will absorb ultraviolet rays. Take care, too, to shield your children from the sun because 80 percent of lifetime sun exposure is received before the age of 18.

While being outdoors can be a terrific boost to a fitness program and an active life, be aware of the negative effects of long-term sun exposure and protect yourself accordingly. As with all elements of being healthy, moderation is the key to success.

⇌   *Tip for the Day*   ⇌
Take sensible steps to protect yourself from the sun's harmful rays whenever you are exercising outdoors, even if it's only for a short period of time.

*"The most wasted of all days is that in which
we have not laughed."*

SEBASTIEN R. N. CHAMFORT

When the blues strike and you want to avoid turning to food,
here are some quick mood boosters:

- *Laugh.* If a certain comic strip always makes you chuckle,
have it close by. Or if you have a friend who never fails to
elicit a giggle, call that person.
- *Get into the light, or a "brighter" atmosphere.* Go outside, even
if it's cold, and expose yourself to sunlight. Change the
lightbulbs in your environment so that you have less fluo-
rescent and more full-spectrum light. Consider painting or
wallpapering walls so that you are surrounded by brighter
hues.
- *Do something you do well, like write a letter, play a computer
game or draw a picture.* The sense of accomplishment can
outweigh negative feelings.
- *Visualize a pleasurable scene,* such as riding a bicycle down a
wooded path.
- *Sit next to a fish tank.* "Aquarium staring" has been shown
to lower blood pressure and invite relaxation.
- *Play music that makes you feel happy.*
- *Walk up and down a flight of stairs until you break a sweat.*
Ten minutes of brisk exercise can induce a feeling of pleasure and also burn off calories.

∞ *Tip for the Day* ∞
*Decide right now what you will do the next time you need
to lift your spirits.*

"Summer has set in with its usual severity."
SAMUEL TAYLOR COLERIDGE

When you are playing or working outdoors in the hot summer sun, be careful to guard against heat cramps and dehydration. Before you leave the cool comfort of your home, check the weather report for the heat index, which is a calculation that factors in humidity as well as temperature. It is important because high humidity makes a hot day even hotter.

Get your body used to the summer heat by taking a brisk walk every day for at least a week before you plan to work out. Start with a 15-minute walk and build up to an hour. Bring a bottle of water with you and drink a cup every half hour. If you get cramps in your abdomen, legs or arms, stop and rest in the shade. Drink several glasses of water and stretch (don't massage) the affected muscles.

After being in the heat for a prolonged period of time, you may feel tired and have a headache. If so, you are probably dehydrated. Drink three to five glasses of water and the symtoms should start to diminish. If you have a fever or feel dizzy or nauseous, you need medical attention, so call your physician right away.

Remember that there are foods that are mostly water. Watermelon, for example, has a water content of 93 percent. Honeydew, cantaloupe and strawberries have a water content of 90 percent or more. And don't forget vegetables; watercress, bell pepper, cucumber, summer squash and some varieties of lettuce have water contents of at least 95 percent. Eat these delicious foods to quench your thirst and refresh yourself.

⟿ *Tip for the Day* ⟾
During the hottest days of the summer, schedule your outdoor exercise so you can avoid the midday sun as much as possible.

"[Water is] the only drink for a wise man."
HENRY DAVID THOREAU

There are several principles that are essential to succeeding at weight loss: eating balanced meals, engaging in regular physical activity, having a support system and learning new behaviors to replace unhealthy ones. Another often overlooked guideline is to drink plenty of water. Water quenches thirst and helps to stave off hunger pangs. One woman says that she used to stack up peanut butter cups next to her computer to keep her company while she wrote. Now she says she's so busy drinking her eight glasses of water each day that she doesn't crave them anymore. Others say that drinking plenty of water has restored balance to their digestion and improved their skin. And anyone who exercises knows that replenishing lost fluids with water before and after workouts prevents dehydration.

Be creative in the ways you drink enough water. If tap water doesn't taste good to you, invest some money in a water filter or high-quality bottled water. Flavor a glass of ice water with a slice of lemon or lime. Or add a fruit-flavored extract if you're looking for a new twist. And keep a bottle of fresh water at your desk so it's as easy to reach for as a cup of coffee or a soda. You'll find that your body will benefit from boosting your intake of water, and you'll also have a valuable way to feel full without adding any calories.

Tip for the Day
Try drinking bottled water this week. If you like it, investigate having regular deliveries to your residence or look into the cost of a filtration system for your home.

*"Some people have a foolish way of not minding, or
pretending not to mind what they eat."*

SAMUEL JOHNSON

A high-fiber diet is naturally low in fat and rich in nutrients,
and it has been shown to lower cholesterol and prevent cancer. The two types of fiber you need are soluble fiber, found in
fruits, vegetables and oat products, and insoluble fiber, found
in plant grains and seeds. Yet most Americans consume only
half the amount of fiber they need—20 to 30 grams per day,
according to the American Dietetic Association. Here are some
easy ways to add fiber to your diet:

- *Serve more grains.* Bulgur wheat, couscous, lentils and bar-
  ley have 3 to 5 grams of fiber per half cup; tabbouleh has 8
  grams per half cup. Insoluble grains like these also help prevent colon cancer.
- *Add wheat bran.* A half-cup of wheat bran has 12 grams of
  fiber. Add it to the bread crumbs when you're breading
  chicken or fish to increase fiber without adding a lot of
  extra calories. It's also good in meatloaf recipes or sprinkled
  over yogurt, hot cereal and applesauce.
- *Eat your fruits and vegetables fresh instead of processed.* Citrus
  fruits, apples, peaches and pears are all sources of pectin, a
  soluble fiber, and the rind is an excellent source of cellu-
  lose, an insoluble fiber. An apple and corn on the cob each
  have ten times more fiber than canned applesauce or
  creamed corn. A baked potato with skin has more fiber
  than a peeled potato. The peels are valuable sources of insoluble fiber.

 Tip for the Day
*Look for a book that lists the grams of fiber in common foods. Then add up the
number of grams of fiber you ate today.*

"Old habits are strong and jealous."

DOROTHEA BRANDE

As any smoker who has tried to quit will tell you, one of the biggest obstacles to kicking nicotine is dealing with the many cues that are associated with smoking. The same is true of food. If you've always munched popcorn in a movie, candy bars in the car or leftovers while clearing the table, you'll have the urge to eat when you do those activities. To be successful in weight loss requires that you find ways to overcome habits like these and replace them with better ones.

A key to overcoming bad habits is simply being aware of them. Stan found that he had the habit of eating breadsticks and crackers whenever these were placed on his table at a restaurant. His solution was to ask that they be removed from the table as soon as he sat down. Similarly, Jill always snacked while she cooked, so now she chews sugar-free gum and munches on cut-up vegetables when she's in the kitchen. By being aware of these habits and using aggressive strategies to fight them, both of these people have achieved success over them.

What are the old habits that trigger your desire to overeat? Is it walking by a bakery, shopping in a certain grocery aisle or being with a certain person? Be aware today of which habits are stubborn and think of ways to overcome them with new activities.

⟻ *Tip for the Day* ⟼
List any habits you have that are undermining your efforts to live more healthfully. What can you do to combat them?

"Sir Christopher Wren / Said, 'I am going to dine with some men. / If anybody calls / Say I am designing St. Paul's.'"
EDMUND CLERIHEW BENTLEY

There are times when a solitary meal is enjoyable because the silence allows you to gather your thoughts, appreciate the textures and flavor of the food and eat at whatever speed you desire. On the other hand, some people prefer to eat in the company of others, particularly if they are trying to lose weight and they have a tendency to overeat when no one else is looking. If this is the case, ensuring that you have a family member or friend with you whenever you are preparing or eating meals is one of the best preventive measures you can take.

Sally finds that she rushes through her meals whenever she eats alone, so now she invites a work colleague to join her for lunch. She says that she's learned to pick her friends carefully, though. Some acquaintances who weren't supportive of her weight-loss efforts encouraged her to share rich foods with them, and others made so many comments about her sensible meals that she felt uncomfortable eating with them. Eating a meal with friends who are interesting and supportive, she says, is the best condiment anyone can add to a meal.

If you frequently find yourself overeating when you're alone, take steps to prevent yourself from sabotaging your own success. Try to prepare meals with another family member, eat only when others are present and invite friends to join you when you are alone. While there are many solitary pleasures in life, your meals may not be among them.

Tip for the Day
Schedule at least one meal this week with a person who encourages your efforts and who will make the time enjoyable.

> *"Guilt is a rope that wears thin."*
> AYN RAND

At a neighborhood party one night Miriam felt that her husband was chatting with everyone but her. That night, and during the next few weeks, Miriam's fears blossomed. As she tossed and turned through sleepless nights, she blamed herself for her husband's apparent disinterest, guiltily telling herself that she'd gained too much weight in recent years. She was convinced he was restless in their marriage and it was her fault.

Overweight people often tend to make their weight the scapegoat for everything that isn't right in their lives. When Miriam finally confronted her husband, he was surprised. He explained that he had been passed over for a promotion at work and was worried about losing his job. Her weight hadn't been a factor in his unhappiness.

If you find yourself feeling guilty because you think your excess weight has created problems, give yourself a break. Quite often, as Miriam's story demonstrates, upsetting situations have nothing to do with you. Taking the blame for other people's problems and saddling yourself with unnecessary guilt will only keep you mired in the role of victim.

Tip for the Day
Instead of feeling guilty about the problems you believe your weight has caused, ask yourself whether the burden should rest somewhere else instead.

"We owe something to extravagance, for thrift and adventure seldom go hand in hand."

JENNIE JEROME CHURCHILL

When you live a busy, errand-filled life, it's easy to forget to pamper yourself. You may feel guilty about spending money or time on yourself, but it's important that you remember to bolster your well-being, particularly if you can do it creatively and inexpensively. Here are some ways to take care of yourself and boost your self-esteem and contentment:

- *Light candles at dinner.* The soft atmosphere helps you relax, so you can enjoy the taste of the food you've prepared and the fellowship of your dinner companions.
- *Take a candlelit bath with scented oils and soft background music.*
- *Order from a catalogue one item that you've been meaning to get.* It's always fun to get a package in the mail, even if you sent it yourself.
- *Trade back rubs with a spouse, friend or significant other.*
- *Put a bowl of potpourri next to your bed so that you can go to sleep and wake up inhaling a heavenly aroma.*

Remember today that self-indulgence isn't something to feel guilty about; it's a way to give yourself a treat. The better you feel about yourself, the more energy and enthusiasm you'll bring to making your life energetic, healthy and joyous.

Tip for the Day

Think of at least one free or inexpensive way you can give yourself a treat today, such as sitting down, closing your eyes and relaxing to your favorite music.

*[Medicine is] a collection of uncertain prescriptio
the results of which, taken collectively, are more fatal
than useful to mankind."*

NAPOLEON I

Many people take prescription and nonprescription medications without giving much thought to whether or not they can combine them with their normal meals. Being unaware of how certain combinations interact can affect your health and emotional well-being. Here are some things to be aware of:

- *If aspirin, acetaminophen (Tylenol) or ibuprofen (Advil, Motrin) cause you stomach irritation, it is okay to take them with food.* However, be aware that food will also inhibit the rate of absorption.
- *Never take any medication with alcohol.* Alcohol by itself causes stomach irritation, and it usually interferes with your body's ability to utilize medications effectively.
- *Most antibiotics have a tendency to cause diarrhea.* To avoid dehydration, be sure to drink plenty of water while you're taking them. If your doctor has prescribed tetracycline, do not take it with milk. Dairy products limit your body's ability to absorb this antibiotic. If your medicine is causing constipation, increase your fiber and fluid intake.

When medications are recommended, whether over the counter or by prescription, make sure you understand how these drugs work in your body so you won't hinder their effectiveness. Your doctor and pharmacist will be glad to answer your questions because they want you to get well as quickly as possible. And be sure to read the instructions to patients that often accompany the prescription. While it's possible to lose weight successfully while being on medication, it will be more pleasant if you are prepared ahead of time and you know how to counteract any negative reactions.

➤ *Tip for the Day* ➤
Check with your doctor or pharmacist every time you take a medication so that you know how it can affect your vitality and eating habits.

*"To will is to select a goal, determine a course of action
that will bring one to that goal, and then hold to that action
till the goal is reached. The key is action."*

MICHAEL HANSON

For most of us, selecting a weight goal means working every day toward success, even though success may not happen for quite a while. Because this may feel discouraging at first, even overwhelming, you must lay out short-term goals to help you get closer to your ultimate goal. Perhaps more important, short-term goals will provide an encouraging feeling of accomplishment and build self-confidence to help keep you motivated over the weeks and months ahead.

Setting a reasonable goal for yourself that is attainable every day can go a long way toward preventing overeating. This is because succeeding at several small tasks is more satisfying than filling up with food. For example, every morning Maria used to write out a "To Do" list of many large jobs. Because the tasks were difficult to complete, she was left with a sense of failure that she sated with late-night snacking. Now she is careful to keep her list to three reasonable items, such as going to the dry cleaner, making a dental appointment and writing a letter. By the end of the day, she has feelings of accomplishment, not discouragement. And she is sure this has helped her stick to a sensible eating regimen.

Have you overburdened yourself with a long list of what you hope to accomplish today? If so, pare it down to several items that you know you can accomplish with some moderate action. The more you can string together days of fulfilling, successful accomplishments, the less likely you'll be to lose hope before you reach your long-term goals.

⋙ *Tip for the Day* ⋘

List three things you can do today and then make sure you do them. At the end of the day, assess how satisfied you are with yourself and whether those feelings helped you to adhere to your eating and exercise plans.

"Our feelings are our most genuine paths to knowledge."

AUDRE LORDE

In the past you may have used food in a variety of inappropriate ways: to celebrate success, to mourn a loss, to mask feelings of guilt and shame or to just ease boredom. If you are to lose and control your weight, it's important that you learn what motivates you to crave food. Then, satisfy that craving with something you truly need or that will benefit you, not just something you want.

Anne says she realized one day that when she craved junk food, what she wanted was to read romance novels and tabloid newspapers. Now, instead of reaching for potato chips and candy when she feels hungry between meals, she indulges herself with several hours of pulp fiction and celebrity profiles.

If you find yourself craving food as an inappropriate response to various situations, stop before eating and ask yourself if another activity would bring you a similar feeling of pleasure. For example, would a ride through the country, listening to your favorite song or calling a close friend help you cope with your emotions better than eating? Instead of giving in to emotional eating today, examine your feelings. Once you learn what it is you truly need you will have invaluable knowledge that will help you cope with life without adding unnecessary calories.

Tip for the Day

Close your eyes when you are tempted to eat and ask yourself what you'd like to do instead. Perhaps the answer is to take a nap, drink a cup of tea or watch an old movie.

"Life itself is the proper binge."
JULIA CHILD

When Joy was in high school she began to eat compulsively. She did so partly out of fear of dating and partly because she was afraid to face the next step in her life—college and independent living. Food soon became the focus of her whole life. She skipped numerous social occasions and opportunities for travel because she felt overweight and frightened of new experiences. Since joining a weight-loss program, Joy is learning how to live life without fear. She's discovering that experiencing new situations can still be intimidating, but it's better than a life of hiding behind food.

Nearly everyone has endured difficult times in life, and part of becoming a mature, responsible adult is accepting the fact that life is hard. If eating has been your way of coping with stress, you will have to learn that setbacks occur in everyone's life. Turning to food for comfort, distraction or some other personal emotional need gives you more things to be unhappy about. Once you can see this, you are free to feel happiness more intensely.

Today, enjoy life, not food. Remind yourself that it's better to be feeling your emotions than to be numbing them with mountains of food. When you have learned how to take pleasure in what happens to you, then you'll have learned the secret to living a vibrant and successful life.

Tip for the Day
Be fully present for one experience today, such as a walk, a warm hug, a telephone call.

"Don't go to the hardware store for milk."
ANONYMOUS

Sometimes you know what is best for you but you act against your best interests anyway. Dan, who had long had a rocky relationship with his father, called him for advice, even though his father had never been warm or sympathetic in the past. After yet another unsatisfying conversation that left Dan feeling unloved and abandoned, he asked a wise friend for advice on how to get the nurturing and support he needed. In answer, the friend reminded Dan of the old saying "Don't go to the hardware store for milk."

This is sage advice for those who are routinely disappointed by the actions of people close to them, but who nevertheless continue to seek those people out. If you've never had the support of certain family members or friends when trying to make positive changes in your life, think twice before going to them for something they can't provide. Likewise, if you're looking for self-esteem, you'll never get it by focusing only on professional rewards. Self-esteem comes from learning to love yourself because of who you are, not what you produce.

Are you still going to the "hardware store" for something you can't get there? If you are repeatedly falling into the trap of being disappointed by a certain person or situation, think about alternative, healthier ways to get your needs met. Whether it's support in losing weight or the companionship of a loving relationship, a big part of success is knowing where to turn.

≈ *Tip for the Day* ≈
Think of a situation where you're frustrated by the outcome. Were you going to the wrong place or person for an answer? Is there a better place to go for resolution?

> *"It is a mistake to regard age as a downhill grade toward dissolution. The reverse is true. As one grows older, one climbs with surprising strides."*
>
> GEORGE SAND

Because society is obsessed with youth, those who are middle-aged and older might begin to develop the attitude that their best years are behind them, that they are sliding toward senility and decrepitude. Fortunately, this isn't true. Those who choose to fight this misperception are often rewarded with fuller lives, an improved outlook and happiness that previously may have been unimaginable.

Carolyn decided to join Weight Watchers and tackle her weight problem at the age of fifty. In the process, she eventually lost 53 pounds, melted inches off her body and made a number of new friends who gave her support. Carolyn's daughter marvels at the change, saying she can't remember the last time she had seen her mother so full of energy and happiness. When Carolyn wears a new outfit, she comes downstairs and twirls around to show it off for the family, states her daughter. Carolyn has proven that it's never too late to improve your life.

Whenever gloominess about the aging process creeps into your thoughts or you find yourself making excuses for yourself because of age, fight this attitude with a determination to succeed at whatever you want to do. Age, as you have probably seen in others, is usually a function of attitude, so make yours as positive and forward-thinking as possible.

⇜ *Tip for the Day* ⇝
*Whenever you hear yourself saying, "I'm too old to ——,"
challenge yourself to disprove it.*

"[Memory is] a man's real possession.... In nothing else is he rich, in nothing else is he poor."

ALEXANDER SMITH

If you suddenly forget where you put your keys, the name of the man just introduced to you, the name of the book you finished last week or the plot of the movie you saw recently, you may worry that you're getting senile. But in fact your meals may be the culprit. For example, a recent study showed that iron and zinc are an important part of a balanced diet. When these minerals are taken together as supplements, they can interfere with each other's absorption; absorption is not affected when these nutrients are coming from natural food sources.

There are legions of benefits in eating a variety of foods. With a wide variety you increase your chances of meeting all your nutritional needs and keeping your body in top form. If you are feeling more forgetful than usual, look at your meal plan. Are you are eating enough iron- and zinc-rich foods such as leafy green vegetables and red meat? Are your meals lacking important nutrients? Spend some time learning a little about which foods can offer you the most benefits and how you can work them into your meals. Although it takes some effort to be educated about the properties of food, not just their calorie or fat content, having this knowledge can dramatically enhance the quality of your health and life.

∽ *Tip for the Day* ∾
Make a chart of the basic food groups and what each group does for you. Keep it handy in your kitchen so you can prepare balanced meals more easily.

"[Exercise] is health."

JAMES THOMSON

It's been well established that exercising does more than promote health and well-being. Exercise is essential in
any weight-loss plan. Any form of exercise is helpful, from
walking to dancing to playing soccer, but some are more effective at trimming fat levels than others. So to receive
multiple benefits from your workout time, consider the
following:

- People who use more than one muscle group in their workouts burn more calories than those who simply
  isolate one area. So if you're going to exercise your legs on
  the stair machine, do something afterwards to work your
  arms too.
- A study of five hundred exercisers showed that those who
  jogged or bicycled for 20 minutes and then did 20 minutes
  of weight work three times each week were two and a half
  times more fit than those who just did aerobic exercise.

While all forms of exercise are beneficial, try to keep some
variety in your routine to eliminate boredom and maximize
the number of calories you can burn in each session. And if
you can combine or supplement those activities with resistance
training, you'll reap more benefits than you once thought
possible.

Tip for the Day
*To make the best use of your time, regularly use weights to build
strength and get rid of fat.*

J u l y   3 0

"This is my answer to the gap between ideas and action—
I will write it out."

HORTENSE CALISHER

Sometimes it's easier to do something if you've made a note
somewhere that you intend to take action. This is why it's helpful to write down meals ahead of time and to have a daily journal filled with your thoughts, affirmations, hopes and accomplishments. Not only can a journal serve as an impetus to make
needed changes, it can remind you of previous triumphs when
you're feeling discouraged about your progress.

If there seems to be a lag between your intentions and your
accomplishments, use your journal today to make notes about
what you'd like to do and how you are going to go about it. If
you've had difficulty staying away from your
favorite bakery and its wares, for example, write down what
you'd like to do (stop unplanned eating), how it makes you
feel (guilty and out of control) and steps you're going to take
to make sure you don't do it again (take another route home
that bypasses the store). Gradually you'll find that writing your
desires in a journal reduces them to a more manageable level.
This makes it easier for you to take action and change whatever is bothering you. In the future when you are struggling
with similar problems in your life, your journal will also remind you that you have coped with similar frustrations in the
past and solved them to your satisfaction.

Tip for the Day

Ask yourself what actions you should be taking today to improve
a situation. Write down what you should do, then follow your own
advice and take those steps.

"It is better to wear out than to rust out."

BISHOP RICHARD CUMBERLAND

Most people who have struggled with their weight will tell you that their body "wants" to stay at a certain weight. Now there's research to show that indeed this is true. A recent study shows that when you start to lose weight, your metabolism will slow down so that you'll burn fewer calories. But the reverse is also true: Your metabolism will increase as you start to gain weight and you'll burn more calories. In short, it's easier to stay at the same weight than it is to lose or gain. The data also appear to support the idea that constantly losing and regaining weight doesn't do any harm. However, most experts agree that yo-yo dieting is bad for your self-esteem, if not your body.

The study also shows what happens to the calories you consume. Most calories, 65 to 70 percent, are used to keep your heart, liver, kidneys and the rest of your body organs working. Eating and digesting food uses another 10 to 15 percent of the calories. Your muscles use up the remaining calories as they exercise. And exercising your muscles, say the researchers, is the key to losing weight.

Remember today that research confirms what your common sense already knows—that one of the best ways to lose and control weight is a moderate eating and exercise regimen.

❧   *Tip for the Day*   ☙
*Honestly evaluate your exercise program today. Be sure that you're burning
calories as well as improving your flexibility and strength.*

*"I really do believe I can accomplish a great deal with a big grin.
I know some people find that disconcerting, but
that doesn't matter."*

BEVERLY SILLS

Overweight people don't often feel very good about themselves or their appearance so they frequently look sad or angry. Your facial expression can then become a self-fulfilling prophecy. If you look unhappy, others may unconsciously avoid you, which is quite likely to make you unhappy. On the other hand, if you have a cheerful expression and erect body posture, others will turn to you to share stories and friendly conversation, which will no doubt make you feel good about yourself.

Damon heard a Weight Watchers leader speak about the importance of personal appearance and facial expression as key indicators of how you feel about yourself. The leader urged Damon to smile and meet others' eyes more often because he tended to scowl and look unhappy. After working on his smile, Damon noticed that people were friendlier to him, which helped him feel better about himself. And he says the better he feels about himself, the easier it is to stick to his program.

Be aware today of how you appear to others. If you find that you usually adopt a downcast attitude as a defense mechanism, try at least to put on a happy face to see if it will help to change your mood. You'll find that the more you can radiate optimism, good cheer and self-assurance, the more likely you'll be to actually embody those qualities. A smile will open the door to interactions that help you have a successful and rewarding day.

⟐ Tip for the Day ⟐
*Smile in a heartfelt way at other people whenever
you have the opportunity today.*

"His sleep was a sensuous gluttony of oblivion."

P. D. JAMES

There are many things you can do to make yourself more attractive as you tone your body and lose weight. During the day, you can work on improving your posture, smiling more and dressing in flattering clothes. You can also indulge in such luxuries as facials and manicures. When you aren't busy, set aside time to pamper yourself with long baths, stretching exercises or special moisturizing treatments for your hair and scalp.

Your improvement efforts don't have to stop when you turn out the lights to go to bed. Sleep time is the perfect opportunity to slather lotion on your hands and feet and wrap them in cotton gloves or socks. To minimize morning eye puffiness, put a dab of rich moisturizer under each eye. And to keep your subconscious on an even keel, try drifting to sleep listening to soothing relaxation tapes of waves lapping a beach shoreline or birds chirping in the woods.

Be creative in your efforts to take care of your body and soul today. Don't overlook the good work you can do at night. As you develop a fondness for your body you'll find a lot of new ways to reward yourself for your weight loss. Remind yourself that you deserve to look as good as you feel 24 hours a day.

⟶ Tip for the Day ⟵
Think of at least one nice thing you can do for
yourself while you sleep tonight.

"That man is the richest whose pleasures are the cheapest."
HENRY DAVID THOREAU

Many people go through a period when money is tight and making every penny count is essential. While this can be a scary and upsetting time, it can also be a time when you learn important values and lessons, such as gratitude for even having a place to call home, or finding out who you can count on for support and understanding.

If you're struggling now to make ends meet, it's important to think of ways to save money while still eating nutritious meals and exercising. To lower food costs, some people grow their own so that they always have a garden to turn to for nourishment. Others join food cooperatives and buy food in bulk, which can cut a food budget significantly. Exercise equipment can be found at bargain prices at flea markets, garage sales or secondhand stores. Sherry, for example, wanted a stationary bike but couldn't afford it. But she found a nearly new one at an exercise exchange store, where she paid a fraction of what she would have paid elsewhere.

When money is tight, remember that you can live healthfully while still being frugal. By planning your meals ahead of time and shopping for bargains, you can eliminate impulse buys at the supermarket. In this way you can learn valuable cost-cutting tips that will stand you in good stead in every area of your life.

Tip for the Day
Remember that a meal prepared in your own kitchen is always less expensive than the same meal at a restaurant.

> *"What other dungeon is so dark as one's own heart!*
> *What jailer so inexorable as one's self!"*
>
> NATHANIEL HAWTHORNE

Sometimes we fall victim to wanting to be perfect: having perfect children, the perfect job, the perfect house and the perfect spouse. This same unbending attitude is often applied to weight loss, too. Impatient with anything but the most exacting standards, people seek to be perfect dieters, successful only if they've followed their meal plan to the letter, exercised for an allotted period of time and have had no slips with food.

This rigid attitude can spell disaster if you're trying to develop healthy eating and exercise routines. If you've been overweight and sedentary for many years, old habits will have to be changed gradually so that the new ones can become routine. On the way, even the best-intentioned are likely to succumb to a bout of emotional eating, skip a workout, gain weight or even fall off the wagon completely. If you're wedded to perfection, you'll be tempted to throw in the towel and declare your situation unsalvageable if you have an unsuccessful weight-loss experience. If you're patient, though, you'll remember that every slip is an opportunity to grow and learn better ways of dealing with difficult situations.

Lighten up on yourself today if you're on a quest for perfection. Everyone who has ever met with success has had disappointments and failures along the way, so there's no reason why you should be any different. Remember that while it's a good idea to set high goals for yourself, taking detours along the way can still take you where you're going if you can forgive yourself. Persevere and allow yourself to be human.

⇜ Tip for the Day ⇝
If you have a slip with food today, remind yourself that it's getting back on track that counts the most.

"Of course there is no formula for success except perhaps an unconditional acceptance of life and what it brings."

ARTUR RUBINSTEIN

When Pat joined a weight-loss program just before she turned 30, her goal was to lose the 24 extra pounds she was carrying around so she could be more comfortably active with her children. Within three months Pat was two pounds under her weight goal and was able to buy size 8 jeans in a store where she had previously only bought size 16. Her celebration was short-lived, however; three months later she was diagnosed with cancer.

Instead of using her illness as an excuse to lapse into old eating habits, Pat used her weight-loss experience to help her fight back, because having a sound diet often gives a cancer patient a better chance of recovery. She was determined not to be self-pitying, so she put on makeup and a wig before each chemotherapy appointment. "Since I was determined to be a survivor, I refused to look the part of the victim," she explains. Today Pat's prognosis is excellent and she credits much of her success to her determination to eat and live as healthfully as possible before and after the diagnosis.

Because life throws everyone curve balls, it's important to cultivate an attitude of acceptance toward whatever comes your way, both positive and negative. If you can do this and retain the discipline to eat well and exercise during even your hardest periods, you'll always have sufficient energy to deal with your challenges.

⌘ *Tip for the Day* ⌘
*Don't allow setbacks to prevent you from adhering
to your food and exercise plan.*

"A ruffled mind makes a restless pillow."

CHARLOTTE BRONTË

Quite often when sleep eludes us, it's because we're upset or anxious and our thoughts keep us awake. There are also times, however, when our minds are "ruffled" with headaches because we've eaten or drunk something that caused a bad reaction. If you suspect that something you are eating is responsible for sleep problems or other adverse medical reactions, it's important to analyze what you're eating to see if you can identify and eliminate an ingredient that might be the culprit.

Johanna gets such painful migraines that she has to stay in a darkened room until the aches pass. She's found that aged cheeses and chocolate will usually trigger an attack, so now she avoids these foods. For women who have headaches during ovulation or their period, it's advisable to avoid caffeine and salt. Foods often associated with headaches include bananas, chocolate, cheese, preservatives, caffeine and alcohol.

If you frequently get headaches, examine your meal plans for a pattern. Keep a log of every single morsel you eat to see if there's a pattern. Perhaps you eat certain foods before your headaches strike, for example. Experiment with eliminating and reintroducing those substances. While weight-loss goals often dictate food choices, you must also eat foods that bring you physical and mental well-being.

⊷ *Tip for the Day* ⊷
Start a food log today. Monitor yourself regularly to become aware of how certain foods affect you and whether they are helping you to feel stronger and more vital.

*"[Optimism is] believing that what will come, and
must come, shall come well."*

ADAPTED FROM EDWIN ARNOLD

There's little doubt that your mind has a powerful effect on
how successful you are in life. People who envision themselves
at a certain weight, in a certain job and living in a joyful way
are far more likely to achieve their dreams than those who are
pessimistic and cynical. Now there's even evidence that people
who tell themselves that they will enjoy their workouts are
more confident and self-assured than those who don't give
themselves pep talks.

The next time you are dreading your workout because you
don't have enough energy or you just don't want to do it, tell
yourself how much stronger, energetic and happy you'll feel
afterward. And in any other situation where you find yourself
being negative, such as "I don't want to go to work because my
job is boring," reverse your thinking with some positive self-
talk like "I will go to work today to see what new thing I can
learn." You'll find that the more you can expect good things to
come to you, the more likely it is that they will.

Tip for the Day
*Before you do any physical activity today, tell yourself that you will feel
wonderful and confident afterward.*

> *"Even if you're on the right track, you'll get run over*
> *if you just sit there."*
> WILL ROGERS

Sometimes when people join a weight-loss program, they will lose a lot of weight quickly, followed by months of more reasonable 1- or 2-pound drops each week. If you have a lot of weight to lose, this can make reaching your weight goal seem impossible. You may begin to slack off and allow yourself bigger food portions or skip your exercise session. When this happens and your weight hits a plateau, it's important to find ways to remotivate yourself and get back on track.

Monica was at a frustrating plateau for four months. During this time she gained and lost the same pound over and over. Finally, with the help of friends, she redesigned her menus to vary the foods she ate and found ways to feel excited about her goal again. As a result, she broke her plateau and resumed a steady weight loss. Susan lost half of the 180 pounds she needed to lose and then began to get discouraged about losing the rest. Fortunately, she stumbled across a letter in a fitness magazine from a woman who'd had the same struggle but successfully overcame it. This was all Susan needed to fire up her enthusiasm again.

If you are stalled in your fitness routine, it's time to reactivate your motivation. Post inspirational stories on your refrigerator and enlist a friend to exercise with every day. Analyze whether you want to lose weight for yourself or someone else. Remind yourself that those who succeed at losing weight do so because of their own inner drive. Once you make the commitment to become healthier, take care not to slack off. If you take your progress for granted, you may indeed get "run over."

↬ *Tip for the Day* ↫

Review your progress. Have you gotten into a rut in your exercise routine?
If so, try to increase the intensity of your workout.

"Progress in civilization has been accompanied by progress in cookery."

FANNIE FARMER

In the last 50 years the world has made astonishing progress in the fields of technology, communications and trans-portation. The same is true in the area of cooking. Elaborate dishes that once took hours of preparation and careful measuring, dicing and mixing can now be completed in a fraction of that time using a food processor. A woman who was a Weight Watchers member in the 1970s rejoined the program 20 years later and was delighted to find that the advent of the microwave oven, other cooking utensils and new sugar substitutes made staying on her food plan much easier than it had once been.

Tasty, low-calorie meals can be purchased in the frozen food section of the grocery store. It's possible to eat a product that tastes identical to ice cream but doesn't contain high levels of fat or sugar. Even fast-food restaurants have updated their menus. Instead of just getting a greasy hamburger, it's now possible to get plain baked potatoes, salads and grilled chicken at a drive-in window.

If time has passed your kitchen by, consider investing in some innovative items that will make meal preparation easier. Bread makers, pasta machines, steamers and microwave ovens can add speed and variety to your day. Learning how to cook "light" can help make meals delicious and low-fat. You'll find that the more you can be aware of progress in cookery, the greater will be the techniques available to you to help you be successful.

    ➦ *Tip for the Day* ➧

Find out where you can take a class in low-fat cooking, or treat yourself to a cookbook featuring light and healthful recipes.

"Where is there dignity unless there is honesty?"
MARCUS TULLIUS CICERO

Heidi's first attempt at weight loss failed because she thought that if no one saw her eat, she really hadn't eaten anything. Although she would follow the plan religiously during the day, after her husband and children went to bed at night she'd curl up in front of the television with bags of sweets and chips. Finally, unable to deceive herself any longer, she acknowledged her nighttime nibbling. She began to be honest with herself about food and soon lost 22 pounds. And she's kept it off.

To be successful at weight loss, you must be conscientious and honest about your attempts and challenges. The most important way to do this is to record accurately what you are actually eating at and between meals, not what you intend to eat. You may be unaware of ways you are hurting your program, so check these areas if your weight loss has slowed significantly or stopped: Are you weighing and measuring your food correctly? Are you snacking while preparing food or cleaning up? Have you changed your exercise regimen?

Remember today to be honest with yourself about how you are going about losing weight. Keep your scales and measuring cups easily accessible so that you always have an accurate account of quantities. Exercise with a friend if that makes it easier to fulfill your commitment. Acknowledge your slips immediately and take action so they won't occur again. You'll find that when honesty is the cornerstone of every aspect of your life, you'll always have the dignity that comes with peace of mind.

❦ *Tip for the Day* ❦
Double-check your meal and exercise planning against what you actually do today, and take steps to correct any discrepancies.

"The wheels of justice... they're square wheels."
BARBARA CORCORAN

There are many injustices in life, one of which is discrimination against overweight people. Studies have shown that obese women are particularly vulnerable to this type of pressure. For example, they are 20 percent less likely to get married than normal-weight peers and their socioeconomic status is likely to be worse than that of other women. Overweight men suffer, too, but not to the same extent. While their socioeconomic status isn't affected, they are 11 percent less likely to get married than normal-weight men.

In an ideal world, being overweight wouldn't be a barrier to getting work or being loved. Unfortunately, that type of society doesn't exist yet. Instead of merely complaining about injustice, use your energies to improve your life. If you are aware that your excess weight is more than just unhealthy, and that it's also a barrier to professional advancement or emotional fulfillment, you have a number of concrete reasons to stay committed to a weight-loss program.

Do you think that being heavy has held you back in various areas of your life? If so, acknowledge to yourself that it's not fair. But remember that success sometimes involves making peace with the world you live in. So instead of arguing about the unfairness of weight discrimination, remind yourself of the many ways your life will improve both personally and professionally as you lose weight. Remain committed to reaching your goals.

Tip for the Day
Make a list of ten things that will improve for you if you remain committed to reaching your weight-loss goals. Be sure to include these three: look better, feel better, reduce risk of heart disease.

"Popcorn [is] the sentimental good-time Charlie of American foods."

PATRICIA LINDEN

Just about everyone grows up going to movies, the circus or a fair and munching on a bag of popcorn. As a result, popcorn is a food that many associate with enjoyment. It is a good weight-loss snack because it's a wholesome sugar-free food. It's a good idea to work foods such as unbuttered popcorn into your meal plan, especially if its texture and the memories associated with it make it easier to stick with your program.

One way to make weight loss successful is to match your food choices to your moods. For example, crunchy foods like popcorn can be good selections if you're frustrated or angry or want to crunch something forcefully. Soft, creamy foods like yogurt can be soothing if you're sad or longing for the comforts of childhood. By the same token, spicy foods can be just what's needed if you're feeling adventurous and want to add excitement to your meal plans.

Be aware today of how what you eat can help you emotionally as well as physically. Foods and textures affect us all in different ways. Use that knowledge to your advantage and make the food selections that will create the most harmony at your meals.

≈ *Tip for the Day* ≈

Assess your mood as you sit down to your meals today. Will what you've planned meet your emotional needs, or should you alter it slightly to give yourself more satisfaction?

"Keep away from people who try to belittle your ambitions."
MARK TWAIN

It is unfortunate that whenever you try to alter your lifestyle in order to improve yourself, there may be people around you who will resist your efforts to change. Perhaps a change in your schedule causes a flip-flop in an established routine, or your determination may threaten someone else's comfort. Whatever the reasons, you must learn to deal with saboteurs in order to be successful, especially when it comes to losing weight.

If you find a few too many monkey wrenches thrown your way, acknowledge that someone you love isn't supportive. Be aware that you must resist attempts by that person to make you fail. Speak up and explain that you would like to be supported. For example, ask saboteurs to refrain from criticizing your appearance and suggest instead that they praise your efforts to eat healthfully and moderately. Another alternative is to take a time out and avoid their company for several weeks. Soliciting ideas and support from other encouraging friends during this period can make dealing with this type of situation easier.

If you feel unsupported in your efforts at weight loss, spend some time thinking about how it has affected your resolve. And if you haven't yet taken action to address the sabotage, write down what you'd like to say to the person and practice in front of the mirror. Whatever you do, don't allow your ambition to fizzle. Possessing the determination to succeed is a critical factor in achieving success.

Tip for the Day
Spend time today with a friend who celebrates your achievements
and is proud of your efforts to change.

"I know of no more encouraging fact than the unquestioned ability of a man to elevate his life by conscious endeavor."

HENRY DAVID THOREAU

Too often we are overwhelmed when faced with a task such as weight loss. We tend to think that we're not strong enough, not disciplined enough or not good enough to accomplish this task. When we find ourselves falling prey to this kind of negativity, it's wise to remotivate ourselves with stories of feats by people who have overcome severe odds to reach their goals.

John is one such inspirational person. When he was 28 he lost his sight to an eye disease. As a way of coping he drank heavily until he was almost 50, at which point he began to recover from alcoholism. Shortly afterward, during a camping trip with his son and grandson, he decided to take on an almost-impossible task: hiking the entire 2,167-mile Appalachian Trail, something that is successfully done by only about 10 percent of those who try. Accompanied by only his seeing-eye dog, he set out from Georgia. Over the next eight months he endured dangerous cliffs, bears, loneliness, a broken rib and blizzards. When he finally arrived in Maine at the end of the trail, 18 members of his hometown church greeted him and sang "Amazing Grace" as a testament to his ambition and faith in himself.

Whenever you take a path that looks difficult, you are saying you believe in yourself enough to take a risk. Remember today to persevere in whatever you want to accomplish, even if it feels overwhelming and scary. If you can nurture your self-confidence and just put one foot in front of the other, you'll succeed in hiking any trail you want to take.

≈ Tip for the Day ≈
Take a risk today that will take you one step closer toward one of your goals. For example, if you want to enlarge your circle of friends, call someone and invite them to share a meal or movie with you.

"Ah, there's nothing like tea in the afternoon."

AYN RAND

Habitual tea drinkers know that taking a break to sip this soothing drink doesn't just quench thirst, it soothes the soul as well. In fact, in Japan the complete tea ritual takes over an hour and is often performed in silence. For the person trying to lose weight, a somewhat shorter break can fulfill various needs including stanching hunger cravings.

Now there's evidence that a few cups of tea each day can be good for the heart. Flavenoids, a type of antioxidant found in various fruits and vegetables, is also found in tea and it is thought to lower the risk of heart attack. In a five-year study of eight hundred elderly men, those who got a significant amount of flavenoids from tea, apples and onions were far less likely to have heart attacks than those who didn't.

If you rely on sodas or coffee to quench your thirst or give you a lift, consider drinking tea instead. If you're avoiding caffeine, try one of the many herb teas that have no caffeine to begin with. Tea comes in a variety of flavors and can be drunk hot or cold. It is also a social drink that can make visiting with a friend that much more pleasant. So the next time you are looking for a way to calm yourself and put something warm into your stomach, try some tea.

❧ *Tip for the Day* ❧
Drink at least one cup of tea today, either iced or hot,
as an afternoon pick-me-up.

*"On close scrutiny, the beast within us looks
suspiciously like a sheep."*

SARAH J. McCARTHY

There are many excuses for being unable to lose weight. Some people blame their lack of willpower. Others take a different approach, passively letting others dictate what happens at mealtimes and avoiding responsibility for their own behavior.

Sandy has lost a great deal of weight and now helps others to do the same as a Weight Watchers leader. She encourages people to avoid being a passive victim of what others do with food. Victims say, "The waiter brought me sour cream on my baked potato," or "My husband wanted cake for dessert." To change this kind of attitude, she says, people who are working on losing weight have to learn to speak up for themselves. No one can force you to eat something you don't want, so be more assertive and send back the potato or push away the cake. Not only are you more likely to achieve the goals you set for yourself but being assertive will raise your self-esteem and give you more incentive to stay on the program.

Don't be a victim today. If you find yourself frequently letting other people lead you to a lapse, examine ways you can avoid this type of occurrence in the future. Practice speaking up with your family and friends so that it's easier when you are in a work or restaurant setting. Consider taking assertiveness classes if your behavior is deeply ingrained. You'll find that when you can stop letting other people and circumstances decide what happens in your life, not only will you feel more empowered to make necessary changes in your life, you'll have the self-confidence that makes it possible.

Tip for the Day

*Take note of how you react to challenges to your weight-loss plan. If you
find yourself allowing others to make decisions about what you eat,
envision yourself being proactive in these situations so you'll
know what to do or say the next time.*

"The farther behind I leave the past, the closer I am to forging my own character."

ISABELLE EBERHARDT

Sometimes it's hard to say farewell to a certain period of your life. Many women lament the end of their children's younger years because they are no longer needed as intensely. Going through menopause can trigger the same kind of sadness because it signals the end of childbearing years and the beginning of another chapter in life.

By the same token, some of us may cling to our past behaviors and the feelings we had when we were overweight because it's safer to be anonymous, sedentary and quiet than vivacious, slender and active. To change this mindset, use pictures of yourself as reminders of your past and present self. One way to do this is to take a full-length picture of yourself when you begin your weight-loss program and then take another one after 16 weeks. Place these pictures side by side on your refrigerator. Seeing yourself in this way is a concrete reminder that you are closing the door on the past and opening the door on a more active and enjoyable future. Keep a current picture of yourself in your wallet to remind you of how much you've changed and how good you look now.

Have you fully shut the door on your past as an overweight person? Are you still clinging to activities or a self-image that isn't consistent with your success? See yourself more positively. As you develop a self-image that accurately reflects your new life, you'll have more enthusiasm and energy to apply toward achieving the goals you set for yourself.

◈ *Tip for the Day* ◈

Stand in front of a full-length mirror today. If you're starting a weight-loss program, say good-bye to the person you see. If you're near or at your weight-loss goal, say hello.

"A restaurant is a fantasy—a kind of living fantasy in which diners are the most important members of the cast."

WARNER LEROY

One of the greatest pleasures in life is eating at a fine restaurant. We all enjoy relaxing meals that are cooked to perfection and served with flair. Also, dressing up and being pampered is an indication that we value ourselves and enjoy the rites of a special occasion.

When people make a commitment to lose weight, they often assume that they can no longer dine at their favorite places. That's not necessarily the case, though. Many restaurants serve meals that are low in fat and nutritious, including entrée-size salads, vegetarian and pasta dishes. Most will honor special requests to serve sauces on the side or will broil food instead of frying it.

Remember today that losing weight doesn't mean forgoing meals at restaurants. It does mean being choosy about what you order, or taking home part of an extra-large portion for another meal. With practice and selectivity you'll find that it's easy to eat a healthy meal, even at a restaurant.

&? *Tip for the Day* ?&

Enjoy a skillfully prepared healthy meal at a restaurant today. Decide in advance to forgo dessert and ask for sauces and dressings served on the side.

"I think I should have no other mortal wants, if I could always have plenty of music. It seems to infuse strength into my limbs and ideas into my brain. Life seems to go on without effort, when I am filled with music."

GEORGE ELIOT

Incorporating exercise into your program is essential for long-term weight loss and to develop a healthy lifestyle. There are many ways to do this, but one of the most popular is to select an activity that is accompanied by music. In fact, studies have shown that exercisers who listen to music while working out feel happier and more relaxed than people who don't.

Walk or jog with a pocket-size cassette or CD player, listening to music you find uplifting and inspirational. Or enroll in aerobic dance classes where you can do movements that match various rhythms. Some people also find that swing dancing is a fun way to get their bodies moving. One woman says that her stationary bike rides are always easier when she turns on a music video channel during her workouts.

Find a way to bring music into your exercise routine today. Make a tape of your favorite songs to listen to while walking, buy an aerobic dance video or subscribe to a music channel. Just as remaining committed to sensible eating requires that you make meals as diverse and enjoyable as possible, adhering to an exercise plan is going to be easier if you add music that makes you smile and puts a spring in your step.

≈ *Tip for the Day* ≈

Exercise while listening to music today. At the end of the session analyze whether your workout was easier and more enjoyable with the music.

"To be able to fill leisure intelligently is the last product of civilization."

ARNOLD TOYNBEE

Boredom can be an enemy of the person who is trying to lose weight. If you have too much time on your hands you may find yourself straying to the kitchen for a snack or visiting the vending machine at work. Long-term success at weight loss means learning how to utilize your spare time so you'll keep away from nibbling.

One of the best ways to fill extra time is with exercise of any kind—walking, jogging, aerobics, bicycling or any activity that will elevate your heart rate. If you still have free time after exercising, though, there are a variety of other activities you can pursue. Some people enjoy volunteering, some fill their spare time with reading or taking classes and others like to meet with their friends. One person who is prone to snacking keeps the Sunday paper and gardening magazines handy so that when she has a few minutes she can catch up with the news and plan her garden.

Make sure today that you have a list of activities you can do if you suddenly are faced with a free block of time and the refrigerator is beckoning. Leave needlework in a handy place, have an enticing book on the nightstand, dump the contents of your purse out and reorganize it and always have the phone numbers of supportive friends with you. If you plan carefully and devise ways to always be busy, you'll be sure to fill your leisure time intelligently and make it easier to reach your goals.

⋙ *Tip for the Day* ⋘
Jot down three things you can do if your plans suddenly change and you don't want to eat for several hours.

"You see what power is—holding someone else's fear in your hand and showing it to them!"

AMY TAN

If you have ever tried to lose weight and found that certain foods led you to abandon a healthy routine, you may have assigned a lot of power to those particular foods. For example, if eating peanut butter is a trigger for you to overeat, you may think that your willpower is no match for peanut butter. Or if baking cookies usually results in your eating the dough, this activity may induce feelings of powerlessness in you as well.

One woman says that she used to be wary of bagels. One morning she ate five bagels and over time went on to gain 68 pounds. In her memory, she assigned that morning's overeating as the trigger for her weight gain. She became fearful of eating bagels because she assumed having a bagel would relaunch the cycle of excessive eating and weight gain. Even after reaching her weight goal she was still afraid of what effect bagels might have on her. One day she tried an experiment. After packing her children off to school, taking the phone off the hook and putting on some music, she ate a single bagel. To her surprise, she realized that a bagel had no power over her. She had learned to manage the food, not let the food manage her.

Are there any foods to which you assign too much power? Do you avoid them because you've eaten too much of them before? If the answer is yes, it might be time for you to put your fears in your hand and look at them honestly. With the support of a friend or family member, try to include that food into one meal this week and remind yourself that there is no bad food. You have the power to eat and live in a healthful way, so don't allow a small piece of food to take that away from you.

Tip for the Day

Pick a food—or even a restaurant—you've been avoiding and affirm that you will not allow fear to dictate what you eat or where you eat any longer.

"*Courage and perseverance have a magical talisman, before which difficulties disappear and obstacles vanish into air.*"
JOHN QUINCY ADAMS

Pamela didn't have a weight problem as a child, but when she got her driver's license she began to make late-night forays to pizza parlors and diners, which resulted in poor eating habits and excess weight. By her twenties Pamela was 60 pounds overweight and spending all her money on takeout food. When she went shopping and couldn't find a pair of pants that fit, she decided to take action and change her unhealthy ways.

Pamela's approach was slow and steady. She gradually cut back on her fat intake and slowly increased her exercise routine as she felt stronger and more energetic. She remembers that her first aerobics classes left her panting for breath, but that within several months she could keep up with the instructor. It took Pamela almost two years to lose 57 pounds. But she persevered and says that at that pace, she was confident that she would be able to control her weight.

Remember today that changes in your lifestyle—like exercise and nutrition habits—will probably take time to adjust to. The resulting weight loss may be slow, but it will give you the opportunity to become accustomed to living healthfully. Pick the pace at which you are most comfortable and begin to make changes today. If you can build on daily success, you will have years of a healthy life ahead of you.

≈ *Tip for the Day* ≈
Persevere in your eating and exercise routines no matter how slowly you are advancing toward your goal.

"A life lived in chaos is an impossibility…."
MADELEINE L'ENGLE

One of the best ways to ensure success is to be organized. By knowing what you want to do and having a plan to achieve it, you eliminate the possibility that disorder, forgetfulness and chaos will throw you off track with weight loss or any other task you set for yourself. And with leisure time continually shrinking—it has sunk 20 percent for the average American since 1973—using time wisely is of paramount importance.

To save time in the supermarket, prepare your grocery list ahead of time and sort your coupons by aisle, strategies that will also keep you from impulse buying. You can also buy food in bulk and create an organized space in your kitchen where you can keep track of what you have and how fresh it is. Organize your closet as well by grouping together similar items. Get rid of outfits that are too old, unflattering or unworn. Other ways to save time include shopping by catalogue or keeping a file of birthday cards ready to be sent whenever the time is right. Above all, practice the TFA principle—throw, file or act on every piece of paper you receive. Doing this diligently prevents clutter from accumulating. Use these tips today to organize a chaotic area of your life. Whether it's streamlining your kitchen or making your desk cleaner, your errands more efficient or your phone calls swifter, getting better organized can be a big boost toward being successful and reaching your goals.

≈ Tip for the Day ≈
If you aren't in the habit of writing a shopping or errand list, make one today. Or make a list of tasks to accomplish on the job today.

*"That is what learning is. You suddenly understand something
you've understood all your life, but in a new way."*

DORIS LESSING

Sometimes people really don't know what good nutrition is, so
they inadvertently eat the wrong foods. For these people, reading nutritional literature and learning correct portion sizes of
healthy foods is what helps them return to a comfortable weight.

Cathy is one such person. For most of her life she didn't
have to watch what she ate because she was naturally thin, but
then she gained a lot of weight during pregnancy and couldn't
lose the last 20 pounds after delivery. She laughs when she
tells how she once thought a nutritionally balanced meal meant
fried chicken, cornbread and a milkshake. But once she learned
what a well-balanced meal was, she had no trouble getting to
her weight goal.

Make sure that you read as much as you can about how you
should eat. Check out some library books on nutrition and
watch television programs that address the principles of healthy
eating. Once you can understand this familiar subject in a new
way, you may be surprised to find how easy it is to create an
environment of health around you.

Tip for the Day

*Make a chart of food groups and portion sizes and post it on your
refrigerator, food cabinet or pantry door.*

> *"At the worst, a house unkept cannot be so*
> *distressing as a life unlived."*
> Rose Macaulay

A best-selling book by a female therapist says that too often we focus on managing trivial aspects of our lives—pruning the bushes, getting the laundry done, mopping the kitchen floor or sweeping the garage—at the expense of exploring new, possibly more creative interests. Once we allow ourselves to express our creativity regardless of our household chores, we can free ourselves to live richer and more rewarding lives.

As you work toward attaining your weight and fitness goals, it's a good idea to set goals for yourself in other areas of your life, too. If you've always had a secret desire to be a painter or writer, for example, you owe it to yourself to pursue those dreams to see where your efforts can take you. This may mean the house is unkept temporarily or you don't rake your leaves promptly, but it's important that you see yourself as a dynamic achiever, and not trapped by day-to-day routines.

Are you living as full a life as you can? Do you dream about learning how to use a potter's wheel, teaching a course or organizing a political campaign, but day-to-day drudgery is holding you back? If so, liberate yourself from some of your mundane duties and take steps to pursue one of your goals today. The more you delegate or ignore tasks that prevent you from pursuing your dreams, the more you can fill your life with activities that bring you joy and enthusiasm.

Tip for the Day
Replace one household chore this week with an activity
that challenges your creativity.

"She endured. And survived."

ANNE CAMERON

For most people there is a period during the year that is particularly and personally challenging, especially as it affects your food and exercise plans. This can occur on different types of occasions, such as summer vacation, a family reunion, the holiday period at the end of the year or during winter months when you may have fewer opportunities for outdoor exercise. If this applies to you, it's important to have some guidelines prepared to help you survive the period that gives you the most trouble.

If holidays are difficult, plan to be lenient with yourself when it comes to sampling a colleague's homemade treats or eating a family favorite. The same is true of summer vacation or winter doldrums. If you've "always" had taffy at the seashore or you "always" have hot chocolate on cold winter nights, either allow yourself the treat by carefully parceling out your calories, or adapt the recipes so that you can enjoy them without gaining weight. Also, remind yourself that after every difficult period comes a break, and you won't have to struggle forever.

Whether the occasion that often derails your eating and exercise regimen is a summer visit to a relative's house or your birthday, remember that taking one day at a time is your best offense in times like these. With a positive outlook, determination and creative preparation, you will survive and overcome every challenging time that comes your way.

❧ *Tip for the Day* ❧
Identify the time of year when you feel most vulnerable to poor eating habits. Think of at least one thing you can do to make the next time easier.

"Most people don't realize how great an influence the foods they eat have on their chances of getting certain types of cancer."

DR. PETER GREENWALD

Obesity and a sedentary lifestyle put people at a health risk. An illness that may be affected by what we eat is cancer. Excess estrogen has been linked to breast cancer, and high estrogen levels are often found among postmenopausal women with high body fat percentages. Obese men also usually have a diet heavy in saturated fats and low in fiber, which has been linked to increased risk of colon and prostate cancer. Being inactive slows the body's digestive tract, increasing its exposure to harmful food-borne carcinogens.

The good news is that losing weight, exercising regularly and eating a diet rich in certain types of foods can significantly cut your risk for certain types of cancer. Dietary fat should make up no more than 30 percent of your total calories. You can reduce your fat intake by eating less red meat and more poultry and fish. Fiber in the form of cereals, legumes and bread should be a significant part of each meal. Eat at least five servings of fruits and vegetables each day, particularly those that are high in beta-carotene and vitamin C.

Be sure that your lifestyle is geared toward preventing the onset or spread of any disease. You are, of course, more than what you eat, but your food and lifestyle desires have a big impact on your quality of life.

≈ *Tip for the Day* ≈
Remember that if you follow a healthy eating plan today and every day, you are working to reduce your risk of some cancers.

"There can be too much communication between people."
ANN BEATTIE

The telephone is our link to the rest of the world. It can be your best friend when you're making business contacts, need help or are searching for specific information. But the telephone is also a mixed blessing because for many of us, the phone is a trigger to eat. We're linked at home from our kitchen phone, which puts anything in the fridge within reach. And at work, while we're talking on the phone we know there's a vending-machine snack in our desk drawer.

To make sure that the telephone doesn't inconvenience or control you, here are some important steps you can take:

- The best days to make calls about problems with some type of service—electricity, insurance claims or post office—are Thursday and Friday. Most people call Monday and Tuesday between 10 A.M. and 2 P.M.
- Decide how much time you are willing to spend on the phone and keep a timer nearby.
- Get to the point quickly. If you have to leave a message, make it as detailed as possible to eliminate a follow-up call.
- When asked if you mind being put on hold, say yes and ask to be called back.
- Use an answering machine. When the phone rings, don't automatically jump to answer it. Decide whether it's an appropriate time to stop what you're doing.
- Cut solicitation calls off quickly by saying you're not interested or that you'd like to be called at a different time.
- Get a nonstop talker to come to the point quickly by saying you have no time to talk.

∽ Tip for the Day ∽
Use the time you save on the phone to do something pleasurable, such as garden, take a walk or eat a leisurely and nutritious meal.

"It is strange indeed that the more you learn about how to build health, the less healthy Americans become."

ADELLE DAVIS

For many years it has been trendy to improve our health by eating more fiber, jogging, quitting smoking and lowering cholesterol. Now, however, it's been reported that Americans are more interested in "pleasure revenge." Tired of heeding so many admonitions to change their ways, Americans have returned with a vengeance to smoking, overeating and avoiding exercise.

Part of the reason why bad habits have regained their popularity is because maintaining a healthy lifestyle is simply more difficult. For example, the proliferation of fast-food restaurants has made it easy to get a high-fat meal, and our reliance on cars means we walk less. To develop a sensible eating and exercise plan you may have to go against an established way of life. This may mean learning new cooking skills, getting up earlier or being more assertive.

Keep in mind today that starting any new regime entails some work that may feel awkward at first. But as soon as you become accustomed to cooking healthy meals, setting aside time to exercise and avoiding stimulants like coffee and cigarettes, it will begin to feel natural to live healthfully. While pleasure revenge may mean indulging in bad habits for some, make sure that your pleasure revenge is doing what makes you feel healthiest and happiest.

◈ *Tip for the Day* ◈
Even if those around you aren't making an effort to build or keep their health, affirm to yourself that you will continue to improve your lifestyle.

"There is no need to go to India or anywhere else to find peace.
You will find that deep place of silence right in your room, your
garden or even your bathtub."

ELISABETH KÜBLER-ROSS

Despondency strikes many people at various times during the
year. Such feelings can occur for a variety of reasons: a death, a
major disappointment, a failed relationship or even the stress
of dealing with a number of small setbacks. Whatever the cause,
it's important that you devise ways to avoid turning to food
when you're feeling blue. You must learn ways to nurture yourself that won't result in creating additional problems.

Experts have long observed that sadness may be helped by
rewarding yourself with small pleasures that induce feelings of calmness. For some this means finding time to
meditate, listening to a favorite piece of music or taking a
solitary walk in nature. For others, though, this means
taking the time to soak in a warm bath where you won't be
disturbed. A bath is not only noncaloric; if you scent the water
with a fragrance that reminds you of a happy time, you can get
the added benefit of letting a wonderful scent distract you from
your immediate concerns.

If you tend to want to eat when the blues strike, make sure
that you have coping strategies in place. Through past experience you probably know that there is something that makes
you feel better—like a manicure or a massage—so have the
resources available to arrange it on short notice. You may not
be able to predict when your spirits will be low, but with some
planning you can always have a solution on hand that will
support, not hinder, your efforts.

◆ *Tip for the Day* ◆
If sadness usually leads you to overeat a specific food, keep that item out of your
house and work on finding better ways to soothe yourself.

*"Friendship… is an Union of Spirits, Marriage of Hearts,
and the Bond thereto Virtue."*

WILLIAM PENN

Being part of a supportive community like Weight Watchers makes weight loss simpler, and it imparts other satisfactions as well. When you watch others struggle and succeed and you share your own triumphs and trials with them, it's easy to develop friendships. By allowing others to see you at your most vulnerable and knowing that they accept you just as you are, you learn to love yourself and to give of your time and care unselfishly.

At Nina's first Weight Watchers meeting, the leader opened by saying that her daughter had just been diagnosed with a serious illness and that being with other members was where she was best able to receive, not just give, love, encouragement and support. Many years later Nina became a Weight Watchers leader herself, and she was able to derive the same feelings from her friends at meetings.

Be sure to attend meetings regularly to benefit fully. Be proactive about meeting people and exchanging advice, and open yourself to the love you can receive from those who have faced similar struggles and who have your best interests at heart. When you can do this, you'll find that giving is a two-way street. You'll learn that everyone to whom you give support will be there to provide you with support as well.

➨ *Tip for the Day* ➩
*Remember that friends from your weight-loss program will celebrate your
successes because they too shared your struggle.*

"Turbulence is life force. It is opportunity. Let's love turbulence and use it for change."

RAMSAY CLARK

It can be tempting to use a turbulent period in life, such as a divorce, loss of a job or death of a loved one, as an excuse to avoid making positive changes. But instead of thinking of this difficult episode as a cause to withdraw and retrench, why not think of this as a time to stretch your limits?

This is exactly what Elizabeth did. Married at 16 and divorced at 31, she moved to a new town and was unsure of herself alone and in a new setting. Instead of retreating into herself and staying home, she took up rock climbing. There were times when she felt the sport was too risky and difficult, but by persevering she gained confidence in herself. This self-confidence in her physical capabilities carried over to her role as a single parent. She realized that if she could climb a mountain, she says, she could do other things that she once thought impossible.

Athletic tests of skill and endurance can teach you that it's indeed possible to move beyond your physical limitations. That realization can spur you to make other changes, but excessive eating due to discouragement or anxiety will prevent you from taking advantage of this special period. By embracing turbulence and using it to take responsible, life-enhancing risks, a situation that looks difficult, such as losing weight or becoming athletically fit, can be transformed into a benefit.

⋘ *Tip for the Day* ⋙
Remember that personal or professional turmoil can be an opportunity to take a bold step in a new direction.

*"Some television programs are so much
chewing gum for the eyes."*

JOHN MASON BROWN

Watching television can be relaxing, but for many people it is also a trigger for mindless snacking. Instead of zoning out, dozing off and eating, use TV time to your benefit. Here are some ways to control the TV instead of letting it control you.

Television makes exercising time go by very quickly. Ride your stationary bicycle or jog on a treadmill or jump on a mini-trampoline while watching your favorite shows. Treat yourself to a different show every day without feeling guilty. If you're tired and need to relax, give yourself a manicure or pedicure. Or brush and groom your dog and cat. To keep your hands occupied with something other than food, build something in your workshop or learn a new needlework technique. You'll still be able to follow a TV program. If you absolutely must eat in front of the TV in the evening, then sip something hot, such as a cup of bouillon with a celery stick, mint tea with a drizzle of honey or decaffeinated coffee with skim milk and a dash of cinnamon. You'll satisfy your hunger and be relaxed and ready for a good night's sleep.

Remember today that television can be more than just an invitation to nibble. It's a way of building time into a busy day, time for you to relax, exercise and play.

Tip for the Day

*Tape a late-night talk show on your VCR, then watch it the next day
while you're getting ready for work or preparing dinner.*

"Bad backs are as common as colds."
MICHAEL COCCO, M.D.

One of the most common and debilitating of all physical problems is an aching back. In fact, studies have shown that 80 percent of Americans will suffer from back pain at some point during their lives, and back pain trails only childbirth as a reason for hospitalization. Bad backs account for much of the absenteeism in the work force, and women suffer most when it comes to needing bed rest to recuperate.

When grappling with a bad back, you're liable to avoid exercise, which will hamper you in weight-loss efforts. You may even feel so sorry for yourself because of the pain that you turn to food for comfort. To avoid this problem and keep your back in peak condition, consider some of the following tips from health professionals:

Stretch before and after exercise sessions, do simple yoga postures that build lower back strength and try to sit and stand without slumped shoulders. If you're already experiencing back pain, heating pads and some gentle stretches, such as pulling your knees to your chest while lying down, can ease your symptoms. A chiropractor can also be an invaluable resource for the person whose back is troublesome.

If lower back pain is keeping you from a fitness routine, try to address your problem with nutritious foods and gentle stretches. Also, take time to meditate and visualize a strong, supple back. With the right preventive care and careful exercise, you won't have to let your back be the weakest part of you.

Tip for the Day
Do one exercise each day to strengthen your back.

"I consulted the moon / like a crystal ball."

DIANE ACKERMAN

In many cultures women use the moon to mark the phases of their monthly fertility, particularly because the moon can affect menstrual cycles and even moods. At different times of the month it's not uncommon for your food cravings to change and for your body to respond differently. In fact, many premenstrual women report that their desire for carbohydrates rises sharply in the week before their periods and that their weight usually plateaus or goes up, even if they are eating carefully and exercising.

Many women find that limiting their salt intake, reducing caffeine consumption and continuing to exercise regularly helps curb cravings, eliminates water weight gain and eases cramps. Menstruation isn't the only phase that affects weight gain or loss. Pregnancy and menopause each require specialized meal plans because both of these conditions can change a woman's metabolism and the needs of her body. Unless special care is taken, weight gain can become a significant problem.

Just as the moon waxes and wanes, so do the seasons in a woman's life when signals of fertility cause marked physical and emotional changes. If you find yourself having trouble with any of these periods, be sure to educate yourself about these unique times of life. Try to adapt your meals to these potentially difficult times. Just as your needs change from time to time, it's smart to use the flexibility of a sensible meal plan to make those times as comfortable and successful as possible.

≈ *Tip for the Day* ≈

Women should take note of any special nutritional needs at different times of the month and be prepared to eat properly with each monthly cycle.

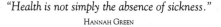

> *"Health is not simply the absence of sickness."*
> HANNAH GREEN

Most people who decide to lose weight do so because their clothes are too tight, they don't like how they look in a bathing suit or they want to look as young as they feel. While these are all good reasons to develop healthy eating habits, it's important that you recognize that losing weight brings many physical benefits as well. Dropping as little as 10 to 15 pounds can reduce the risk of developing heart disease, diabetes, high blood pressure, gallbladder disease and some types of cancer.

When Jane began a weight-loss program she was on disability leave from her job because her obesity had severely weakened her knees to such an extent that she couldn't walk. As her weight gradually dropped, she began to walk without pain, her blood pressure went down and she was able to stop taking several medications. Altogether Jane lost 150 pounds, rejoined her company full time and became more active than she'd ever been before. Delighted that she can wear small sizes again, she says she is also thrilled to be healthy and fit.

Has your weight caused you any physical problems? If so, remember as you lose weight that you are doing more than transforming yourself externally, you are also becoming healthier. While it's always gratifying to like what you see in the mirror, health is weight loss's most precious reward.

⤳ *Tip for the Day* ⤳
Make a list of any physical ailments that are related to being overweight. Have any of them improved or become minimal since you started to lose weight?

"The boughs of no two trees ever have the same arrangement. Nature always produces individuals; She never produces classes."
LYDIA MARIA CHILD

Linda joined a weight-loss program at a low point in her life and successfully lost 25 pounds. This boosted her self-esteem tremendously. All of her new-found confidence evaporated, however, on a trip to the beach with a friend who is naturally model-thin. Linda felt fat and frumpy next to her friend, she remembers, so she gave up on her diet during that trip because she knew she'd never look that thin.

We all know someone who is naturally thin and who can apparently polish off a five-course dinner without gaining a pound. Instead of moaning about the unfairness of life, you must accept your individual differences and do your best to cope with them. Linda reawakened her pride in her own accomplishments by standing in front of a full-length mirror once a week and finding something about her body to admire. She learned to wear pieces of clothing to accentuate a part of her body that made her feel good about her weight loss.

Remember today that everyone is unique. Comparing yourself unfavorably with others will only make you lose sight of what is special about you. Take a moment today to think of things you've accomplished in the last year that make you feel proud of yourself. You'll find that if you love yourself unconditionally you'll have more love available to share with others.

☙ *Tip for the Day* ☙
List three things you like about yourself that you consider special to you.

"A simple enough pleasure, surely, to have breakfast alone with one's husband, but how seldom married people in the midst of life achieve it."

ANNE MORROW LINDBERGH

Jeanne was a classic "people pleaser" who always put others' needs ahead of her own. Losing 55 pounds helped her to find her own voice and become more assertive, she says. One of the things she learned was that the most important person at the dinner table was herself. Jeanne realized that unless her top priority was eating properly and being in a supportive environment that enabled her to do so, her disappointment would affect everyone around her.

If you are to enjoy losing weight, it's important that you create the right ambiance for yourself. One way to do this may include scheduling a private breakfast with your spouse on a regular basis. Lara discovered that going to school and raising two active children was preventing her from having quality time for herself and her husband. Now she sets aside every other Saturday morning to have breakfast in bed with her husband while her children watch a video.

Has your active life prevented you from having a quiet breakfast with your partner recently? If so, try the breakfast-in-bed option or look into going out for a meal at a restaurant where your weight-loss needs can be met. If you can carve out regular periods when you can catch up with someone you love while meeting your meal plan needs, it will help you remain enthusiastic about losing weight. And you'll be helping your relationships with others, too.

Tip for the Day

Buy a tray that you can take to bed with you and make a "date" to share a meal this weekend with someone you love.

"A grandeur in the beatings of the heart."

WILLIAM WORDSWORTH

To improve your heart's health and reduce the risk of a heart attack, it is important to lower cholesterol and cut down on dietary fat. A recent study showed that lowering your blood cholesterol is worth the effort. For every 1 percent decrease in cholesterol, heart attack rate is lowered by 2 percent. The kind of fat most damaging to your heart is saturated fat; it is found in foods such as butter, coconut and palm oil, chicken skin, sausage, bacon, salami, whole milk dairy products and baked goods like cookies and crackers. Health and nutrition groups recommend that saturated fats provide a maximum of 10 percent of your day's calories.

Cutting saturated fats from your diet is easier than you think. Use skim milk in your coffee and tea instead of cream or powdered cream substitutes. Skim milk is also a better choice than whole or 2-percent milk, and part-skim ricotta and light cream cheese have less saturated fat than whole-milk ricotta and regular cream cheese. Try marmalade or jelly on your toast instead of margarine or butter. Lean ham is better for you than all-beef bologna; moisten it with mustard instead of mayonnaise. Granola is fine—but get the low-fat kind. A whole-wheat dinner roll has less fat than a refrigerator crescent roll.

There are many other benefits of a low-fat diet besides preventing and treating heart disease, including a lowered risk for developing breast, colon and prostate cancers and improved immune function. Remember the importance of prevention today. To reap the maximum benefit of a healthy, low-fat diet, follow these guidelines before heart disease begins to develop.

❧ *Tip for the Day* ❧

Examine your meal plan and look for ways to reduce saturated fats today. Be sure to remove the skin from roasted chicken, and you can substitute three egg whites in most recipes that call for a whole egg.

"[Self-defense classes are] potentially life-changing.
Instead of dread and despair and hopelessness,
[it's] taking an action-oriented approach."

MELISSA SOALT

When people make the decision to lose weight and then follow through with healthful activities, they discover new confidence. After reaching her weight and fitness goals, one woman
realized she used to have a very narrow view of what she could
do with her life. But now, she says, anything seems possible.

Another activity that may create these same feelings of
empowerment is taking self-defense courses. The goal of martial arts is to instill a sense of power in movement and control
of your body. Many of the movement combinations are meditations in motion. One woman who timidly began a three-
week course found that at the end of the sessions she had more
self-confidence knowing that she could defend herself if necessary. Men echo her feelings.

If your excess weight has prevented you from developing
self-confidence or assertiveness, consider taking a self-defense
class. By learning how to defend yourself physically, you'll also
get the powerful psychological boost that you are worthy of
care.

∞ *Tip for the Day* ∞
Make arrangements to watch a self-defense class. If it appeals
to you, sign up for an introductory class.

*"The happiness of a man in this life does not consist in
the absence but in the mastery of his passions."*

ALFRED, LORD TENNYSON

For most of her life Cynthia allowed sweets to rule her. Because she was a heavy child, sweets were forbidden, which only increased their allure. As an adult, Cynthia gave in to her cravings with massive overeating, and then she'd berate herself for being "bad." Then the obsession would start again and it wouldn't be long before Cynthia was sneaking sweets between meals, causing her weight to increase steadily.

In Weight Watchers Cynthia learned how to master her passion. She discovered she can include occasional sweets in her food plan in a guilt-free way and still lose weight. In fact, the more she has allowed herself "forbidden" foods, the less important those foods have become to her. She marvels that sneaking a candy bar isn't even tempting anymore.

Be aware of any foods that may be controlling your life. If you learn how to plan ahead for special taste treats, you'll discover they will lose their power over you. Remember, you are the master—not the slave—of your passions.

Tip for the Day

*If there is a food you're passionate about, think about how to incorporate
it into your meal plan without derailing your weight-loss efforts.*

"We turn not older with years, but newer every day."
EMILY DICKINSON

As you get older, you can look at your birthday in two different ways—as dreaded proof that you are aging, or as an opportunity to grow. If you are successfully losing weight and changing your lifestyle, you're probably feeling and looking better with every passing day. And if your last birthday was marked by overeating, shame and inactivity, this birthday can be a celebration of a healthier approach to life.

If your birthday is near, take stock of ways you have improved your life since your last birthday. Perhaps you are working on becoming healthier and happier. Or you have explored new interests and met new friends. Or you are committed to living a full and rewarding life. Congratulate yourself for all your positive changes. Promise yourself that the coming year will bring you even more growth, joy and appreciation for the healthy life you have created.

⮞ *Tip for the Day* ⮜
*Think of several ways your upcoming birthday can be a celebration of
new and healthy behaviors instead of a reminder that you are one year older.*

> *"Touch is a human physiological need that, when left
> unsatisfied, has profound psychological consequences."*
> MEREDITH GOULD RUCH

Many years ago it was shown that hospitalized infants did better when they were touched and held. Subsequent research has shown that touch also has a profound effect on adults. For example, people have consistently lower levels of stress-related hormones after a 30-minute massage and are more alert, less restless and better able to sleep than before.

One overweight woman who used to turn to food for comfort says that massage makes her feel lovable and nurtured. In addition, massage helps to reduce tension, improve circulation, increase energy and raise self-esteem. As these positive emotions surface, it becomes easier to avoid turning to food to feel loved.

Investigate how supportive touch and massage therapy might help you in your weight-loss efforts. There are many different schools of therapy, so try to find someone with whom you feel comfortable and whose technique makes you feel most relaxed. Although massage may feel frivolous at first, supportive touch can make the difference between feeling empty inside and feeling satisfied enough to avoid overeating.

Tip for the Day

Look into getting an appointment with a massage therapist today.

"I must govern the clock, not be governed by it."
GOLDA MEIR

A recent poll of a magazine's female readers showed that 68 percent wished they had more time to spend on themselves but they felt guilty taking any time out of their already busy schedules to attend to their own needs. But taking time for yourself, whether you're female or male, isn't frivolous—it's a necessity and an investment in yourself. A study of 3,400 U.S. workers found that setting aside time for personal pleasures resulted in a heightened sense of mental and physical well-being.

Here are some experts' tips on how to carve out more time for yourself, time that can be spent working toward achieving your weight and fitness goals:

- Use an egg timer to put a limit on phone calls, vacuuming and other time-consuming chores.
- Instead of saying "maybe" to a request, say "yes" or "no" so that you don't waste time reconsidering it.
- Make extra meals on weekends and freeze them for use later in the week.
- Invest in extra food storage space so you can save time by buying larger quantities and shopping less often.
- Set up a food station in the kitchen so children can help make their own meals.
- Carry a large basket around the house for picking up anything that's out of place. Two round-trips should do it.
- Ask for help; don't do everything yourself.

Once you've created extra time for yourself, use it wisely. Spending your newly found 30 or 60 minutes watching television may not improve your life, but exercising, meditating or going to a group support meeting will.

Tip for the Day
Employ at least one time-saving device today. And ask for help.

> "We improve ourselves by victories over ourself.
> There must be contests, and you must win."
>
> EDWARD GIBBON

The newcomer to Weight Watchers may chafe at the program's insistence on weighing and measuring food, keeping a food diary and finding time to exercise regularly. "I don't want to!" or "I don't have time!" are two often-heard excuses by people who want to be in the program, but only on their own terms.

Nancy is a leader who emphasizes the importance of discipline in order to reach goals you set for yourself. She credits losing 36 pounds and keeping it off for eighteen years to weighing and measuring her food—no matter what—faithfully, every day of her life. Weighing her food only takes a minute or two, she explains, but it gives her 24 hours of being thin.

Remember today that you must sometimes do things that you don't want to do in order to achieve something you desire. So if attending meetings, exercising, weighing your food or planning your meals feels like an unnecessary burden, resolve to win by overcoming at least one of those challenges today. The more you can persuade yourself to do something that initially feels hard, the more you'll find that genuine contentment often flows from enjoying the fruits of this type of discipline.

Tip for the Day
Do at least one thing today that you don't want to do
but that is beneficial for you.

"If you can organize your kitchen, you can organize your life."
LOUIS PARRISH

So much of your success in losing weight is in being organized, especially in the kitchen, where most of your meals are probably prepared. If you aren't organized—you don't have the right ingredients for proper meals or the right utensils to prepare and measure them, for example—you'll sabotage your efforts right from the start. For that reason it's essential to reorganize your kitchen when you join a weight-loss program.

Start with your drawers. Check to see if you have a complete set of measuring cups and spoons. Slotted spoons are handy for stirring pasta, and nonstick pans and spatulas are essential for sauteing with very little oil. Make sure you have one or more recent cookbooks readily available to give you ideas for healthy meals. If needed, clean the vegetable drawers in your refrigerator and check that you have enough room in your freezer to stock up on sale items. Clear your counters so you have enough open and clean counter space readily available.

Think of ways to streamline your kitchen today. Some people find that putting up a spice rack, taking clutter off the front of the refrigerator and hanging pots on a pretty rack make their kitchens more pleasant. Others find that rearranging the cabinets and cleaning the floors make the biggest difference for them. Whatever you decide to do, keep in mind that how you feel while working with food has a big effect on how much you enjoy your meals. Make your kitchen work space as pleasant and organized as possible so meal preparation is an enjoyable and successful experience.

    Tip for the Day
Do something to organize your kitchen today, such as
putting all of your recipes in a file box or binder.

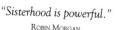

"Sisterhood is powerful."
ROBIN MORGAN

A group of five working women who found evening mealtimes very difficult to manage came up with an unusual solution: They formed an arrangement to cook meals for each other one night each week. For the time and cost of preparing a dinner for over 20 adults and children once a week, these women have the ability to come home from work on the other four nights and relax until a hot meal arrives at their door. These women say that the arrangement has helped them to streamline their efficiency, have more time for themselves and devote more hours to their husbands and children.

Consider making this type of arrangement if you are so short on time at the end of the day that you aren't preparing a hot, healthy meal for yourself and your family. One way to do this is to ask four other people who live nearby to try this idea for a month. Meet to review the recipes beforehand so your weight-loss needs are met. Later, get feedback about which dishes were the most successful and whether it's an arrangement you'd like to continue. The more you can use your creativity to make your mealtimes healthy and enjoyable, the more time you may free up for yourself and your family.

Tip for the Day
*Think about sharing cooking duties with a friend at least
once a week to give you time away from the kitchen.*

"One hour with a child is like a ten-mile run."

JOAN BENOIT SAMUELSON

Penny was young when she married and started having children. She began gaining weight right away. When she turned 45, she was five-foot-five and 191 pounds. Her excess weight caused her to become easily winded so she couldn't play comfortably with her grandchildren whenever they visited. Unhappy that she was missing out on one of life's greatest pleasures, she joined a weight-loss program and lost 60 pounds over 18 months. Now she says with pride that people who meet her can't believe she's a grandmother. She walks three miles every day now, feels good about herself and no longer has the health problems she did when she was overweight.

People have many different reasons for wanting to lose weight, but one of the most compelling is a desire to keep up with children or grandchildren. Being available to children means having stamina and enthusiasm, but you'll never have enough if you're unhealthy and overweight. By giving yourself the gift of health you also give children the gift of your energy and presence, something they'll treasure for a lifetime.

Ask yourself honestly if your weight interferes with your relationship with your children or grandchildren. If so, redouble your commitment to losing weight. Your health and vitality enhance your life as well as the lives of those around you, especially the children.

Tip for the Day

Think of ways that losing weight makes it easier for you to deal with children. Remind yourself that being energetic is a benefit of eating and exercising wisely.

"All happiness depends on a leisurely breakfast."
JOHN GUNTHER

One of the ways you may have undermined your weight-loss efforts is by eating meals in a hurry. For some this may have meant stopping at a fast-food place for drive-through meals, grabbing something off a pastry cart at work or eating while standing up. When you rush you're likely to misjudge portion size, eat whatever's convenient or finish other people's leftovers. This rarely adds up to a balanced meal, much less a satisfying one.

As part of starting off your day on the right foot, try to set aside some time every morning for a relaxed and sensible breakfast. Eating this way enables you to focus on feelings of hunger and fullness more easily. When you allow enough time, you can measure your food and eat a nutritious meal. Getting through the first meal of the day without having a slip will give you the self-confidence to stay on your program for the rest of the day.

Be aware of how you eat your breakfast today. Are you stressed and distracted, or are you enjoying your meal? Do you finish with a feeling of satisfaction or anxiety? Try to make sure that every day starts with success. When you get your day off to a good start, it's more likely that you'll carry a winning attitude through the rest of the day.

☙ *Tip for the Day* ❧
Set aside enough time to make and enjoy a nourishing breakfast today.

"'Tain't worthwhile to wear a day all out before it comes."

SARAH ORNE JEWETT

Stella lost 28 pounds and maintained her weight for two years. But then she experienced a setback and regained the weight. Although she wanted to rejoin the program that had helped her to be successful, she was too embarrassed to walk into a meeting and admit that she had "failed." She was also depressed about how long it would take her to reach her weight goal again, berating herself for having "wasted" several years of her life.

With the help of a good friend, Stella began to put the experience in perspective. She began to focus on what she *could* do to make the necessary changes and learned to stop berating herself. She knew from her previous success that the effort of losing weight by herself would be hard and lonely, whereas being part of a support group would be more encouraging and empowering.

Whether you are rejoining a weight-loss program after an absence, joining one for the first time or maintaining your weight goal, remember to start each day with the positive belief that you will do the best you can, one day at a time. It's useless to worry about the past or what the future holds for you. When you learn to live in 24-hour segments, you can focus your energies on being enthusiastic and self-confident during that brief period. Then you'll find that you will reach your goals more easily, and you'll have more enjoyment getting there, too.

∞   *Tip for the Day*   ∞

Start today with this affirmation: I will focus on being as successful as possible for the next 24 hours, and I won't worry about yesterday or tomorrow.

"[Economy is] a great revenue."
JOHN RAY

A group of chefs in one large city regularly meet with mothers on public assistance to teach them how to stretch their food dollars while still shopping healthfully and nutritiously. One single mother of four children had initially despaired that she could accomplish both goals on her limited means. But she learned that if food looks different and interesting, children will eat it. The chefs taught her that people eat with their eyes.

One of the first things the cooking professionals stress is using the right tools, such as a sharp paring knife, a cutting board, a meat thermometer and a vegetable peeler because these make food preparation easier and more pleasant. They also teach not to throw out useful food, such as ham or chicken bones, which can be used to make stock. "One of the things your grandparents knew is that they could use every single piece of the chicken," one chef says, "so you need to ask yourself if you got four dollars' worth out of the chicken you bought."

Remember today to keep your food budget low by getting as much as you can out of every item you buy. And make your dishes appealing to the eye so that you're less likely to have waste. One mother says her children switched from chips to fruit after she created skewers of grapes, pineapple and bananas. The more economical and creative you can be, the more money you will save. And you can improve your family's health at the same time.

⚮ *Tip for the Day* ⚮
Ask yourself if there are leftovers today that can be used to make another meal tomorrow.

"The world stands aside to let anyone pass who knows where he is going."

DAVID STARR JORDAN

June is a classic overachiever. She excels in her competitive career, devotes quality time to her toddler, cooks gourmet meals and participates in numerous worthwhile charities. Although she is highly disciplined and motivated when it comes to managing her work and her family life, June can't work up the initiative to lose the ten extra pounds she's been carrying around for several years. She laments that while she can rack up achievement in most areas of her life, being successful at weight loss eludes her.

June isn't alone. Experts say that it's very normal to be motivated in some areas and not others. To succeed in reaching a goal, they counsel, a person must embody several qualities. First, there should be compelling personal reasons to want to change. You're unlikely to lose weight, for example, if you are doing it for someone else's approval. Winners also set goals that are one step ahead of themselves, which keeps them challenged. Also, they don't treat setbacks as failures. If they have eaten some "bad" foods during a vacation, for example, they don't berate themselves. Instead, they remind themselves how far they've come, then get back on track.

Are you motivated to succeed at weight loss? Examine your motives for wanting to lose weight. Ask yourself if you have what it takes to reach and maintain your goal. Once you can apply your energy and drive in a positive way, you will lose weight, and the world will "stand aside to let you pass" in other areas of your life, too.

Tip for the Day

Write down where you are going today, personally and professionally. Are you completely committed to reaching these goals? Whom will you please by meeting them?

"[Food is] the commonest cause of domestic strife."
ANONYMOUS

For some people, the dinner table of their childhood was fraught with emotion. Here are some examples: Pleasing a parent meant cleaning the plate. Food equaled love. Desserts were frequently used as rewards. Vegetables were food that only had to be tolerated. To control a parent, refuse to eat.

Because you have adopted a sensible attitude toward food now, it's essential to create a healthy family dynamic around meals so that food won't become such an emotional issue for your children. Experts say that the best way to prevent strife from occurring is for the parents to take responsibility for providing nutritious meals and healthy snacks. But the children are allowed to have control over how much they eat. For example, instead of ordering a child to clear his plate, allow him to eat until he's full. By the same token, have only low-fat snack foods in the house so that whenever your child is tempted to eat, the only choices will be beneficial ones.

Food doesn't have to be the cause of arguments if you and your family have the right approach. If you are still using food as a way of punishing, rewarding and controlling a child or significant other, adopt a less judgmental attitude. When you focus on keeping yourself well and not forcing another to conform to your wishes, you might be surprised at how much harmony you'll have in your house.

Tip for the Day

Remember today that food is simply nourishment. Food is neither a tool to control others nor a measure of love.

"They are committing murder who merely live."
MAY SARTON

Joining Weight Watchers is a big step to take toward creating a healthy and active life. If you follow the eating guidelines and increase your level of exercise, a new world is certain to open up to you. In fact, according to national health statistics, changing your diet and exercise patterns is one of the best ways to lengthen your life and improve its quality.

As part of this effort, you owe it to yourself to take charge of your health. For example, become aware of the risks of tobacco and alcohol. According to the Institute for Health Policy, in 1990 deaths from cigarettes alone numbered 419,000. So it's wise to avoid tobacco altogether—and that includes secondhand smoke, too. Alcohol is another factor that contributes to disease and poor health. In 1989, alcohol could be traced as a direct cause of death in 19,594 cases and as an indirect cause in another 88,864 cases. And in 1991, it was estimated that 47.9 percent of all traffic fatalities were alcohol related. Other areas where you can be proactive about your health include seeing the dentist regularly and getting an annual prostate exam or mammogram.

Be sure to enhance your weight-loss efforts by keeping up to date on the latest findings on nutrition and fitness, and scheduling time each day to reflect on your goals. Take steps to change unhealthful situations so you won't undo the positive changes you make. While it's commendable to succeed at weight loss, you will indeed be committing "murder" if you ignore unsound areas of your life.

Tip for the Day
Scrutinize areas where you could be more responsible,
such as wearing a seatbelt whenever you're in a car.

"Enjoyment is not a goal, it is a feeling that accompanies important ongoing activity."

PAUL GOODMAN

Many people mistakenly associate losing weight with starving themselves, overexercising or feeling deprived. When you are in a sensible weight-loss program, though, it's possible to eat your favorite foods and have fun while still losing weight. This may seem impossible to those who previously have had unpleasant experiences, but with planning and determination the process of achieving a fit and slender body can be enjoyable.

If you think that cooking is a bore, there are several ways to introduce fun into the kitchen. Invest in a new piece of cooking equipment, use a cookbook with easy and nutritious recipes or join a cooking class with a friend. Exercise doesn't have to be painful or dull, either. Go to an exercise class at your local fitness center, listen to a book while you walk, pedal a stationary bicycle while you catch up on your favorite TV shows or work out to a popular exercise video in the privacy of your own house.

Remind yourself today that it's important to enjoy the process of working toward your weight goal, not just achieving it. Affirm to yourself every morning that you will have fun eating and exercising healthfully, and that you'll ask others for advice whenever you feel bored, deprived or depressed. If you consciously seek out ways to bring laughter and imagination into your dining and exercise routines, you'll be surprised at how quickly and easily you'll be able to reach your goal.

Tip for the Day
*When you go for a walk today, listen to a tape of
Jack Benny's old radio shows.*

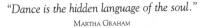

"Dance is the hidden language of the soul."
MARTHA GRAHAM

People who are unaccustomed to exercise might be intimidated at the idea of working out and breaking into a sweat. But there are many ways to incorporate exercise into your daily routine that are fun, such as roller skating, in-line skating, water aerobics and power walking. One of the most popular activities, however, is dancing because it doesn't involve buying a lot of equipment. It can be done by yourself or with others, and it's enjoyable.

There are many different forms of dance to choose from. Some people are swing-dance devotees, some love dance aerobics and some are square-dance enthusiasts. If you are too embarrassed in the beginning, work out by yourself with a videotape. When you feel more confident, join a class and dance with others. If you want to try something different, try the Non-Impact Aerobics (NIA) Technique. This dance form combines ballet, jazz, modern dance, yoga and the martial arts. Practitioners say it promotes feelings of strength and control while fostering grace, agility and a sense of serenity.

If your exercise routine is dull or nonexistent, consider including some form of dance today. There are many videotapes and classes available, geared to all levels of ability, so it's possible to find something that suits you. By giving your fitness routine variety and making sure you have fun at the same time, you'll help your weight-loss efforts, and you'll give your emotions a boost, too.

⮞ *Tip for the Day* ⮜
*Look for a dance aerobics show or videotape that can
jazz up your exercise routine.*

> *"Self-respect is the fruit of discipline; the sense of dignity grows with the ability to say no to oneself."*
>
> ABRAHAM J. HESCHEL

One of the most difficult things to do when trying to lose or maintain weight is to socialize without going off your weight-loss program. It's almost impossible to avoid snacking on tempting hors d'oeuvres or rich desserts if you go to parties with an empty stomach or if you think that the only way to be gracious is to eat everything that is offered to you. But at Weight Watchers you learn that part of being successful is learning how to say "no" to foods and situations that aren't good for you.

Here are some suggestions on how to have a social life that complements your weight-loss efforts: To make it easier to refuse food that is offered to you at a party, take the edge off your hunger by having some juice or vegetables at home before going to the party. If someone offers you wedding cake or champagne at a reception and you don't want any, politely say that you've had enough already. When being assertive doesn't do the trick, take the food and simply put it down on another table.

An important aspect of being successful is learning how to say "no" to unhealthy foods when part of you wants to say "yes." Make it easier for yourself to withstand temptation by arriving at parties with a plan and internal resolve. Instead of socializing with anxiety, you'll make these types of occasions work for you by using them to strengthen your resolve and self-respect.

Tip for the Day

Practice saying "no" before you go to your next party. Look at yourself in the mirror, then imagine you're at a party and are being offered food that isn't part of your meal plan. Now smile pleasantly and say, "No thank you."

"When it comes to Chinese food I have always operated under the policy that the less known about the preparation the better."

CALVIN TRILLIN

It used to be assumed that Chinese food was a dieter's dream: low in fat, high in fiber and tasty to boot. Unfortunately, that's not always the case. Restaurant surveys have found that certain Chinese dishes are as high in fat and salt as some fast-food fare, and thus eating at a Chinese restaurant may be more dangerous to a healthy routine than some other cuisines.

There are numerous magazine articles and books on how to select your dishes carefully when eating out. One tip for Chinese restaurants is to select dishes that are made with vegetables instead of dumplings or pancakes. And instead of spooning the food directly onto your plate, it's wise to pour it over a mound of rice so that some of the oil can be absorbed. Then spoon the "drained" food onto fresh rice and eat it. Being assertive with the chef about whether you want salt, soy sauce or MSG added can make a big difference in whether the meal is nutritious. Finally, avoid fried items like egg rolls because they contain a lot of saturated fat; order steamed vegetables instead.

Losing weight means you can indulge your love of Chinese food or any other cuisine. But it's essential that you know how to make the meal work within your nutritional guidelines. Instead of listening to reports about what you should and shouldn't eat, educate yourself so that you can make wise choices and still enjoy your favorite foods.

Tip for the Day
Whenever you order carry-out food or go to a restaurant, ask specific questions about how the food is prepared and what ingredients are used. Be sure to avoid fried food and order items like steamed vegetables instead.

> *"Life shrinks or expands in proportion to one's courage."*
>
> ANAÏS NIN

As Sheila's weight ballooned, her husband became more and more abusive. He rebuffed her attempts at intimacy, saying her body "disgusted" him. He mocked her when she had trouble fitting into airplane or movie theater seats and when she once leaned over and her pants split, he embarrassed her by telling all his friends about it. Sheila finally decided to do something about her weight, hoping that if she lost weight her husband would stop berating her and calling her names. When Sheila finally reached her weight goal, though, her husband remained abusive, accusing her of losing weight to attract other men. Emboldened by her weight-loss success, Sheila filed for divorce and started a new life for herself.

It takes courage to make big changes in your life, but when you do, your life expands. If you're low on courage, successfully changing your eating and fitness habits can increase feelings of self-confidence that lead to courageous actions. So use the weight-loss progress you're making as incentive to help you address something else that is troublesome. By taking one such action at a time, you'll build up enough courage to have a limitless and joyful future.

Tip for the Day

Your success in losing weight has undoubtedly expanded your view of what you can do. But have you acted on this new confidence yet? If not, do so today.

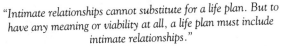

"Intimate relationships cannot substitute for a life plan. But to have any meaning or viability at all, a life plan must include intimate relationships."

HARRIET LERNER •

Being overweight might be a hindrance in developing intimate relationships. When you are ashamed of your body, bereft of self-esteem and low in confidence, it's difficult to radiate the good feelings that can draw a loving person to you. Therefore, when you lose weight, you may be ready but uncertain how to meet people and nurture close relationships.

If you've been away from the dating scene, try to meet people in places where you can get acquainted without pressure, such as a health club or church. By developing a friendship first, you can gradually open yourself to intimacy. The process of becoming close to people can feel scary at times. Instead of turning to food, ease the awkwardness through such avenues as counseling and expressing yourself through writing, art and music.

Remember today that losing weight and developing a healthy lifestyle is only part of becoming fulfilled. It's important that you have a satisfying emotional life, too. If you've created a solitary life because of your weight, work on socializing and developing relationships that will help you to open up your heart. By doing this you will develop self-confidence and increase your ability to give love to yourself and others.

⇝ *Tip for the Day* ⇜
*If you aren't in a relationship or you feel isolated and friendless, think
of one new place you can go to meet people who share common interests.
Check your newspaper or library bulletin board for activities like a
book club, computer class or public lecture.*

"One picture is worth a thousand words."
FRED R. BARNARD

If you've been overweight for many years, you may have grown accustomed to seeing a certain image in the mirror or wearing a certain clothing size. If this is the case, it may be hard to accept a slim body. One woman who lost 30 pounds ten years ago says she's still surprised when she passes a window and sees the reflection of a thin woman. She says it sounds crazy, but there are days when she's convinced that she's still a fat person.

Similarly, Ruth has lost five dress sizes but still has the ingrained belief that she is unattractive and overweight. She still reaches for a size 22 dress in the department store even though she has been a 12 for several years, she admits. To fight her misperceptions, she keeps a special picture in her wallet. One side is a photo of herself at her top weight, but taped on the reverse is a current picture of herself. She says the only way she can grasp intellectually that she's not heavy anymore is to look constantly at the pictures, proving she's changed a lot.

If you believe you are heavier than you really are, take concrete steps to change your thinking. Carry current pictures of yourself in your wallet. Sometimes it's difficult to imagine yourself as others see you. But when you are armed with actual evidence that you are thinner and healthier today than you once were, you're one step closer to achieving the healthy frame of mind you need to be successful.

≈ *Tip for the Day* ≈
Stand in front of the mirror and compliment yourself about areas of your body that have changed since you lost weight. Perhaps your arms and legs are more defined, for example. Is your belt on a notch you only used to dream about?

"My heart, which is so full to overflowing, has often been solaced and refreshed by music when sick and weary."

MARTIN LUTHER

When you're tired, your day hasn't gone well or you're avoiding dealing with a problem, you're a candidate for emotional eating. Emotional eating is what happens when you use food to hide from your real feelings or distract yourself from doing something important. It also occurs when you want to comfort yourself during a hard time or temporarily escape from your cares.

Although there are many ways to attack emotional eating, experts stress that learning how to cope with stress without turning to food is one of the most important skills you can learn. One inexpensive and effective way to do this is through music. Nearly everyone can be soothed by a string quartet or a favorite melody. By losing yourself in the music, anxiety slips away, your heartbeat slows down and your mind becomes clear.

Use your love of music to help you deal with stress today and avoid the downfall of emotional eating. Put a tape player or radio in the kitchen while you prepare and eat your meals, and make a point of listening to a beautiful piece of music. Use this and other techniques to replace your urges to eat when stressed; you'll find that a new world of effective and beneficial solutions has opened up to you.

∼ *Tip for the Day* ∼

Find a classical music station on your radio and listen to it while you drive, eat, meditate or go for a walk.

"Flying may not be all plain sailing, but the fun of it is worth the price."

AMELIA EARHART

An actress and Weight Watchers member who travels often for her work says that flying used to be her weight-loss downfall. Whenever she was on tour, she'd eat the heavy airline food and plentiful snacks, which added up to excess weight and lethargy. When she turned 40, she decided to join the program and change her life. She was determined to lose weight despite the difficulties presented by her itinerant lifestyle.

One of the first things she learned was to call ahead and order a special meal that fit her nutritional requirements. She brought raw vegetables to snack on instead of the airline treats, and she carried needlework and crossword puzzles to distract her from thoughts of food. Once she landed at her destination, she booked rooms only at hotels that had exercise facilities, and she would always call ahead to restaurants to make sure they served healthy food.

Traveling can be a fun and enlightening experience if you are armed with strategies to support your weight-loss efforts. If you will be flying somewhere soon, make a note to call the airline a day or two ahead and order a special meal. Carry reading material you can refer to for inspiration and try to attend a meeting or be among people who will help you achieve your goals. Although the challenges presented by traveling may not be clear sailing, successfully navigating this tricky course can give you self-confidence to survive other difficult passages, too.

                Tip for the Day

Call an airline or hotel you use often and ask about healthy meals they serve and how much advance notice they need to provide special preparations.

"*Oh sleep! it is a gentle thing, / Beloved from pole to pole.*"

SAMUEL TAYLOR COLERIDGE

Being tired is one of the most common excuses people give when they have a slip in their weight-loss programs. "I was so tired that I didn't have the energy to put together a good meal," or "I'm too exhausted to exercise today." The less rested we are, the more irritable, tense and impulsive we're likely to be—all of which are common triggers for overeating.

Too often we sacrifice sleep to keep up with other demands in our lives, such as work, parenting, socializing and caring for elderly parents. We don't realize how detrimental these demands are to our health and well-being. But people who chronically deprive themselves of enough sleep are more prone to depression, accidents and misjudgments than those who get at least eight hours of sleep. When you're tired, it's hard to do anything diligently, including exercising or following a healthy food program.

Look at your evening schedule to see if there are some activities that could be streamlined or eliminated. For example, can you return phone calls during the day instead of after dinner? Do you really need to watch a certain late-night TV program? You could tape it and watch it at a more convenient time. Learn to be vigilant about getting enough sleep as regularly as possible. Soon you'll find that you are more rested and have more energy to apply toward reaching all your goals.

≈ *Tip for the Day* ≈

Simplify your nightly routine so that you can enjoy a relaxing dinner and enjoyable evening activity and still get to bed at a reasonable time.

*"The cinema, like the detective story, makes it possible
to experience without danger all the excitement, passion
and desirousness which must be repressed in a humanitarian
ordering of society."*

C. J. JUNG

As you reach new milestones in your weight-loss program, it's important to find new and innovative ways to reward yourself for hard work and success. A popular way to do this is to go to a movie theater to immerse yourself in drama, adventure, laughter and romance. Movies can engage all of your senses and enable you to express joy or sadness too. Sometimes you can even draw upon the courage of a hero or heroine to make changes in your own life.

The next time you are looking for a way to reward yourself for weight loss or a positive behavioral change, go to a movie or rent a video and plan an afternoon or evening around enjoying it. Skip the extras like buttered popcorn and candy. Make the session an instructional one if you want. For example, if you want to become more assertive, watch movies with strong leads, such as *Run Silent, Run Deep* or *Gone With the Wind*. Or if passion is missing from your life, find a movie that will awaken those emotions in you. If you allow movies to take you and your emotions on a wonderful adventure, you'll have found another way to savor life without turning to food.

⟿ *Tip for the Day* ⟼
*Ask yourself which qualities in yourself you'd like to reinforce and then rent a
video or see a movie that will model that behavior for you.*

"Is it sufficient that you have learned to drive the car, or shall you look and see what is under the hood? Most people go through life without ever knowing."

JUNE SINGER

For many years you may have blamed a whole range of negative behaviors on everything from your relationship with your parents to frustration at work. When food becomes a scapegoat for all of your problems, however, you usually fail to address the real issues troubling you. It is important to learn that extra pounds aren't the source of all life's pain. The key to living a successful and fulfilling life is to improve your attitudes, your behavior and your health.

Beth had always thought that her overeating was the reason she and her husband fought frequently. When she joined a weight-loss program and lost weight, she realized that their marital problems were rooted in a lack of respect for each other's needs, not her overeating. In therapy she and her husband learned new ways of communicating that enhanced their relationship. This new-found support from her husband enabled Beth to continue to be successful in the program, too.

A weight-management program is a wonderful way to change your body, and in doing so other aspects of your life may change as well. But losing weight can't fix everything in your life that may be unsettled. Seek the services of a supportive, informed friend or a professional counselor if your weight loss has triggered the desire to resolve some personal issues. Be flexible about making changes in your lifestyle. Although getting a healthier body helps in looking good on the outside, it's always good to look "under the hood" with someone who can help with problems that need professional attention.

Tip for the Day

If you have some unresolved issues that are draining your emotions, look into finding a counselor or support group that can help you continue with your personal growth.

"The one thing more difficult than following a regimen is not imposing it on others."
MARCEL PROUST

If you have made some beneficial changes in your lifestyle and you're losing weight and enjoying the positive effects of exercise, you are probably eager to help others achieve the same kind of success. You may be dismayed, then, to find that your efforts to promote your newfound way of life aren't always met with appreciation. Instead of being grateful, family and friends may be offended by your overtures to help them.

Studies have shown that people who are most successful in losing weight and keeping it off are those who are "sick of feeling fat." Those who are motivated most to change their behavior do so because of internal, not external, prompting. While it's possible to pressure people into joining a weight-loss program, if their heart isn't into eating healthfully and making permanent changes in their behavior, it's unlikely that they'll maintain their weight loss or stick with an exercise routine.

As thrilled as you might be by your success, keep in mind today that you have made headway because you were at a point where you were prepared to make changes in your life. Instead of proselytizing and trying to convert others to your thinking, allow them to approach you for advice instead. Learn to inspire and motivate by example, not by instruction. Respect the choices that others make, even if you disagree, and concentrate on continuing your own program of improved health and well-being.

  Tip for the Day
Work on being a silent example of success today and resist attempts to broadcast it to others.

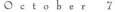
"He who laughs, lasts!"

MARY PETTIBONE POOLE

Ted grew up in a family of overweight people where portion sizes were routinely enormous. Despite being heavy both as a child and a teenager, Ted never felt that his excess weight stood in the way of his career goal of becoming a professional singer. As he went to more and more auditions, however, he was told again and again that he needed to lose 50 pounds if he hoped to be hired. Consequently he joined a weight-loss program and worked to reach his weight goal.

Ted now helps others to lose weight by leading Weight Watchers meetings. He shares his success by telling humorous anecdotes about his struggles to lose weight. Susan, another leader who believes in the importance of laughter in weight loss, often will dress up or perform a skit to emphasize a particular point.

Remember today that if you're not having a good time in your efforts to lose weight, you may become disheartened and give up. Make a conscious effort to bring laughter into your life and your mealtimes by being with people who have a light-hearted approach to life. Or treat yourself to an entertaining pastime when you know you will enjoy a good laugh, such as a favorite radio or television program. The more fun you can create in your life, the more energy you'll have to apply toward reaching your goals.

Tip for the Day

Find something to laugh about today. Remind yourself that serious endeavors like weight loss are made easier when you take time to enjoy lighter moments too.

"Order is the shape upon which beauty depends."

PEARL BUCK

If you frequently find yourself skipping breakfast or throwing some food together in the morning because you're short on time and burdened with other activities, it's essential to create order in the kitchen so that pulling a sensible meal together is as simple as possible.

One successful way is to make your own prepackaged meals. For example, instead of fumbling around for measuring cups in the morning, measure a week's worth of cereal portions into resealable plastic bags and put them in the pantry or freezer for easy retrieval. If traditional breakfast foods turn you off, have vegetable soup or a baked potato ready to reheat in the morning. It's also a good idea to have a coffee maker plugged in and set to brew, utensils already on the table and dishes out of the sink so that you aren't distracted by the previous night's meal.

Think of ways to simplify your morning routine so that you don't have the excuse that there's not enough time to eat or exercise properly. By making small adjustments—like having your walking shoes waiting for you next to the door or making your children's lunches the night before—you'll find that your mornings can be the most productive time of the day.

Tip for the Day

Think of at least one activity you can do tonight so tomorrow's morning routine will be more orderly.

"Smell is a potent wizard that transports you across thousands of miles and all the years you have lived."

HELEN KELLER

Before joining a weight-loss program, you may have rewarded yourself with fattening snacks and treats. As part of learning a new lifestyle, it's important that you find other ways to bring pleasure and contentment into your life. One way that you can do this quickly and inexpensively is to use the power of scent.

Research shows that some fragrances, like vanilla, have the universal ability to lift a person's mood. Other fragrances are calming, like orange or honeysuckle. If there's a scent that reminds you of a happy time in your life—perhaps the smell of sea air or the scent of roses or baby powder—it can also have the power to soothe you when you're tired or in need of a treat.

Try rewarding yourself today with a wonderful aroma that harks back to a happy time in your life. Whether it's the aftershave a lover wore or the mesmerizing smell of a pine forest, surround yourself with these nonfattening treats. Scents can help you feel special and give you a boost when you need it most.

    ∽ *Tip for the Day* ∽
Spritz on a perfume or take a relaxing bath with scented oils today. Let the aroma transport you to a special place.

"The results of philanthropy are always beyond calculation."
MIRIAM BEARD

It is now well established that being philanthropic is one of the best indicators of mental health, and that those who volunteer regularly are happier and healthier than those who don't. For the busy person, finding time for charitable activities is often a major challenge. If you are committed to getting enough exercise each day, carving out extra time to fit in volunteer activities can be difficult.

There are many creative solutions to this challenge. One man who stays in shape by bicycling makes a point of entering at least four bike-a-thons every year to benefit his favorite charities. Another woman who likes to walk enters two annual walkathons in her area to benefit local causes, raising a lot of money and awareness through her activities.

If you want to become more active with charity but your time is tight, consider taking part in the many athletic activities that assist the less fortunate. You will be doing your body a favor, and you'll be improving your mental health at the same time.

∞ *Tip for the Day* ∞
Ask your friends for ideas on walkathons or exercise marathons you can participate in at your own level.

> *"Know thyself."*
> THALES

In one study of ten chronic dieters, researchers discovered that overweight people who blamed their inability to lose weight on a slow metabolism or some other factor out of their control were actually eating more and exercising less than they reported. One of the researchers said that this piece of evidence wasn't proof that heavy people were less truthful than thin people; he said it underscored the gap between how people perceived themselves and what was actually the case.

One way to discover why you are heavier than you want to be is to carry around a notebook and record every morsel that passes your lips. If you do this you'll probably notice that you sliced an extra piece of bread at breakfast, sampled a neighbor's coffee cake while visiting, had a slice of pizza after doing errands or ate a bowl of ice cream while watching television. If you monitor your physical movements, too, you might be surprised to discover that you walked less and sat more than you would have liked to believe.

If you are gaining weight or have stopped losing, spend a day recording everything you eat and drink, as well as how much exercise you do and how intensely you do it. If you are faithfully writing your meal plan and sticking to it, you may be at a plateau that will correct itself. But if you find that you are sneaking bites here and there, you'll have identified the source of the problem.

❧ *Tip for the Day* ❧
Instead of "guesstimating" what you are eating and drinking each day, be as accurate as possible so that you can achieve your fitness goals without wasting time.

"I have always felt that the moment when first you wake up in the morning is the most wonderful of the twenty-four hours."

MONICA BALDWIN

Do you like to stay up late and sleep late? Are you more likely to see the late shows or the morning news? If you are a night owl, you may be sabotaging your efforts to lose weight without even knowing it. A national poll has shown that nearly half of all Americans get up well after sunrise and have significant differences from their early-bird peers. For example, morning people eat better, have more energy, lead more active lives and are more optimistic than those who sleep late.

If you are having trouble following through with your daily eating and exercise plan, consider whether your sleep habits might have anything to do with it. If so, start trying to become more of a morning person by moving your bedtime earlier by a half-hour and getting up a little earlier. While you may never feel completely comfortable seeing the sunrise, the benefits you'll gain from getting an early start on the day will undoubtedly make any discomfort bearable.

⤿ *Tip for the Day* ⤾

If you are a late-night person, take a step toward going to bed 30 minutes earlier. Eliminate caffeine, skip a late show or put off some chores around the house to make it easier for you to get to bed at a more reasonable hour.

"Give me the splendid silent sun with all his beams full-dazzling."
WALT WHITMAN

For some people overeating is a seasonal behavior. Jenny is one such person. Every fall she begins to sleep more, feel lethargic and irritable and crave sweet foods. Like clockwork she gains 30 pounds between October and March and then spends the summer months trying to get back into shape. She complains that she feels like a bear going into hibernation every October. She knows she shouldn't be eating so much but she can't seem to control it.

Jenny is not alone. Many go through a regular weight gain and loss cycle each year as the days get shorter and there is less sunlight. Jenny's craving for sweets and lack of energy is typical of a problem known as Seasonal Affective Disorder (S.A.D.), which can vary in intensity depending on a person's body chemistry. Even if this specific condition doesn't affect you, being indoors during winter months with time on your hands can make weight loss difficult. To combat cold weather blues or boredom, try to be involved in regular activities such as a bowling league, a church study group, a mother's play group or an indoor exercise program. If you have regularly scheduled activities with other people, getting out of the house will lift your spirits and help keep you away from eating. Another very successful way to boost your spirits without eating is to maximize your exposure to sun through outdoor walks or skylights in the house; always protect your skin with sunscreen.

If you suspect you have S.A.D., check with a medical professional for advice. Get the proper treatment so these winter months will make weight management simpler. No matter what your personal situation is, plan ahead to find ways to get more light and activity into your life.

∞ *Tip for the Day* ∞
Ask yourself if you have an interesting activity scheduled for the winter months.
If not, plan one today that will take you outdoors
for stimulation and fulfillment.

"Nature is just enough; but men and women must comprehend and accept her suggestions."

ANTOINETTE BROWN BLACKWELL

Novelist Paul Theroux was vacationing on a small island off New Guinea when he observed that the natives were in excellent physical condition with strong white teeth, unusual vigor and taut physiques. He learned that their meals revolved around natural foods such as fruit, grains, honey and salads. Theroux experimented on himself, swearing off refined, high-fat and caffeinated foods, eating only those foods that could have been available many years ago.

Just like these islanders who hadn't been exposed to processed foods, Theroux became much healthier on this meal plan because the foods were naturally low in cholesterol and high in fiber and nutrients. Now he dines on fish, vegetable soups, hearty breads and little meat, and he says he has never felt better.

Sometimes the best meal plans are those that involve the simplest foods, those that are closest to nature. Because our ancestors didn't have to worry about obesity, we might take some hints from their meal plans. Try to eat more like your ancestors did, if only for a week, to see how that diet affects you. Make your meals heavy on grains, dried and fresh fruit and fiber-rich vegetables. You may well discover that nature's suggestions are exactly the advice you need to follow.

⁓ Tip for the Day ⁓
Eat meals that are as fresh and unprocessed as possible and take note of how much more energetic and regular you are.

"Human beings, by changing the inner attitudes of their minds, can change the outer aspects of their lives."

WILLIAM JAMES

One way to increase your odds of success in weight loss is to be realistic about when and why you're going to start. For example, the odds of success are less if you're just starting a new job or leaving on a long-awaited vacation. But don't procrastinate, either. Although there's never a perfect time to begin any project, finding a window when you are relatively stress free is a much better way to begin. Your motivation for change should also come from a desire to look and feel better, not just to impress another person.

Remember today that anything you wish to accomplish in life must first be preceded by the inner belief that you can be successful. So if you're just starting a weight-loss or exercise program, make sure that you are beginning at a time when you're likely to be armed with self-confidence and determination. By doing this you will be embarking on a project in the right frame of mind. And at the same time, you'll be increasing the odds of success.

Tip for the Day

Before starting any project today, ask yourself if you're prepared to devote time and energy to accomplishing it with enthusiasm.

"Variety is the soul of pleasure."

APHRA BEHN

One of the biggest strengths of a sensible and healthy weight-loss program is the variety offered in meal planning, exercise options and the kinds of meetings available. A good program recognizes that once boredom sets in with any part of a program, slips may not be far behind. You are provided with ways to keep your days varied and interesting and encouraged to think of new ways to keep you motivated.

There are many ways to add variety to a healthy exercise program, including cycling, swimming and dancing. Some people who start their exercise program with a basic walking routine may branch out into more vigorous sports like downhill skiing and ice dancing. Others may opt to vary their workouts with activities that promote breathing and flexibility, such as yoga. By changing exercise routines and challenging yourself in different ways, you maximize your fitness capacity and ensure that boredom won't cause you to give up.

If your program feels stale in any area, try to add variety. Meals can always be varied by incorporating new cooking techniques or seasonings. Walking routines can be altered by adding hand weights or simply by changing the route. Remember that while much of your success will come from adhering to the sensible suggestions you get from other weight-loss achievers, tailoring those ideas to your lifestyle is what will provide the variety you need to sustain your interest and enthusiasm.

∾ *Tip for the Day* ∾
If your exercise routine consists of walking only, add variety by trying a new activity like swimming or cycling.

"No one can make you feel inferior without your consent."
ELEANOR ROOSEVELT

One of the problems many overweight people share is a desire to be liked by everyone. But when you defer too often to others because you are ashamed of yourself or you believe you're inferior to others, you are selling yourself short. If you're a people pleaser, you make the mistake of always deferring to others' opinions, being silent when you should be assertive and allowing others to dictate what you do. To be successful at promoting yourself and at weight loss you must work on better self-assurance and practice assertive behavior that will help you reach your goals.

One place where you may begin speaking up for yourself is in a restaurant. For example, if you want your food prepared simply and without added sauces, you may have to stand up to an imperious or impatient waiter. But you deserve to enjoy the food you pay for, so it's important that you not allow others make you drop your request or deter you from your goal in this situation. No one should make you feel uncomfortable for asking.

Take note of whether you are assertive in personal and professional situations today, or whether you still find yourself feeling inferior and trying too hard to be liked. If you fall into the latter category, practice making your requests. Consider taking an assertiveness-training class or reading some books on the subject. You deserve to be taken seriously and respected for your opinions, but you must first believe in yourself.

Tip for the Day
Be conscious of how often you defer to others today. Practice more self-assured responses so you'll be ready for the next similar situation.

"She did not talk to people as if they were strange hard shells she had to crack open to get inside. She talked as if she were already in the shell. In their very shell."

MARITA BONNER

Stephanie remembers clearly the first Weight Watchers meeting she attended. She was scared and didn't want anyone to know how much she weighed. But she says the moment she walked into the room and met the leader, she knew she'd found the right place. The leader told her that she was happy Stephanie had had the courage to take the first step toward turning her life around.

Now, 40 pounds lighter, Stephanie emphasizes that her leader was an integral part of her success because she always tried to say something that Stephanie could relate to and that might help her improve her program. When she hit a plateau, her leader told her what steps she had taken to get moving again; whenever Stephanie had a good week, her leader celebrated with her. Stephanie says she always felt like she had a friend supporting her and that she wasn't in this alone.

Be sure you attend your weekly meetings because Weight Watchers leaders are one of the most important and effective tools the program offers. You'll find that weight loss doesn't have to be a depressing and lonely task anymore. By using the wisdom of your leaders and the camaraderie of your group, you'll have excellent resources to support you.

Tip for the Day
Think of ways that your leader's enthusiasm has helped your program and share your gratitude at the next meeting.

"Appetite, with an opinion of attaining, is called hope; the same, without such opinion, despair."

THOMAS HOBBES

Hopeful people have an appetite for success. Their motivation and control come from within, so they believe they can succeed at whatever they attempt, including weight loss. They have a positive outlook about their future and can visualize their goals. They are optimists.

Pessimists lack faith in themselves. They don't easily see themselves in successful situations and find it difficult to visualize changes. They may overeat to allay anxieties or fears. They set rigid eating standards, then abandon their weight-loss plans because they see any falter as the inevitable failure of their efforts.

Optimists turn to friends for advice. They retain hope that things will improve even when conditions look bleak. They tackle large tasks by breaking them into small steps. Optimists believe they can succeed, so they allow flexibility in how they attain their goals. Optimists who go off their weight-loss plans rebound successfully. Because they see the relapse as an isolated episode, they are able to devise a new strategy to avoid the same situation in the future.

If you're not optimistic by nature, you can still learn the skills. Anticipate problems and have alternative solutions prepared. Seek the counseling of supportive people whenever you're down and need advice or encouragement. To shore up your resolve, give yourself time to relax and unwind. Surround yourself with other upbeat people. If you develop an optimistic outlook, you'll be well on your way to achieving your goals.

Tip for the Day
Practice optimism today. If you believe in yourself, you can achieve your goals.

"The fragrance always remains in the hand that gives the rose."
HEDA BEJAR

You always make yourself feel better when you forget your own concerns and do something to help someone else. There are many ways people weave this type of selflessness into their lives. Some regularly give their time to a good cause, some participate in church outreach programs and others just practice the policy of being a good neighbor. One of the ways you can have the most impact on changing your attitude toward food, though, is to become active in providing food for the needy.

Several people who successfully lost weight have found that this type of activity brought home the truth of Benjamin Franklin's words: Eat to live, and not live to eat. After years of worrying about eating too much, Carmen found it helpful to organize a fund-raiser that would pay for food baskets for Christmas week. This reminded her that many people never have the opportunity to have "too much" food. Another woman, Adora, makes regular contributions to an overseas fund that helps to feed the needy. It's gratifying to know, she says, that while she maintains her weight goal and eats sensibly, she can make a difference in someone else's life by donating money for food.

Consider becoming involved in a local food bank or an organization that provides meals to shut-ins, impoverished families or needy children. Not only will you have the benefit of retaining the "fragrance" of your actions, you'll help others who can demonstrate that food is for nourishment, not just pleasure.

⇝ *Tip for the Day* ⇜
Fill a grocery bag with nonperishable items and take it to a shelter, a soup kitchen or a family that could benefit from your generosity.

"Autumn is the bite of the harvest apple."
CHRISTINA PETROWSKY

The changing seasons can remind you of foods that we've usually enjoyed during these times. Spring and summer are usually associated with fresh fruits and vegetables, which are helpful in weight-loss efforts. During the fall and winter, though, you may have memories of heavier stick-to-the-ribs dishes that can mean disaster for weight-loss efforts unless the recipes are adapted to your needs.

There are several clever ways to make hearty dishes lighter in fat and calories. Mashed potatoes can be made with low-fat buttermilk instead of butter and cream. Chili and even meatloaf can be made using lower-fat meats like turkey or chicken breast. For an even healthier, low-fat version of some of your favorite recipes, substitute grains like bulgur for some of the meat required in the recipe. Use nonfat cottage cheese in lasagna and on baked potatoes. Soup made from lean cuts of beef and lots of vegetable are easy, nutritious and very low in fat; chill them and remove the fat before eating.

Be aware of your changing needs when the seasons shift and the weather turns cold. Instead of responding by eating high-fat foods, make this the year that you cuddle up with nutritious meals that don't wreak dietary havoc. If you are resourceful during this period and keep sight of your fitness goals, you'll emerge from the winter months without the usual excess poundage that hibernation often brings.

≈ *Tip for the Day* ≈
Pick a fall or winter favorite and think of a way you can adapt it to your meal plan by substituting low-fat ingredients.

"What is food to one man is bitter poison to others."
LUCRETIUS

One goal of a weight-loss program is to help you get in touch with your body. You can learn to be more aware of when you are and are not hungry and whether certain foods have an adverse effect on you. You may have some food allergies that you were previously ignoring. It's important to remember that you are a unique person with your own body, and foods that work for someone else may not be as successful for you.

Two well-known food sensitivities are to wheat and corn. While one person may lose weight eating judicious amounts of bread, another person might develop skin rashes, fluid retention and nasal congestion because of allergic reactions to the gluten in bread. Some people are also more susceptible to the effects of caffeine. While one person can drink coffee up until bedtime and still get a good night's rest, another may toss and turn all night because of a morning cup. Artificial sweeteners may have an adverse effect on some but not on others. Several varieties of fruit, particularly if they are treated with preservatives, can result in hives. Milk, which is tasty for many, can produce gastronomic distress in others.

The best way to devise a healthful meal plan is to eat foods that make you feel good and don't cause adverse physical or emotional reactions. Some medical professionals can perform tests to isolate troublesome foods, but the best way to know what works best is to observe your reactions after ingesting certain substances. Knowing what makes your body special and giving it the fuel that will produce the best effects is one of the most important keys to having enjoyable and successful weight loss.

≈ Tip for the Day ≈
Note any reactions you have to certain foods and see if
eliminating them makes you feel better.

"Silence is more musical than any song."

CHRISTINA ROSSETTI

It's become increasingly difficult in today's busy, high-tech world to find places where you can enjoy silence and not hear cars, planes, music or other distractions. Even when you are alone, the silence is often broken by the noise of a television or radio. If you are surrounded by constant noise, however, you lose the ability to retreat within yourself. Silent meditation and introspection is a valuable way to gain perspective on your life and what you are doing.

Many mental health experts say that meditation is an easy and efficient way to create healthful silence and lower levels of stress and anxiety. A simple ten-minute session of quiet and regular breathing can regulate heart rate, increase endorphins and provide the same physical benefits as a nap. Barbara says that a brief meditation session before lunch each day keeps her from eating too quickly and helps her identify the emotions that might trigger overeating.

Although everyone has a busy life, it's imperative that you slow down occasionally and allow time for introspective thought. Make a point of carving several minutes out of today to relax and let your thoughts flow. If you can introduce an oasis of calm into your day, you'll find that you'll have the clarity and energy to accomplish your goals more efficiently.

Tip for the Day
Take a moment of silence in the middle of the afternoon to take stock of how you are feeling today.

"What may be done at any time will be done at no time."
SCOTTISH PROVERB

There are many factors that come together to make a person successful in his or her weight-loss efforts. Several of the most important include following a sensible eating plan, exercising and making long-term changes in behavior. A key element that is often overlooked, however, is having the right mindset and being focused and determined. One popular TV talk-show personality, who has successfully lost 80 pounds, stresses that you have to be prepared emotionally, mentally and physically before you can win the war against your fat cells.

Some individuals knew they had a weight problem but put off dealing with the condition until they were forced to look at it. Amy finally joined a weight-loss program when her doctor told her she'd have permanent knee and back problems unless she lost weight. Another woman said her daughter begged her not to drive her to school because she was afraid her friends would laugh at how fat her mother was. The mother had always told herself she had to lose weight but she'd never followed through. Her daughter's comment led her to join a weight-loss program that day.

Perhaps you have promised yourself that you'll lose weight, exercise, be more assertive or try something new someday, but you haven't taken any steps to make the necessary changes. Take stock of the areas in your life that need improvement and ask yourself what it will take for you to commit to taking action. Try to get into the habit of doing things *now* instead of making vague promises to do them someday or waiting for a crisis to force you into action. Once you act, you can leave behind any regrets about not having tried, and the sooner you begin, the sooner you'll achieve more of your dreams.

Tip for the Day
Do you have any promises waiting for "someday" to arrive? If so, do something that you can take steps to achieve today.

"I reached for sleep and drew it round me like a blanket muffling pain and thought together in the merciful dark."

MARY STEWART

Whenever you become overly tired, you suffer in more ways than you may realize. Not only will you become sleepy during the day, but if you use caffeine or food as stimulants, the odds increase that you'll have another night of restless sleep. Lack of sleep has been shown to result in irritability, anxiety, depression, lack of ability to concentrate and a loss of creativity.

Although it's not always easy to leave the ranks of the sleep deprived, taking certain steps can help. Experts say that if you lose sleep one night you should try to get it back as soon as possible, so that the average amount of sleep each night is eight hours. They also say daily physical exercise is optimal for restful sleep at night. In addition, it's best to go to sleep and awaken at the same time every day, and get your sleep in a continuous block rather than in segments.

Don't underestimate your need for sleep tonight, especially if you have found yourself dozing off during the day or getting an extra cup of coffee to keep up your energy. You may have to forgo some activities in order to reduce your sleep debt, but if giving up a nightly TV show results in more vitality and satisfaction, it is a worthwhile improvement to your life.

⟶ *Tip for the Day* ⟵
Think of ways you can get a better night's rest than you are getting now, so that tomorrow you won't be too tired to exercise or need food to stay awake. Try changing your exercise time, eliminating stimulants from your beverages and taking a hot bath before going to bed.

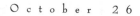

"Live life in day-tight compartments."
DALE CARNEGIE

Many people who have successfully lost weight and kept it off often say they only need to consider their meal plan one day at a time. When they can focus on taking each day as it comes and not think about the prospect of being tempted next week, next month or even next year, many find that eating healthfully is easier than they once thought.

If you make a goal every morning to just stick to a sensible meal plan for 24 hours, the task of losing weight becomes more manageable. In the same fashion, if you are trying to settle into an exercise routine and you've been a couch potato for many years, it's a better idea to think about walking briskly for ten minutes one day at a time rather than training to run a marathon. It's easier to stay committed to your program when your sights remain focused on goals that are reasonable for you today.

Be sure today that you are focused only on today. If you find your mind wandering toward what the future holds for you, what you'll eat for dinner next weekend, or how you'll survive a visit from your mother-in-law next Christmas, remind yourself that your primary task is to be as successful and happy as you can be during the next 24 hours. By staying narrowly focused and keeping your goals manageable, you will achieve more and you'll be happier while doing it.

Tip for the Day
Examine your goals for today. Make sure they are reasonable and manageable.
Remind yourself that tomorrow will be easier
if you have been successful today.

"If you're in harmony, you know what to eat."

DEEPAK CHOPRA, M.D.

People who are overweight sometimes lose touch with their bodies. They eat out of habit or emotional need rather than physical need. They may no longer know what their bodies want or what will make them better. Marie says she sometimes had mild abdominal cramps but ignored them. After she started keeping a food journal, she recognized that there might be a connection between her discomfort and eating. Eventually she discovered that she was allergic to certain foods.

Take the time to listen to your body. Sit quietly for a few moments, then place your hands on your abdomen. Is it really hungry? Let it tell you when to start eating and when to stop. Think about what foods you need to eat to make your body feel better. Now place your hands on your heart and check on your emotions. Is anxiety triggering a desire to eat? Does your body hurt when thinking about a certain person or situation? Learn to listen to your body and the messages it is giving you, and it will tell you what it needs.

Respect your body and the signals it sends you today. If you have lost touch over the years, spend some time talking to your body today and try to follow whatever healthful directions it is suggesting. When your mind and body are working together as one, shedding excess weight won't be a struggle.

≈ *Tip for the Day* ≈

Before every meal today, take a few moments to get in touch with your body. If you are craving a certain food, ask yourself whether you want that item in order to ease your mind or nourish your body.

"[The television is] an invention that permits you to be entertained in your living room by people you wouldn't have in your home."

DAVID FROST

It's true that watching television isn't conducive to living an active life because sitting down to watch and be entertained means you aren't moving your body or entertaining yourself. There are times when television can be helpful in losing weight, though. Public broadcasting stations have shows that demonstrate low-fat and healthful cooking techniques, and it's easy to find aerobics shows in the early mornings and on weekends.

You can also use the television to play Weight Watchers stretching and exercise videotapes. For those who are uncomfortable working out in public, this can be the ideal way to ease into aerobic activity. It's essential to follow a recommended program, however, instead of just buying a video because it features a model or famous person. Some fitness trainers advise taking at least one aerobics class with a certified instructor so that you know correct body positions when you exercise at home. They also say it's wise to select a supple, nonskid surface like wood—not concrete or linoleum—to protect your joints while you exercise. You also might want to rent a variety of tapes before committing yourself to a purchase to make sure you have a workout that feels right and will keep your interest.

Instead of watching television out of habit, use it to help you enhance a healthy lifestyle. Look at the television listings for aerobics and yoga shows and take advantage of the many tapes that exist on exercise and weight training. Learn to turn the passive sport of television into an active participant in helping you get fit.

Tip for the Day
Rent a different workout tape every day this week. Which one is best suited to your level of fitness?

"[Selfishness is] taking care of number one in all situations."
ANONYMOUS

Selfishness is not necessarily a personality flaw; it could very well be the quality that determines whether you are successful at weight loss or not. For example, a study has shown that women are 50 percent more likely than men to drop out of work-site fitness programs. Their reasons for doing so often relate to concerns about inconveniencing co-workers or family members. Men who drop out of exercise classes give more pragmatic reasons such as not wanting to wait in line for the machines.

Are you concerned enough about yourself to be a winner in creating a healthy lifestyle? If you avoid going to weight-loss meetings or fail to create exercise time for yourself because you don't want to hire a sitter or inconvenience someone else, you aren't being unselfish, you are being a martyr. Make sure that you are meeting your fitness and nutritional needs today, even if it causes someone else's plans to be changed. Anything you do to make yourself happier and more fit will benefit more than just you; it will benefit those around you, too.

Tip for the Day
Remember today that taking care of yourself also means getting enough rest.
Stopping to rest or sleep is not selfish; it's sensible.

"Men *acquire a particular quality by constantly acting a particular way*.... *you become just by performing just actions, temperate by performing temperate actions, brave by performing brave actions.*"

ARISTOTLE

For a person who has spent many years being inactive and routinely indulging in overeating, the idea of becoming moderate and healthy may seem preposterous. Ramona felt this way when she joined Weight Watchers and surveyed the men and women at the meetings who had already reached their weight goal. She initially thought she could never be like them because she was unable to envision herself as a slim, attractive woman.

The good news is that no matter how negatively you see yourself, you are capable of change. For example, Ramona was advised by another member to just act as if she were already thin whenever she was tempted to go off her meal plan. Amazingly, Ramona found that the more she pretended to be something she wasn't (at least not yet), or possess a quality she didn't yet have, the easier it was to develop that quality. As a result, although she'd never been able to leave food on her plate at a restaurant, when she pretended she was already a thin person, it became easy for her to act like one too.

If you want to embody a certain quality, start acting that way today. Instead of telling yourself you're not athletic, pretend to be an athlete today. Instead of believing that you're incapable of passing up desserts, act as if you've always done it. The more you do the things that lead to what you wish to be, the more likely it is that you'll be that way soon.

❧ *Tip for the Day* ❧
Pick a quality you wish to possess, such as honesty or kindliness, and embody that trait all day.

> *"I've never known any trouble that an hour's*
> *reading didn't assuage."*
>
> CHARLES DE SECONDAT

The person who learns early the joys of reading is someone who always has a ready-made solution to every difficulty: books. Whenever you're feeling discouraged or sad, it's rare for those feelings to overwhelm you if you can immerse yourself in a book that transports you to another place and time. Some people find romance novels do the trick, some like history books and some find picture books to be the most enjoyable. And there are those who like an adventure that engages their mind like a spy thriller or a good mystery.

Reading can be an effective antidote to the emotions that tempt you to eat. Some self-help books can provide assistance in addressing negative behaviors. To select a good self-help book, skim the contents to see if the book promotes actions that result in positive change. Also, look for books that share others' experiences because they can be very comforting and instructive. Keep in mind that a book can't solve your problems, but it may lead you to useful ideas that will be helpful.

Use books to bring healing, adventure and excitement into your life. The more you can find noncaloric ways to enrich yourself and create a balanced lifestyle, the less likely you'll be to allow food to dominate your world.

Tip for the Day
Have a good book next to your bed so that you always have something
to look forward to at night.

"Arranging a bowl of flowers in the morning can give a sense of quiet in a crowded day—like writing a poem, or saying a prayer."

ANNE MORROW LINDBERGH

It's easy to get off track when the day is filled with unpredictable occurrences that knock you off balance, causing you to feel stressed out and anxious. When this happens, it's normal to want to reach for a soothing food treat for comfort. But it's precisely this type of unhealthy behavior that leads to overeating.

An excellent way to avoid falling into these emotional eating traps is to create an oasis of calm each morning. There are many ways to do this, including prayer, meditation, a walk outdoors and arranging flowers. Start the day with quiet activities like these and use this quiet time to strengthen your resolve to eat healthfully.

Do something silent this morning—watch the sunrise or eat a balanced breakfast without interruption—quietly and in a focused way that will give you a sense of calm. Visualize yourself having a successful day and reacting to challenges with determination and clear thinking. If you can be sure to carve this important time out of your busy day, you will be more productive and serene. You'll have more inner resources to achieve the goals you set for yourself.

Tip for the Day

Take five minutes this morning to do something calming and reflective.

"I always wanted to be somebody. If I made it, it's half because I was game enough to take a lot of punishment along the way and half because there were a lot of people who cared enough to help me."

ALTHEA GIBSON

When Mark started to lose weight he expected the support of his girlfriend, but was taken aback when she didn't provide it. Before he went on his weight-loss program, she'd prepare elaborate desserts, but when he started losing weight, he was bewildered because cutting up fruit for salad suddenly became a big deal for her.

It's very common for people losing weight to find that their friends and family become threatened by their success and try to sabotage their efforts, either consciously or subconsciously. Experts say that jealousy and competitiveness are partly responsible for diet sabotage. Spouses may fear that their newly attractive and slim husband or wife is going to leave them or depend less on them. It is often best to confront the issue directly but in a noncombative manner. Reassure your spouse that you are not going to leave, but at the same time point out which behaviors seem to you to be subtle sabotage. When your spouse shows genuine support for your weight-loss program, express your thanks.

But sometimes even your best efforts aren't enough to enlist the support of the people in your life. Accept that in the end you may have to follow your program on your own with little support from your family and friends. You must set limits on how often you see those who don't have your best interests at heart. Use your energy to stay motivated, and be proud that you are in control of your weight and your destiny.

∽ *Tip for the Day* ∽

If someone asks you why you want to lose weight, turn the tables on them and ask why it wouldn't be important to take such a healthy step.

"The only way to get rid of a temptation is to yield to it. Resist it, and your soul grows sick with longing for the things it has forbidden to itself."

OSCAR WILDE

One of the surest ways to derail weight-loss efforts and lapse into overeating is to deny yourself some favorite foods. If you're feeling deprived, you are more likely to give in to what you are missing. By building favorite foods into your meal plan through optional calories and other substitutions, you will enjoy losing weight, and you'll be less likely to feel obsessed by those items.

Although it's almost always possible to include favorite foods in your program, you'll probably find that some things are more trouble than they're worth. Kathleen, for example, designed her meal plan carefully so that she could have fudge once a week. The problem was that the piece was so modest that it always left her craving more than she could reasonably allow herself. Her Weight Watchers leader suggested that she omit the fudge and try to substitute another sweet. In time, the leader assured her, fudge might become less important to her and therefore not occupy so much of her thoughts.

If you are feeling deprived of a certain food today, include it in your meal plan. If that doesn't satisfy your yearnings, consider omitting it altogether until you've reached your goal. Once you know that you never have to say "never" to any food, it will not seem as tempting to you.

⇜ *Tip for the Day* ⇝

If you feel deprived of a certain food, find a way to work it into your meal plan, or make peace with the idea that you will abstain from it for a period of time.

"Consult your friend on all things, especially on those which respect yourself. His counsel may then be useful where your own self-love might impair your judgment."

LUCIUS ANNAEUS SENECA

For many people, weight loss is something they feel was accomplished only because they did it with a friend. For example, Meredith and Dagney talked about joining a weight-loss program together for over a year before they actually did it. But once they committed themselves to changing their lifestyles, they both reached their weight goals in eight months. Joining with a friend was great, both say with enthusiasm. If one needed support, she could always call the other. Having a friend to share progress with served as a built-in support system.

If you lack motivation or support, consider starting a weight-loss program with a friend. Not only can your friend cheer you on when you're discouraged, but watching another's progress can be a mirror of your own efforts if you've lost sight of how far you've come. And when you can't see your own difficulties clearly, a friend can lovingly point you in the right direction and provide solutions you may not have considered. Dagney says her successful effort to lose weight was helped by working with a friend. They are a team success story.

❧ *Tip for the Day* ❧

Ask a friend to join you in a weight-loss program or in making exercise a regular part of your day.

"A sound mind in a sound body is a short but full description of a happy state in this world."

JOHN LOCKE

Anyone who has spent time feeling miserable and lethargic as a result of being overweight can't help but feel happier after losing weight and becoming more active. Countless people say that just waking up and knowing they can wear a size they only once dreamed about brings them joy. Others say that being able to fit comfortably in an airplane seat is a pleasure that never leaves them.

It's unrealistic, however, to think that being thin will automatically make your world happy and perfect. Day-to-day stresses can accumulate and create discouragement, as can occasional setbacks like illness, the death of a loved one or the loss of a job. Because these stressful situations are often unavoidable, it's important to know how to create a sound mind to go along with your sound body.

Some people find that practices like biofeedback and yoga are helpful in creating a calming meditative state when they are upset. Physical exercise is another excellent way to reduce internal stress. If your stress level remains high regardless of what you do, consider seeking supportive counseling with a trained professional. Remember that happiness is not how you look on the outside, but comes from a feeling of peace and contentment on the inside.

≈ *Tip for the Day* ≈

Relax, close your eyes and breathe deeply. Imagine inhaling a cleansing white light, and then see yourself exhaling any stress or anxiety in a dark hue. Do this for several minutes until you feel yourself become mentally calmed and soothed.

"Promises that you make to yourself are often like the Japanese plum tree—they bear no fruit."

FRANCIS MARION

For many people, there have been times when they promised themselves they would stop smoking, exercise more, eat less, get up earlier and be more patient. But despite their best intentions, they've still failed. Quite often this doesn't have anything to do with skills, willpower or worth. It is simply a reflection of the fact that it's easier to be successful when we're part of a group than when we attempt to accomplish something alone.

With this in mind, resolve to do something today as part of a group rather than by yourself. For example, if you want to learn how to knit but you can't decipher the diagrams, sign up for a class. If you're eager to take a vacation, but you're single and tentative about traveling alone, sign up for a group excursion where you can meet more friends and increase your knowledge about a new area of the world. And if your efforts at weight loss have only led to plateaus in the past, join a sensible weight-loss program that offers group support. You'll get new ideas for handling trigger situations, suggestions for recipes that you may not have tried yet, and the camaraderie of other people working toward the same goals.

Resolve that you will do something with others that you've struggled with in the past. While it's always important to be accountable to yourself for your actions, you'll find that having the support of others will bring you additional success and satisfaction.

≈ Tip for the Day ≈
Call your local community college today and ask for a listing of their adult education classes.

"Menopause still has that aura of mystery about it. Every woman kind of keeps it to herself."

EDIE HOGAN

In the past, openly discussing bodily topics like menopause was taboo. As a result, many women entered this pivotal time of their life unprepared for the hormonal and physical changes that awaited them. For example, one of the common side effects of menopause is weight gain. One study showed that 70 percent of thin and normal-weight women gained weight, and 90 percent of overweight women did.

Being successful at weight loss means adapting to the periodic changes of our bodies. During menopause, there can be many different reasons why losing weight is difficult. Hormone replacement therapy can result in water retention. And facing the normal aging process can induce many women to soothe themselves with food. At least one nutritionist says that chronic dieters suffer the most in menopause because the hot flashes and other physical changes make them feel out of control, so they become out of control with food as well.

Instead of entering menopause unprepared about the typical changes you might expect, educate yourself about this time of life. With knowledge, you can weather this period with little or no weight gain or negative feelings about yourself. If you understand your body, you'll have more enthusiasm and vitality to enjoy life after menopause.

∽ *Tip for the Day* ∽

Make an appointment with your physician today. Prepare a list of questions to ask about the changes happening to your body.

*"We are indeed much more than what we eat, but what we eat
can nevertheless help us to be much more than what we are."*
ADELLE DAVIS

Prior to deciding to lose weight in a healthful way, you may
have had little information about what you ate and whether
or not it was good for you. Part of learning how to lose weight
and successfully maintain weight loss, however, is learning
which foods are most nutritious and how they can enhance
your health. One way to do this is by reading about health and
nutrition topics, watching educational shows or videos and
carefully reading and analyzing food labels.

One key piece of knowledge you should have is your daily
requirement for vitamins and other nutrients and how you can
meet those needs through the foods you eat.
Research has shown, for example, that vitamin C helps
reduce blood cholesterol, heart-disease risk and angina, as well
as promote the absorption of iron and combat infection. Because vitamin C is excreted from the body every day, it's important to include foods that will replenish those levels with
such foods as cantaloupe, oranges, cauliflower and green peppers.

Take a few moments today to remember that every time
you eat you are satisfying your hunger and building your health
at the same time, so every morsel you eat should
be packed with as many positive benefits as possible. Vary your
choice of foods and you'll more easily meet your body's nutritional requirements. With a little knowledge and
creativity, your meals will be satisfying and powerful components of a healthy life.

Tip for the Day
*Know what vitamins and other nutrients are in the foods you eat today and
what properties they have to enhance your health.*

"A smiling face is half the meal."
LATVIAN PROVERB

How do you approach your meals? Are you anxious about eating the right thing and worrying about whether or not it will make you fat? Are you tense because you don't have enough time to enjoy it? Are you distracted because you have the television on at the same time?

How you feel while you are eating is an important determinant of how you'll feel after the meal. If you're tense, you may develop indigestion. If you're distracted, you may feel unfulfilled, which can lead to snacking. One nutritionist feels that *how* you eat may even be more important than *what* you eat. No matter how healthy your diet, he says, if you're eating while anxious or upset, you won't digest your meal properly.

Pay attention to your attitude during your meals today. If you are anxious or fearful, do some deep breathing so that you won't abandon your program or overeat. Remind yourself that eating is meant to be a pleasant social occasion. Eliminate distractions and stressors from the area where you eat; for example, keep piles of bills away from the dinner table and turn off the TV. Try to surround yourself with people who bring you joy so that you're sure to have a smiling face to converse with at mealtime.

⤞ *Tip for the Day* ⤝
Make a conscious effort to relax and smile during your meals today.

"Frugality without creativity is deprivation."

AMY DACYCZYN

In an uncertain economy, it's a safe bet that most families live on tight budgets, trying to stretch their food dollars as far as possible. This doesn't have to mean creating dull meals or depriving yourself of foods you enjoy. Careful shopping, experimentation with combinations and a determination to eat healthfully despite constraints on your money can still make pleasant and nutritious mealtimes possible.

One way to save money is to join a food cooperative and buy staples like flour, oatmeal and beans in large quantities. Warehouse shopping and buyer clubs have made this type of bulk food buying easier and more accessible to the general public. Don't overlook inexpensive cuts of meat, either; stewing can make them tender and flavorful. Bean dishes are also tasty and economical; pasta can help make leftovers a meal; and dishes like meatloaf can be stretched with grains and other fillers. If you have a freezer, stock up on foods you like when they are on sale.

If you're unemployed or your food budget is already tight, you can still have interesting, delicious meals. Watch for food sales at supermarkets, use coupons, experiment with grains and beans and make good use of spices and condiments to dress up your main dishes. Look for newsletters and cookbooks with tips on how to make your food money stretch as far as possible. With creativity and careful shopping, you will save money and at the same time discover new ways to enliven your menus.

⇔ *Tip for the Day* ⇔

Analyze where your food money goes. Are you spending a lot on prepared foods that you could make from scratch yourself?

"Dieting is murder on the road. Show me a man who travels and I'll show you one who eats."

BRUCE FROEMMING

Many professionals are required to travel as part of their jobs. But it can be difficult to eat nutritious and balanced meals on the road. It's all too easy to succumb to fattening airline meals, overly generous restaurant portions and snacks. When your routine is disrupted, maintaining a healthy eating program might be difficult. With foresight and planning, however, business travel doesn't have to be an orgy of overeating.

John was a typical, overweight businessman who traveled a lot when he joined Weight Watchers. He learned that there were many ways he could stay on his meal plan without drawing attention to himself when he was eating with his colleagues. For example, he would ask for lean cuts of meat with sauces on the side. He would even have an occasional glass of wine with his Optional Calorie allotments. He called the airlines a day or two ahead and requested special healthy meals.

Traveling—for business or pleasure—need not ruin your food planning. Make advance preparations: Pack fruit or diet dressings and select hotels that have exercise facilities. With determination and flexibility, even the disruptions and demands of traveling can be worked into a successful program.

Tip for the Day
Think of ways you can avoid possible slips the next time you travel.

"Gluttony is not a secret vice."
ORSON WELLES

Whenever Charlotte was in public, she'd eat lightly and refuse second helpings. In the privacy of her own home, though, Charlotte would overeat, devouring baked goods, snacks, casseroles and leftovers. If she wasn't eating in front of others, she felt she didn't have a problem with food, and no one else would think she had a problem, either.

You're fooling only yourself if you think that it's okay to overeat when you're alone. If you aren't taking proper care of your body, you won't be able to hide that from anyone, regardless of whether they see you eating or not. By the same token, if you try to lose weight but overeat when no one is looking, the only person you're hurting is yourself. Being successful at weight loss or any other activity requires total honesty with yourself at all times—not just when someone is looking.

Do you have different standards for yourself when you are alone and when you're in public? If so, make a commitment to yourself today to become honest in all your affairs, and especially with your food program. The more truthful you can be in every life situation, the less likely you'll be to have any private vices.

᪆ *Tip for the Day* ᪆
Scrutinize your behavior today when you're eating alone. Do you fudge with portion sizes? If so, make an effort to be as scrupulous when you're alone as you are when with others.

"You don't have to cook fancy or complicated masterpieces—just good food from fresh ingredients."

JULIA CHILD

When you are in a hurry, you tend to eat whatever is quick and convenient. This often means chips, fast food or sweet treats. If this is your pattern, however, be aware that high-fat, high-sugar items aren't nutritious and usually lead to weight gain. One study demonstrates that people who practice good nutrition are more likely to cook healthy foods from scratch. Those who are less vigilant often use prepackaged, prepared foods with empty calories and high sodium and fat contents.

While it's very possible to follow the Weight Watchers program without spending a lot of time in the kitchen, learning to create tasty meals will boost your odds of eating healthfully. If the prospect of cooking healthy meals is intimidating, remind yourself that twenty minutes is all that's required to assemble a good meal. Buy precleaned, precut vegetables, select meats that are presliced or cubed and use the microwave oven to prepare basics like baked potatoes and grains.

If that still seems too difficult, set aside weekend time to prepare dishes that can be frozen and later reheated. You'll find that the more time you can invest in creating nutritious meals, the less likely you'll be to derail your food plan with unplanned eating.

Tip for the Day
Shop for groceries to make a fresh, healthy meal.

"Self-confidence is the first requisite to great undertakings."
SAMUEL JOHNSON

One dietitian who has counseled hundreds of people in weight loss says that there is a striking similarity among the ones who have successfully maintained their weight goal—self-confidence. These men and women believe that they can be thin and remain thin, and they don't allow themselves to dwell on potential negative influences.

The dietitian says that part of the reason chronic dieters lack self-confidence is because they've lost weight many times but have been unable to maintain their ideal weight. When someone repeatedly loses weight only to regain it, they start to believe that they can never be permanently thin.

If you fear that your success will be short-lived, start dealing with your concerns now. Remind yourself that every day of healthful eating and regular exercise is another foundation block for a permanent lifestyle. Instead of looking at past weight-loss problems as harbingers of your future, study them to learn what *will* work for you. And talk to others who are successful. The more you can emulate the successful masters of weight control, the more likely you'll be to join them.

Tip for the Day
Every time you begin to doubt your future as a slender person, repeat this affirmation: I can maintain a trim body.

"The body is a sacred garment."

MARTHA GRAHAM

If you want your body to serve you well, you need to treat it with respect. Consider, for example, your feet. If you go through the day in shoes that are ill fitting, you're going to be uncomfortable and may even injure yourself. For women, in particular, high heels can be a menace to good health because they constrict the feet unnaturally and put a lot of pressure on the big toe joint of the foot.

When you are exercising, it's important to wear the right shoes. To do this you need to know a bit about yourself. Do you have a high arch or a flat foot? Do your feet and ankles turn in or out? Place your wet foot on a piece of paper and examine your footprint. If the center of your foot is visible, you're flat-footed. To discern if your foot pronates, evaluate whether your foot rolls inward or outward when you walk. The next step is to go to a store that specializes in running shoes to purchase the shoe that best suits you. Take a used pair of walking shoes with you so the salesperson can look at the soles and heels to see where the shoe is worn out. With this information it's easier to determine if you need extra heel or arch support or even extra cushioning. With the diversity of shoes available now that are made for specific athletic activities for both men and women, you can be assured that you will get what you need.

Treat your bare feet right with warm water soaks and pedicures. To eliminate dryness you can slather cream on your feet and sleep in cotton socks. The more attention and care you can lavish on your feet, the more likely it is that they'll perform comfortably for you when you need them.

❧ *Tip for the Day* ❧
Don't wear any shoes that cause pain, regardless of how pretty or expensive they are.

"*[The stomach] is a slave that must accept everything that is given to it, but which avenges wrongs as slyly as does the slave.*"

EMILE SOUVESTER

When you give your body optimal nutrition, you benefit from more energy and emotional well-being. On the other hand, when you eat or drink foodstuffs that aren't healthy and can't fuel your body effectively, you develop subtle—and not so subtle—symptoms that indicate you would be well advised to move on to different foods.

The human body is designed for moderation. Therefore, too much of anything, even if it's healthful, can hurt you. Simone says that even though she always ate lean meat and fish, she gained weight anyway because she was overeating. Roy says that anything sugary leaves him feeling irritable and depressed and that fruit provides a steadier stream of energy. Some people who have food sensitivities say that they often crave the very substances that their bodies can't tolerate, such as nuts, eggs and cheese. When they succumb to temptation, they are plagued with skin rashes, mood swings, respiratory problems and bloating.

Keep in mind today that you can't fool your body. You may think that you can slip some treats into your meal plan because they're too small to matter. Even if there's no weight gain, you might have to grapple with physical and emotional setbacks that affect your weight-loss efforts. If you can remember to be respectful of your body and to put into it only what will bring you the most gains, you'll never have to deal with a stomach that has to avenge wrongs.

↭   *Tip for the Day*   ↭

Concentrate today on the messages your stomach is giving you. Your body will tell you what is good for it if you take the time to listen and feel.

"Change is the constant, the signal for rebirth, the egg of the phoenix."

CHRISTINA BALDWIN

When you set out to lose weight, you may think that achieving a new figure will change only your external appearance and not alter your personality. This isn't necessarily true, however. Deep within an overweight body is often someone who is different—someone who is just waiting for a thin body in order to unleash creative skills and a vibrant personality.

This is what happened to Helen after she lost 60 pounds. When heavy, Helen was painfully shy and insecure, and she shunned social functions for fear people would look at her critically. As a consequence of making long-term changes in her eating and exercise habits, and gaining self-confidence from her success, Helen was transformed. Before she lost weight, Helen recalls that her hobbies were grocery shopping and eating. Now she plays tennis and bridge, gardens, reads, goes to the movies, travels and shops for flattering clothes. Previously unable to speak in front of a group, she now leads weekly classes for people trying to lose weight.

As your weight comes off, allow your personality and habits to change along with your body. You'll probably discover that you're more outgoing, self-confident and willing to take risks, so nurture those aspects of your emerging self. Change is a natural part of life. The more you can benefit from its occurrence, the more likely you'll be to have the exciting and fulfilling life you want.

⁓ *Tip for the Day* ⁓

Watch for signs that your personality is changing and emerging as you lose weight. Continue to push yourself to develop aspects of your personality that may have been hidden.

"The crowd gives the leader new strength."

EVENIUS

When you join Weight Watchers, one of the first people to greet you will be your leader, a person who has met his or her own weight goal, maintained it and been trained specifically to meet all of the challenges he or she may encounter in this important position. You will also meet and be inspired by other members who have long-term success in losing and maintaining their weight. Because these people will undoubtedly play a large role in motivating you, you may see them as larger than life. It's important to remember, though, that they are not infallible.

You are free to choose the advice that fits your lifestyle best. The meal choices that work best for another member may not be the best choices for you and the lifestyle of your family. Listen carefully to members' advice because it obviously worked for them, but understand that the final decision is up to you. If a leader or someone you admire gains weight, it's important to remember that even if he or she has had a slip, it doesn't mean that you will, too, or that your weight-loss program doesn't work.

Absorb all of the strength and wisdom you can from the leaders and members at the meetings. Remember, though, that they aren't any more capable or successful than you can be yourself. Take the time to praise your new friends for their support and encouragement because the more positive feedback you provide, the more strength they will continue to have for you and others.

Tip for the Day

Thank your leader or other friends for something they have said that has made a difference in your program.

"If pregnancy were a book, they would cut the last two chapters."
NORA EPHRON

Some woman who have borne children feel that the nine months of pregnancy are sometimes frustrating and exhausting. The end of the pregnancy is likely to be more uncomfortable because you are at your largest. You may wonder if you'll ever fit back into your clothes. Even after delivery you may still feel and look bloated, which may make you worry about looking thin and toned again.

However, it is crucial for pregnant and nursing women to focus on the importance of good nutrition during the months when weight *gain* is important. For nursing mothers, this is the time when nourishing an infant requires massive energy and caloric stores. Use your pregnancy and nursing months wisely. Learn about and practice good eating and exercise habits. If you accept the importance of proper nutrition while you are pregnant and nursing, any woman can emerge from childbirth in excellent physical and emotional shape.

Instead of using pregnancy as an excuse to overeat and underexercise, use this unique time to properly nourish yourself and your growing child. Although the last two months might possibly test the limits of your patience and energy, remember that your unborn child will benefit most from the care you give yourself.

  Tip for the Day
If you are pregnant, remind yourself to be careful about your meals and exercise. If you know someone who is expecting, encourage her to see this period as a time when she can make lasting, beneficial changes.

"Dwelling on the negative simply contributes to its power."
SHIRLEY MACLAINE

For most people, nothing is as deflating as being criticized. If you are thin skinned, criticism has the power to ruin your day and destroy your self-confidence. And if you dwell on it, you're liable to increase its hold on your thoughts, perhaps driving you back into the comfort of food where you can momentarily soothe your hurt feelings.

The key to coping with criticism is learning how to profit from it. Psychologists say that if you overreact to criticism by rushing to defend yourself or getting angry, you'll miss out on an opportunity to improve yourself. Most criticism, they say, contains a kernel of truth so it's best to avoid reacting until you've had a day or two to process your emotions. Then, if you still disagree with what's been said, you'll be able to let go of it or address it in a rational way. And if you see some truth in the comment after thinking about it, you can thank the critic for drawing your attention to something that needs to be addressed.

Don't allow criticism, however mild or severe, to lead you back into overeating. Retreating into an oblivion of food may temporarily anesthetize you, but you'll still have your feelings to cope with after you eat. Remember that criticism can be a stepping-stone to making yourself stronger. Use it wisely and you'll increase your chances of being successful in a weight-loss program as well as in life.

≈ *Tip for the Day* ≈
Think of how you've reacted to criticism in the past. Do you resent and ignore these kinds of comments, or do you use them to help you see a subject in a new way?

> *"Great services are not canceled by one act or by
> one single error."*
>
> BENJAMIN DISRAELI

Kelly once thought that slipping off her meal plan by eating a piece of chocolate cake meant her entire weight-loss program was a failure. Instead of seeing the situation as a one-time slip, she negated all of her progress by telling herself she'd never succeed and that she was weak. At Weight Watchers, she has learned that events will crop up to challenge her efforts. She says that it's healthier to learn why the slip occurred rather than to see her efforts at losing weight as doomed.

One effective way to deal with eating slips before they happen is to complete the following sentence: I am at high risk for unplanned eating or deviating from my exercise plan when I'm ———. Perhaps your answer is *bored, alone, celebrating* or *anxious*. In any case, it is an important clue. Use it to figure out how to keep the situation from happening again. For example, if you always eat in the car after grocery shopping, you can plan ahead to shop on a full stomach or place the grocery bags out of reach in the trunk. If parties and weddings are occasions for you to overeat, bring a camera and take pictures so you will have something to do besides hang out at the hors d'oeuvres table. Understand that good eating behavior is more likely if you plan ahead.

Remember today that just about everyone has relapses from time to time. The best response is to identify and try to avoid tempting situations. While you may not always behave in the way you want, you'll be more likely to succeed if you keep your slips in perspective and use them to understand yourself better.

⟳ Tip for the Day ⟳
*If you do slip, affirm to yourself you're not a failure and renew your
efforts to achieve your goal.*

"[A chair] is the headquarters for the hindquarters."
ANONYMOUS

Many people sit for long stretches day after day in a car, at a desk, in a waiting room or while on the telephone. Needless to say, this activity doesn't promote fitness because practically the only thing moving is your mouth. With some creativity and determination, though, you can learn how to increase your fitness while sitting, as well as change normal sitting time into calorie-burning time.

The next time you're seated for a long period of time, do some silent exercises. For example, practice deep chest breathing to increase your lung capacity. This is done by inhaling through the nose, holding your breath briefly and exhaling through the mouth. You can also tighten your buttock muscles by holding them together for the count of ten and repeat. Do the same exercise with your stomach muscles. There are also simple yoga exercises you can do as you sit. Try neck rolls, arm stretches toward the ceiling and pushing your feet straight in front of you and flexing your heels. If available, a cordless phone can eliminate sitting time by giving you the ability to talk while walking on a treadmill or exercising on a stationary bike.

Try not to be a prisoner of your chair. Be creative and turn even these passive moments into periods when you can tone your body and improve your health.

Tip for the Day
Think of at least three things you can do while sitting today, such as stretching or deep breathing. Do one of them.

"Thanksgiving is a typically American holiday... The lavish meal is a symbol of the fact that abundant consumption is the result and reward of production."

AYN RAND

For many Americans, Thanksgiving is a time when we spend a lot of time planning a big meal, cooking it, eating it and then complaining about how full we feel. To manage weight loss successfully we must learn to celebrate holidays like Thanksgiving without focusing exclusively on food. Our goal should be to enjoy and celebrate the holiday and feel satisfied with ourselves.

With planning you can still eat many traditional Thanksgiving favorites like sweet potatoes, turkey, gravy, stuffing and pie without going off your meal plan. Beth decided that Thanksgiving dinner usually left her feeling guilt ridden about overeating. So she created an appetizing menu that controlled fat and calories yet didn't make her feel deprived. In the process she discovered that cooking calorie-rich dishes for her family wasn't necessary. By making lighter versions of recipes, she kept herself from slipping and at the same time helped her family eat healthfully, too.

Thanksgiving is a day to give thanks, not overindulge. As you begin the day, silently give thanks for all the blessings in your life—perhaps your family, a home, a job or comfort. Remind yourself that any special meal you eat today should be the condiment, not the main course, of the day.

⇜ *Tip for the Day* ⇝
Celebrate and give thanks today for the blessings of your family, your friends and your country. Let the meal be a symbol of these gifts.

"Anything you fully do is an alone journey."
NATALIE GOLDBERG

Barbara was 70 pounds overweight and miserable in her mid-twenties when her doctor informed her that she had multiple sclerosis. Depressed that life seemed to be passing her by, Barbara joined a weight-loss program at what she considers the lowest point of her life. She admits she had no self-esteem.

Four years later, Barbara's disease is now in remission and she has maintained a 70-pound weight loss that her doctor says was a large factor in her improved condition. Barbara adds that while she benefited from the support of other people in her program, she learned that she was the one who was ultimately responsible for making the changes that led to success. She says she knew she had to make time to exercise if she were going to change her lifestyle in a healthy way.

Remind yourself today that while you can get encouragement, helpful tips and support from friends and at weight-loss meetings, you are the one who must prepare and eat healthful meals. You must set aside the time to exercise and follow through with the plans you set for yourself. Learning to take this important step is what will help you stick to your plan in difficult times when temptation abounds. It is also what will give you the most joy when you reach your weight goal. Then you know that you, and you alone, are the one who did the hard work that led to your success.

Tip for the Day

Ask yourself if you accept that you alone hold the key to being successful in your weight-loss efforts.

"I'm glad I don't have to explain to a man from Mars why each day I set fire to dozens of little pieces of paper, and then put them in my mouth."

MIGNON MCLAUGHLIN

Part of any good weight-loss program is making a commitment to live a healthy life and develop sensible coping behaviors. But if you are still smoking, you are continuing to damage your health. And smoking works against adopting a lifestyle that will help you have the energy and enthusiasm to lose weight and exercise regularly. Secondhand smoke will harm you and can undo your good efforts at trying to live healthfully.

Smoking kills. Chronic obstructive pulmonary disease is a common and ultimately deadly result of smoking. Lung cancer—which is almost always a result of smoking—is the top cancer killer among women. And overweight women who smoke have more difficulty quitting smoking because they often smoke to avoid food. Experts suggest that women who smoke join a weight-loss program and get comfortable with that program before trying to quit. Then, relearn routines that were once synonymous with smoking. Two alternative behaviors are: Learn to have tea with fruit instead of a cigarette, and take a brisk morning walk instead of that first cigarette.

Kicking the smoking habit isn't easy, but it's probably the single most important step you can take toward improving the quality of your life. The feared weight gain is often minimal, too, which is far less dangerous to your health than smoking anyway. Use the tools of a good weight-loss program to conquer an addiction today. It will aid you and make quitting easier, and it will support your weight-loss efforts, too.

Tip for the Day

If you smoke, investigate new ways to quit, such as the nicotine patch or smoke-cessation classes. If you frequently find yourself in a smoke-filled environment—such as a bar or waiting room—remove yourself.

"A handful of patience is worth more than a bushel of brains."
DUTCH PROVERB

By the age of 37 David was carrying more than four hundred pounds on his six-foot-one frame. His excessive weight resulted in such severe joint problems that he couldn't walk a block to buy his lunch without hurting his ankles and knees. At least once a week a stranger would make a rude comment about David's weight and even swear at him. David also remembers that his weight limited his life in other ways. When he used the shoulder harness in his car, for example, he couldn't reach the radio knob.

When David joined a weight-loss program, he was the heaviest member and therefore had the largest amount of weight to lose. He was discouraged about how long it would take him to reach his weight goal. Then he saw a woman in bicycle shorts being recognized at one of the support-group meetings for losing 100 pounds, and her success made David realize he could do it, too. David wisely decided to be patient as he set about losing weight, telling himself that if he just kept up his daily routine, he'd make it through.

David was handsomely rewarded for his patience. Not only did he eventually lose more than two hundred pounds, his efforts to increase his exercise program gradually kept him from injuring himself by overexercising or losing motivation. He is now a regular racewalker. David's success story is one that brings hope to anyone who thinks that his or her goal is unattainable. With patience and a commitment to change your life, you'll find that there is nothing that you cannot achieve.

&ewe; *Tip for the Day* &ewe;
*Do you frequently sabotage yourself by being too impatient to follow through
with a commitment? If so, remind yourself that patience and delaying
gratification usually results in more permanent results.*

"Cheese—milk's leap toward immortality."

CLIFTON FADIMAN

While many people think that cheese is the best thing that can be derived from milk, others might argue in favor of another milk product: yogurt. Studies show that calcium is more readily absorbed in the presence of fermented milk such as yogurt or buttermilk. Another study has found that eating yogurt helps the body fight infection and cancer. And yogurt can reduce blood serum cholesterol and kill the bacteria that foster ulcers and gastritis.

Be careful when selecting yogurt if you want to enjoy these myriad health benefits. Only yogurt products that list "live" cultures are useful, so avoid foods that have been heated to extend shelf life, or frozen yogurt desserts that have only small amounts of live cultures. Also, be aware of the drawbacks to some yogurt products, like the added sugar in fruit-based yogurts or the fat in whole-milk yogurts. As with other foods, if you choose carefully and read labels, you can enjoy this delicious milk product that has been popular for centuries.

Tip for the Day
Include yogurt or buttermilk in your meal plan today.

"I consider being ill as one of the great pleasures of life, provided one is not too ill."

SAMUEL BUTLER

Sometimes being sick is a learning experience. Linda, who had developed walking pneumonia, said that spending time in bed made her realize that she'd been pushing herself too hard and that she needed more balance between work and leisure. When Nancy broke her foot, she found that she was more comfortable doing things for other people than asking them for help. She went to a counselor to find out why she felt so uncomfortable being needy.

In the winter season you're probably going to get at least one bout of flu or a cold, and your down time may be a valuable introspective experience. If you're always getting sick, however, it's probably interfering with getting to work or living healthfully. Take some steps to get yourself into better physical condition and improve your overall sense of well-being. Take vitamins, drink plenty of fluids and get enough rest. It is also important to reduce stress, because stressed-out people develop twice as many colds as those who have more balanced lives. Regular, moderate exercise also builds the body's immune system; inactive women have been shown to get colds and the flu twice as often as women who walk briskly for 45 minutes a day.

Use the down time that a minor illness brings and let it teach you about your body and your lifestyle. But if infection is a constant problem, take some steps to make changes in your life so that you're less vulnerable. Although it may be impossible to avoid all colds and flu this season, it's always possible to reduce your risk.

Tip for the Day

Do one new thing this winter that will minimize your chances of getting sick, such as scheduling a flu shot.

"*Music hath charms to soothe a savage breast / To soften rocks, or bend a knotted oak.*"

WILLIAM CONGREVE

The ancient Greeks believed that musical harmony was the key to the workings of the cosmos. Consequently, ancient scholars such as Plato and Pythagoras advocated the use of music in healing. The harp, for instance, was thought to cure sciatica and was also used to relieve nervous disorders. Whether this instrument contained such healing powers is uncertain. What is clear, though, is that music *does* affect the way you feel, and how you feel has a powerful effect on your health and well-being.

If music isn't a big part of your life, try to introduce it in soothing, beneficial ways. Instead of listening to stimulating sounds or jarring music, turn on music that makes you feel relaxed and at ease with yourself. Experiment with different instruments and composers for the sound and beat that harmonizes best with your internal state. Learning how to elevate your emotions, soothe anxiety and even heal yourself is a tool that can always be used to improve your life.

Tip for the Day

Turn on the radio today if you are feeling sad or uneasy. Turn the dial until you find a soothing melody that reduces your tension level and takes your mind off your worries.

"Perhaps too much of everything is as bad as too little."
EDNA FERBER

Nutritionists have begun to see a new type of client: someone who is afraid of fat. These types of people have taken weight loss and health consciousness to an extreme, counting fat grams as compulsively as they once counted calories.

It's important to remember moderation in all things with your weight-loss plans. Eating moderate amounts of fat will make food tastier and will keep you from feeling deprived. Becoming too focused on cutting back on fat can take the enjoyment out of meals. It can even occasionally result in weight gain. One nutritionist says that she had a client who made poor food choices by severely restricting fats while loading up on low-fat foods that were high in sugar and calories. The client was taught the importance of portion size and how to get enough protein, carbohydrates and fiber in a low-fat meal plan.

Be sensible with your meal planning today, particularly when it comes to balancing nutrients and food groups. While it may seem smart to eliminate fat because it contributes to high cholesterol and weight gain, it's only by learning how to eat all things in moderation that you can lose weight and keep it off.

Tip for the Day
Be sure to read labels on fat-free, low-fat and reduced-fat foods. Are the portion sizes unrealistically small? Are the sugar and sodium contents too high?

"Do give books—religious or otherwise—for Christmas. They're never fattening, seldom sinful, and permanently personal."
LENORE HERSHEY

If you take time to examine the role that food plays in your life, you may be surprised that you use food in places and situations where it needn't be. For example, when you want to give someone a gift, do you automatically think of baked goods or food-related items such as china or cooking utensils? Holidays especially can be a time for inappropriate baking and eating.

If you are tempted to whip up a favorite dessert as a present (while sampling some yourself) or celebrate the holidays with special foods, make this year one in which you will find gifts that benefit others in richer and more stimulating ways. Books are an ideal gift choice. Books cover so many topics, sizes and prices that the gift of a book can be tailored to fit many preferences. If you give rich foods, you may unnecessarily tempt yourself and unconsciously sabotage someone else's efforts to eat in a healthful way.

During this holiday season, try to remember people with gifts that can be treasured long after the celebrations are over. Take the time to find out what really interests them, too, such as biography, traveling, handyman projects or crafts. Then your gift will be more personal and a permanent reminder of your thoughtfulness.

∾ *Tip for the Day* ∾
Make a list of situations where you have used food as a gift and then list acceptable nonfood substitutes.

*"Over the years your bodies become walking autobiographies,
telling friends and strangers alike of the minor and major stresses
of your lives."*

MARILYN FERGUSON

When you are overweight, it is probable that food has been
one of the ways you have comforted yourself and coped with
stress in your life. There are other clues your body
can reveal about your emotions. If you walk with hunched
shoulders, it may be that you are unconsciously protecting yourself. Or if you have persistent lower back pain, it could be an
indication that you don't feel supported.

One special treat you can give yourself as you lose weight is
a session with a massage therapist, or you can even trade a
back rub with a family member or friend. After Julie lost 50
pounds she visited a massage therapist as a reward for her hard
work and success. Not only was it therapeutic to have a massage, it helped Julie see that she was still carrying her body as if
she were overweight. The massage therapist pointed out that
some of her aches were from slouching. Now she says she is
proud of her body, so she walks with confidence.

Take note today of what signals your body is sending out
about you. Try to walk as tall as possible and be conscious of
what areas are painful or that you are unconsciously protecting. As you develop an active lifestyle and toned body, it will
become easier to present yourself in a strong, confident and
assertive way. It's also important to be aware of your feelings
about your body so that you can address any negative emotions that are lingering.

Tip for the Day

*Look in the mirror at your body and observe how you stand. Practice standing
with shoulders back, chin up and eyes facing front. Now add a smile because
your posture is that of someone who radiates ease and confidence.*

"As I see it, every day you do one of two things: build health or produce disease in yourself."

ADELLE DAVIS

When you join Weight Watchers, you make a commitment to yourself to develop a way of living that promotes health and fitness. But eating properly and exercising is only one part. Be diligent about other areas of your health, such as getting annual Pap smears or prostate exams. Having a physician check for possible skin cancers and heart irregularities is important, too. And if diseases like diabetes run in your family, it's prudent to be aware of what the signs are and how likely you are to develop them.

One crucial checkup that most women neglect is a mammogram. In 1992 only 41 percent of women aged 40 and over—the highest-risk class—had this screening, despite the fact that early detection improves the odds of survival. Procrastination and a belief that if you look fine, you must be fine, keep many from taking this important step. Making a regular appointment with your physician is one way to safeguard your health. Health techniques such as chiropractic massage therapy, meditation and acupuncture are alternative ways to help prevent disease from manifesting itself in your body.

Make sure you attend to all areas of your health today. Know your risk factors and look into ways to enhance your health care with safe alternative techniques. By eating well and exercising, you are creating the foundation for good health. Take steps to make sure that what you build supports your efforts. Having regular checkups and routine screenings for disease that you are at risk for is just another facet of a healthy lifestyle.

⟳ Tip for the Day ⟲
Make an appointment that will safeguard your health, such as for an EKG, TB test, flu shot or cholesterol screening.

"[Long hair] is considered bohemian, which may be why I grew it, but I keep it long because I love the way it feels, part cloak, part fan, part mane, part security blanket."

MARGE PIERCY

One of the ways many people hide, particularly women, is by having long hair. If you're overweight, you may feel sensitive about your face size, thinking that short hair will only emphasize your chubby cheeks or double chin. As a result, you may make long hair the security blanket that will shield you from unfavorable comments about your appearance.

If this has been your attitude, weight loss may create problems—and opportunities—for you. After you've bought new clothes and changed your makeup, it may occur to you that you need an updated hairstyle as well, but parting with that familiar, comforting hair may feel frightening. To ease you into getting a shorter, more complimentary cut, study pictures in magazines of makeovers and think of ways to incorporate a new look. Ask friends to give you an honest appraisal of what they think would look best. If you're still unsure, look at your high school or college yearbook to see if you're still wearing the same style. If so, chances are you need something new.

If you suspect you're clinging to an old hairstyle for security, make an appointment to update or change it. Even a subtle shift in layers or color can give you a fresh look and a different attitude toward yourself. Be bold and experiment a bit. A new cut may be just the boost you need to continue to make beneficial changes in your life.

Tip for the Day
Look at both old and recent pictures of yourself. Is your hair the same, even if your body is different? Can you think of a way to change it for a fresher, cleaner look?

"It's odd that you can get so anesthetized by your own pain or your own problem that you don't quite fully share the hell of someone close to you."

LADY BIRD JOHNSON

Anyone who has ever felt the pain of being overweight—through job discrimination, being unable to sit comfortably at a movie or in an airplane or not having any flattering clothes to wear—knows that it can occupy a great deal of your time and thoughts. If you aren't thinking about how unhappy you are with your weight, you're obsessing about losing weight, how embarrassed you are about your appearance or what others say about you when you aren't there.

It wasn't until Jennifer joined Weight Watchers and began to feel good about herself that she had the energy to really care about others. For example, her husband was under a great deal of stress because he had started his own business and was uncertain of its future—something Jennifer hadn't noticed before. All of her energy had gone toward feeling sorry for herself, she admits. Being obsessed about her weight had prevented her from being a sounding board for her husband when he most needed it.

Have you neglected a good friend or spouse because thinking about yourself or your own troubles has consumed all of your energy? If so, remind yourself today that each person in your life has his or her own burdens to bear and that being a good friend means thinking of others. Although it's often hard to see outside your own world at times, learning how to be giving can be the best gift you can give yourself.

Tip for the Day

Take time to be a friend to someone today by asking how she or he is and finding a way to offer support.

*"Nobody speaks the truth when there's something
they must have."*

ELIZABETH BOWEN

For several weeks after joining a weight-loss program, Dora's success was minimal, even though she felt she was rigorously following the suggested menu plan. At her program leader's suggestion, she made a list of what she put into her mouth every day. She was shocked to discover that she'd been unconsciously adding extra bites of food throughout the day. For example, she noted that every morning her daughter left a bite or two of her waffles, which Dora had grown accustomed to finishing. She also regularly had mints from the vending machine, a sprinkling of bacon bits on her salad and the chips her son left in his lunch box. Although none of these were significant snacks, those extra calories made weight loss harder.

If you are having trouble losing weight, it might be good to look for the invisible extras that you are adding to your daily meal plan. Are you adding cream to your coffee, sampling goodies at the supermarket or finishing your children's meals? Once you have detected a pattern of when you have invisible extras, devise a strategy to get yourself back on track. If cleaning up the breakfast dishes always results in some nibbling, delegate this chore to your spouse or pour liquid soap on the leftovers. And if your favorite supermarket always hands free samples when you go grocery shopping, go on a full stomach or find a different place to shop.

Pay attention to the truth of what you're eating during the day, especially if you've had an unexplained weight gain or plateau recently. Invisible extras are common to everyone, but with some sleuthing and new strategies they will become visible, so they won't undercut your success any longer.

⤜ *Tip for the Day* ⤛
*Write down everything that passes your lips today, even the little tastes you
might usually ignore, like mints.*

"I am convinced digestion is the great secret of life."
REVEREND SYDNEY SMITH

When one 75-pound-overweight woman decided to stop her on-again, off-again diets, she joined a weight-loss program designed for people who wanted to lose weight sensibly. She was surprised at how differently she felt when she changed her meal plan from high fat to high fiber. She is also delighted at how much more energy she has now. Whenever she tries some of the things she used to eat, like French fries, she gets tired, finds it hard to exercise and doesn't sleep well. She says she was just sleepwalking through life when she ate all that fat, sugar and refined food.

This woman's experience bears out what scientific study has shown: What you eat has a dramatic effect on how you feel. Judith Wurtman, Ph.D., who has pioneered much of this work, says that eating for health starts in the morning with protein, which makes you feel alert. Complex carbohydrates, such as pasta and potatoes, are mood lifters that steady blood sugar. Too much fat, she says, is like an "emotional anesthetic" because you are likely to become lethargic. She reports that high-fat foods turn off the body and the mind.

As you eat your nutritious meals, observe how different types of foods change your mood and use that to your advantage. If carbohydrates make you sleepy, eat those kinds of foods at night. If eggs evoke alertness, make sure you have protein before sitting down to work. Once you learn to fuel your body with foods that bring you emotional and physical benefits, you'll have the tools to foster joy, energy and concentration whenever you need them.

Tip for the Day
Note how you feel after a breakfast of protein versus a breakfast of carbohydrates. Use this knowledge to help you plan meals that synchronize nutritional needs with your schedule.

"Tradition is a guide and not a jailer."

SOMERSET MAUGHAM

One of the most stressful times of the year, especially for the person who is conscious of eating healthfully, is the period from Thanksgiving to the end of the year. The food temptations are plentiful: Holiday parties usually feature calorie-laden goodies, gifts are often food-related and there is a lot of encouragement to drink and eat too much. There are also stresses that come from last-minute shopping and trying to re-create the magic and wonder of childhood. In fact, therapists say that most of their calls from depressed patients come during this season.

If you want to maintain your emotional equilibrium and control, you must be protective of yourself and your time. Budget calories and food choices ahead of time. It's also a good idea to focus on holiday traditions that don't involve cooking or food. Make ornaments, help those less fortunate than yourself and send personal greeting cards and notes to family and friends. And to help combat the stress created by holiday expectations, it's wise to make exercise a high priority, set aside time for friends and attend supportive weight-loss group meetings.

Don't put so much pressure on yourself this season to create the perfect holiday ambiance for you and your family. Be aware of the many enticements to overdo your limits. You should have strategies in mind to help you deal with those temptations. With proper planning, realistic expectations and dedication to achieving your goals, you can emerge from the holiday season serene, joyous and ready for the new year.

~ *Tip for the Day* ~
Try a new holiday activity this year that involves your family but doesn't include food.

"[The body is] a marvelous machine... a chemical laboratory, a power-house. Every movement, voluntary or involuntary, full of secrets and marvels!"

THEODOR HERZL

Stretching is one aspect of exercise that is often neglected yet is essential to optimal functioning of the body. The tendency for many is to begin exercising without first warming up their muscles or to stop suddenly without giving themselves sufficient time to make the transition to a less demanding pace. To keep your muscles supple and able to recover from vigorous activity, you must allot several minutes each day for stretching.

If you haven't exercised for many years, your range of motion with stretches may be quite limited at first. But even if you stretch regularly, the technique remains the same: stretch the muscle until you feel a slight strain, then hold the stretch steady for at least ten seconds. Be careful not to bounce or you might injure yourself. It is best to warm up each major muscle group one at a time before you work out, and then do the same when you're finished. The more care you can take to prevent yourself from being injured, the greater the enjoyment and benefit you'll derive from your workouts.

Tip for the Day

Before and after you exercise today, devote at least five minutes to stretching.

"The camera makes everyone a tourist in other people's reality, and eventually in one's own."

SUSAN SONTAG

One of the things that often prompts people to lose weight is seeing themselves in a photograph and realizing—perhaps for the first time—that they're carrying around a lot of extra weight. When Kay looked at her summer vacation pictures, she noticed that she always tried to put one of her children in front of herself so that no one could see how fat she was. It upset her tremendously to realize she was going to such great lengths to hide her body, so she joined a weight-loss program that day.

While pictures can be an unhappy reminder of your fat days, keeping those images where you can see them can also motivate you to adhere to your weight-loss program. One expert suggests that you take a picture of yourself every time you lose ten pounds and post it next to a picture of yourself at your top weight. It's a way of reinforcing successful weight loss while reminding you why you were prompted to lose weight in the first place.

Have a picture of yourself taken today and keep it somewhere where you'll always see it—on a mirror or the refrigerator door, for example. Resolve that you will do everything you can to eat sensibly this day. If you can use this technique to motivate you, it won't be long before the picture you want of yourself is right next to the one that once made you so unhappy.

∾ *Tip for the Day* ∾
*Look at pictures of yourself at your top weight. How did you feel about yourself
then compared with how you feel about yourself today?*

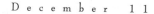
"Food is the most primitive form of comfort."

SHEILAH GRAHAM

One of the reasons many people overeat is because food provides a satisfying and contented feeling, particularly when you are distressed. Crystal said that for years eating brownies was the way she dealt with all her problems. Whenever her children were irritable or she was frustrated at work or upset with her husband, she admits she would drown her feelings in sweet things.

When you decide to lose weight sensibly, you don't give up food; you give up *abusing* it. When stressed by the demands of a busy life, you learn to treat yourself to nourishing meals and activities that give you the perspective and energy to cope with your emotions instead of comforting yourself with fattening unhealthy snacks. By removing a familiar food crutch, you are free to approach life assertively and honestly.

Examine the ways in which you've used food for solace and to numb your feelings. Next, think of ways you could have better dealt with those emotions, like talking with a therapist, taking a walk, or confronting an unpleasant situation directly. You'll find that the more you can cope with discomfort in healthy ways, the more problems you're likely to resolve to your satisfaction. Food will have less power over you in the future.

Tip for the Day

Think of three ways you can comfort yourself without turning to food.

*"If you think about it, everything in life is like a banana.
Nothing is straight or logical."*

THOMAS BAUMGARTEL

If you are searching for a food that tastes rich, is sweet, can be carried in your pocket and doesn't need refrigeration, look no further than the banana. This tasty fruit is the perfect food for anyone who wants to eat healthfully and lose weight. In fact, it is also this country's favorite fruit, far more popular than apples and oranges.

Bananas can add much to your food plan. They are low in sodium, nonfat, rich in fiber and potassium and chock full of vitamins C, A and B$_6$. They are also available year round and come in three hundred different varieties ranging from small and sweet to orange and lemony. Bananas also pack a nutritional punch when they are dried into chips, so they are favored by long-distance athletes who need to keep their bodies constantly fueled with high-energy foods.

If you're short on ideas about how to prepare bananas, consult a cookbook. Bananas can be used in a wide variety of cooking techniques including baking, flambeeing and skewering. Part of the fun of losing weight is making your meals colorful and delicious, two things that a banana will always supply.

Tip for the Day

*Take a banana along with you for a quick snack the next time you're doing
errands or know you will be spending a lot of time in your car.*

"To be without some of the things you want is an indispensable part of happiness."

BERTRAND RUSSELL

When you begin a weight-loss program and you select a weight goal, you should consider several factors, including bone structure, height and previous attempts at maintaining a target weight. When you reach this goal, you will probably be elated and proud of your accomplishment. Some people, however, are not as contented, thinking that they would look better at an even lower weight.

While you might want to weigh less than your weight goal, you must remember that success isn't based on being a certain dress size or conforming to a certain ideal. It means discovering a comfortable weight that you can maintain with a moderate amount of exercise and a healthy meal plan. If you strive to be thinner than your body ought to be, you may feel hungry and irritable, or you may have to raise your exercise level beyond your body's capacity. If this happens, you may find yourself gaining and losing the same five or ten pounds as you struggle to meet an unrealistic standard. Not only is this situation discouraging, it may set the stage for you to give up altogether.

Have a healthy perspective on what your body can handle versus the weight or body shape you might want. If you are dissatisfied after reaching your weight goal, consider carefully whether it's realistic to set a lower goal given your frame and activity level. If not, accept your body as it is and give yourself credit for the energy and determination it took to get this far.

❧ *Tip for the Day* ❧

Resolve today to accept your body ams it is. Honor yourself by providing the nutrients and exercise your body needs to function at its best.

"[A dog is] an exercise machine with hair."

AD FOR THE AMERICAN COUNCIL ON EXERCISE

Mike takes his Doberman, Amy, for a long jog every day. They trot along the trails in a nearby park, Amy in the lead. On days when Mike is not really in the mood, he will show Amy his workout clothes, knowing that she will pester him until he takes her out.

If you have read about all the benefits of exercise, purchased special workout clothes and joined a health club, but you still find it hard to exercise regularly, the solution may be getting a dog. These lovable pets have many special qualities, including offering unconditional love and an element of safety, but they also come with a major condition: They must be walked often. If you are committed to taking care of your dog, you're guaranteed to walk every day, which is a wonderful way to begin your athletic career.

Remember today that *any* type of exercise is going to help you lose weight and lengthen your life. It's estimated that moderate physical activity can add two hours to your life for every hour you exercise. So whether you are cutting the grass, washing your car, walking the dog or taking the stairs instead of the elevator, bear in mind that the key is simply to move your body.

Tip for the Day
If you don't have a dog to walk, borrow one and take it on at least two brisk walks every day this week.

"All things must change to something new, to something strange."
HENRY WADSWORTH LONGFELLOW

When you make the decision to lose weight or address a dissatisfying area of life, the prospect of change can be scary. You may feel haunted by past failures to meet your expectations or you may fear the loss of a comfortable habit. Whatever the reason for your apprehension, it is best to confront it because change is the natural order of life. If you don't allow yourself to evolve constantly, you will stay stuck in old patterns and miss the pleasure that comes with new challenges.

One person who counsels people on creating healthy exercise and eating routines says that if the prospect of change is overwhelming, the answer is to start small. He recalls a woman who gave up cigarettes, sugar, caffeine and fat all at once, only to be overwhelmed by the drastic change and quickly reverted to her bad habits. Instead, he says, begin the task of weight loss by starting a moderate exercise program. The feelings of well-being from exercise can lead to a sense of control, which gives a person more confidence to start to changing eating habits.

If change is hard for you, find one small area of life you can address. Let the success you get from that experience empower you to change other areas. Gradually, as you gain more confidence and see that you are in control of your body, you'll find that there's nothing in life that can't be accomplished starting with the first small step. Remember that change doesn't have to be drastic for the long term.

⋙ *Tip for the Day* ⋘
Choose one small step you can make today to improve your physical fitness.

"Without friends no one would choose to live, though he had all other goods."

ARISTOTLE

Sherry and Ginnie became fast friends when they joined the same dance group in the retirement community where they lived. Despite exercising together and dancing often, neither woman could lose weight. After dance practice one day, they agreed to join Weight Watchers together. Within three months both had reached their weight goal, which they felt was helped by their friendship and their mutual encouragement of each other.

Listening to the information and tips at meetings was encouraging to Ginnie. But she says that she can get discouraged very easily, too, so following the guidelines with a friend helped enormously. Sherry agrees with this assessment, saying it was so much easier to be successful because Ginnie made her go to meetings when she was tired; and when Ginnie didn't want to exercise, Sherry would be the one getting her out the door to go walking.

Do you have a friend who would like to join you in losing weight? If you can create a partnership with someone who can motivate you when you're down and enjoy your success with you, you'll have a great tool to help you reach your weight goal. Losing weight together can be a fun experience with rewards for both of you.

❧ *Tip for the Day* ❧
Ask a friend if he or she would be interested in joining your weight-loss efforts. Emphasize the positive aspects of working together toward a mutual goal.

"Why do some people always see beautiful skies and grass and lovely flowers and incredible human beings, while others are hard-pressed to find anything or any place that is beautiful?"

LEO BUSCAGLIA

There is a housing project in a large city that is overrun with violence, gangs and drugs. In the midst of this despair, however, there are people who choose to see what is positive and good in the world, not what is depressing and tragic. There are parents, for example, who are attending high school with their own children, determined to get the education they didn't receive as teenagers. They are focused on what lies ahead, and they are excited about their future opportunities and the good fortune that has come their way.

Be sure that you are focused on possibilities today instead of obstacles. Open your mind to new ideas that you haven't yet tried. Nearly anything is possible if you want it enough. Instead of looking back at overweight years when you didn't have enough self-confidence to take risks, congratulate yourself for deciding to change your life right now.

Look today for the opportunities in your life and try to see what's possible instead of what's impossible. Being upbeat and positive may not bring you sympathy and attention, but it will open more doors and make more of your dreams come true.

Tip for the Day

If you don't have enough money to join a gym, think of inexpensive ways to get fit, such as jumping rope, climbing stairs and walking.

"One ought, every day at least, to hear a little song, read a good poem, see a fine picture, and, if it were possible, to speak a few reasonable words."

JOHANN WOLFGANG VON GOETHE

Prior to joining Weight Watchers, much of your time may have been spent worrying about your weight or feeling guilty and ashamed of how you look. In the program you may have swung to the opposite extreme, focusing only on what you are eating, how much weight you are losing, whether you are getting enough exercise and checking off every box on your Weekly Tracker.

Either end of the spectrum is unhealthy and incompatible with a fulfilling and successful life. To make sure that your weight is kept in perspective, try to include a variety of activities that bring balance and harmony into your life every day: For example, allow time for quiet contemplation or touch base with a close and supportive friend. Lift your soul with music, and read something that will enrich your mind. Doing the basics—eating, planning meals, working and going to bed—is important, of course, but without additional enrichment life can be one-dimensional and stagnant.

Include a variety of activities in this day and every day. If you have time, browse through an art book or visit a museum. Listen to a beautiful piece of music or play it yourself. Instead of staring at the television tonight, curl up with a book that will teach you something valuable. The more you can strive to make your day diverse, balanced and enlightening, the more zest and intelligence you'll bring to your life.

∞ *Tip for the Day* ∞

Take a break from your routine today with one activity that will help you appreciate beauty or educate your mind.

"Water is the most neglected nutrient in your diet but one of the most vital."

KELLY BARTON

Water is an important component in successful weight loss and exercise. During exercise, water has several important functions. It maintains blood volume and moves nutrients, hormones and antibodies through your bloodstream and lymphatic system. It increases your urine output so that you can get rid of metabolic wastes. And, of course, water is essential in helping you sweat and keeping your body cooled.

Most physical fitness experts advise that you drink water before and during exercise to prevent dehydration. But unless you are doing strenuous exercise over a prolonged period, such as running a marathon, you can replenish your fluids afterwards if you prefer. The best time to ingest foods and beverages with water is *before* you are thirsty. If you're drinking enough water, you will urinate frequently and your urine will be clear, not dark.

Most experts recommend eight to ten glasses of water or other fluid every day. Remember that fruits and vegetables also contain water. However, the water you get from sodas and coffee are poor sources of water because caffeinated drinks act as diuretics, pulling water from your system more quickly than normal. If you don't like the taste of the water that comes through your faucet, try bottled spring or mineral water. You may surprise yourself by discovering that the clear, refreshing taste of water is preferable to any other drink.

Tip for the Day
Try some alternatives to soft drinks this week. Easy-to-find choices are sparkling and nonsparkling waters, flavored and plain waters, club soda and seltzer.

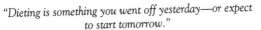

*"Dieting is something you went off yesterday—or expect
to start tomorrow."*

ANONYMOUS

There is a burgeoning movement of people who have decided
to stop dieting and to accept themselves instead just as they
are. These men and women say that ignoring scales, calories
and being a certain dress size has freed them up to be more
creative, loving and happy. They have a point—the word *diet*
suggests to many that eating sensibly is temporary, something
you do only until you lose enough weight. But in fact, eating
sensibly is a lifetime skill you must learn if you want to control
your weight permanently.

Accepting yourself is an important step in emotional health.
But you can also accept that you will be doing yourself a favor
when you change some of your attitudes and behaviors regard-
ing food. You can abolish the word *diet* from your vocabulary
without eliminating the goal of being slender and healthy. A
sensible and balanced approach to weight loss will enable you
to feel satisfied and not deprived, but most importantly it will
give you the means to achieve the figure that you desire.

Tip for the Day

*Remind yourself today that real self-acceptance means you love yourself enough
to take the best possible care of your body.*

"What saves a man is to take a step. Then another step. It is always the same step, but you have to take it."

ANTOINE DE SAINT-EXUPÉRY

Although she was trim at her wedding, Maria began gaining weight on her honeymoon. By the time her first child was born three years later, she was 70 pounds overweight. Maria reluctantly began to research diets, assuming she'd have to eat unappetizing food and exercise if she wanted to lose weight. To Maria's surprise she found that the Weight Watchers sensible meal plans could include some of the foods she liked as well as new main dishes that were tasty and filling. Instead of dreading exercise, it made her feel so much better that she now looks forward to it. She has even become an aerobics instructor and teaches seven classes a week.

The first step in losing weight is making the commitment to follow the guidelines of a healthy program. The next step is to integrate exercise into your life. Finally, you must be diligent about your new lifestyle because each small step takes you closer to your goals. Although you may resist taking a certain step—like exercising regularly—you may be surprised to find that it is exactly that step that leads you to happiness and success.

Tip for the Day

Take a step today that you've been avoiding, a step that you know will make your life healthier. Step out the door and go for a walk.

*"Retirement at sixty-five is ridiculous. When I was sixty-five
I still had pimples."*

GEORGE BURNS

When Al reached his sixties, he realized that he was
extremely overweight. His family history of strokes and heart
attacks made him a prime candidate for sudden illness or even
death. But instead of thinking that he was "too old" to change
his life, he joined a weight-loss program and lost 60 pounds.
Now he walks ten miles each day, plays 18 holes of golf with
ease and buys size 36 trousers instead of 42.

Al is an example to all who wonder if they are too old to
make long-term and healthy changes in their lives. Studies
have shown that if you continue to learn new things as you
age, your brain is more likely to remain vigorous and
active. Similarly, if you change your poor eating and
exercise habits late in life, it's not uncommon for physical problems to ease or disappear. As another benefit, you may experience more enthusiasm and energy than you have for many years.

If you're wondering if changing your lifestyle can still have
benefits for you, remember that age is more a state
of mind than a physical condition. Losing weight and
becoming active can bring a new dimension of vitality to your
life. As one seventy-year-old woman said about her
successful weight loss, "It's never too late for your dreams to
come true!"

⇜ *Tip for the Day* ⇝
*No matter how old you are, make a list of four things that losing weight will
enable you to do.*

"There smites nothing so sharp, nor smelleth so sour as shame."
WILLIAM LANGLAND

As part of becoming athletically fit, it's often helpful to join a health club where you can lift weights, participate in aerobics classes and be around people who share your lifestyle goals. One psychologist has found, though, that overweight women suffer from social physique anxiety and avoid situations where their bodies may be scrutinized by others. Therefore, the people who could really benefit from fitness activities are often unlikely to take advantage of them because they are ashamed of their bodies.

If you have avoided joining a class or health club, summon up the courage to become involved anyway. You may feel intimidated, thinking you'll be surrounded by slim, shapely bodies, but look again. Few, if any, are model-thin. Everyone else is just like you, exercising to get in shape, to look and feel better, to improve their overall well-being.

Although it's possible to become fit through solitary workouts, sometimes it's fun to be part of a group, too. By becoming a member of a class, you'll have the support and enthusiasm of those around you to spur you on. Remind yourself that avoiding activities out of shame will only hurt you. Have the courage to become a joiner, and set an example for someone else.

⇌ *Tip for the Day* ⇌
Analyze your workout style. Are you exercising alone because you don't want to be seen? Would becoming part of a group help you to reach more of your fitness goals?

"Americans are always looking for a magic bullet."
WILLIAM CASTELLI, M.D.

With the proliferation of health-food stores and knowledge about nutrition, taking vitamins and supplements has never been easier or more popular. Unfortunately, when reports appear that certain vitamins found in foods are linked to lowering the incidence of disease or that certain supplements are responsible for increased vitality, some people prefer to take those supplements in pill form.

It's important to note that the value of using supplements is becoming well established. For example, one study found that men who took a 500-milligram vitamin C supplement had a 42 percent lower death rate from heart disease and stroke than men who didn't. However, the human body is designed to get its nutrients from food rather than supplements, so it's smart to eat as wide and varied a menu as possible to maximize your chances of health instead of just hoping that a vitamin pill will be your magic bullet.

Make your top priority today getting varied meals so that you won't have to rely on pills to make up for nutritional deficiencies. If you do choose to take vitamins or supplements, be knowledgeable about them because too much of some substances can be toxic or dangerous. Moderation is the watchword, even when it comes to taking vitamins, so be educated about your options and be responsible for what you do.

∞   *Tip for the Day*   ∞
Today talk to a health professional who is well informed about vitamins and supplements and ask which ones would be helpful to you.

"What soon grows old? Gratitude."

ARISTOTLE

If you have joined a sensible weight-loss program and made steady progress toward reaching your weight and fitness goals, you may have begun to lose the sense of relief and gratitude you initially felt when the weight first started to come off. Gratitude is important because it helps you appreciate the past as well as the present. Gratefulness for healthful living today helps to remind you how you felt when you weren't treating your body well. When you appreciate your present achievement, you can remember that success in weight loss takes time and requires daily focus and attention.

Have you begun to take losing weight for granted? Are you no longer grateful that you have the ability to walk a mile or fit through a turnstile? If gratitude has grown "old," remind yourself today of several things that you worked hard to achieve and give yourself credit for your efforts. Whether it's having a roof over your head, being thinner and more active than you were one year ago or having a job that pays the bills, you must remember to give thanks for your blessings regularly. When you are grateful for past and present successes, future challenges seem easier.

Tip for the Day

Fill in this blank: "I am grateful today for having ––– in my life."

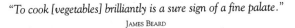

"To cook [vegetables] brilliantly is a sure sign of a fine palate."
JAMES BEARD

Many people who want to lose weight are unhappy that they can't eat meat at every meal. Accustomed to roast beef sandwiches, hamburgers, hot dogs, lamb chops and bacon, they fear that their new meal plan will be uninteresting and unsatisfying. Without substantial servings of meat they are concerned they won't get enough protein in their diets.

The person who wants to lose weight need not fear that the process of doing so will be unpleasant. It's possible to tailor a menu to incorporate the foods you like, within moderation, but you might be surprised to find that eating *less* meat may make you feel better. One study showed that people who lowered their intake of fatty foods, especially meat, and replaced them with complex carbohydrates, such as legumes, potatoes and rice, were happier than those who didn't. Another benefit is to lower the risk of heart disease. And complex carbohydrates like beans, sweet potatoes, pasta and squash cost far less than even inexpensive cuts of meat.

If you've always eaten large quantities of meat, consider foods that have higher levels of fiber and complex carbohydrates. Make meat an appetizer or side dish. Not only will you probably learn to enjoy a diet that gives you more energy, but you might be surprised to find how much better you feel in countless other areas of your life.

Tip for the Day
Make a hearty soup for dinner today. Reduce the amount of meat by half and add twice as many vegetables.

"For now I am in a holiday humour."

WILLIAM SHAKESPEARE

Many people find the post-holiday period to be disappointing, especially concerning their weight-loss efforts. Although you may have stuck to a sensible eating and exercise routine during most of the holiday period, there may have been several occasions—such as an office party or neighborhood gathering—where your resolve evaporated and you allowed yourself more food than you should have. As a result you may enter the new year with a few excess pounds, not to mention guilt, remorse and a fear that you will never get yourself back on track.

Experts say that this type of setback is not unusual, and that the best way to overcome negative feelings about yourself is to get right back into your food and exercise plans. In addition, you should forgive yourself for overindulging. Accept that you are human and imperfect. Then learn from your setbacks. You can also take note of the situations in which you had your lapses and devise solutions so that similar situations in the future will be easier for you to handle.

If the joy of the holidays is diminished because you are feeling disappointed in yourself, banish those feelings immediately. Make today the day that you start back with your eating and exercise plan. Be careful that you're not blowing your relapse out of proportion. For example, weigh yourself and you may be surprised to find that you haven't gained as much as you assumed. As soon as you can learn to love yourself despite your setbacks, there will be no situation you cannot handle—even the holiday festivities.

Tip for the Day
Don't wait for January 1 to make a fresh start on any holiday slips.
Remember that success comes by focusing on each day as it occurs,
not on the past or future.

*"If I knew what I was so anxious about, I wouldn't be
so anxious."*

MIGNON MCLAUGHLIN

Anxiety and stress are cited most often as the causes for snacking, which women do more often than men. One study showed that 46 percent of women snack when they are nervous, 40 percent when they are frustrated, and 34 percent when they are angry. Crunchy items like popcorn are favorites, but the most popular snack food was ice cream.

If you find solace in snacks, you need to plan ahead. One woman who is trying to lose weight says that having a bowl of cut-up carrots and celery in her refrigerator prevents her from turning to high-fat alternatives like potato chips. It also satisfies her need to relieve tension by crunching something. Depending on your mood, you may want to choose fruits that are solid, like apples, or softer foods, like bananas.

Although it's always better to alleviate tension through physical exercise, it won't hurt you to snack occasionally *if* you turn to healthful alternatives. To prepare ahead, keep vegetables and fruits in your refrigerator at all times, and banish high-fat snacks so that they don't tempt you. If you know your tendencies and accommodate them in a healthful way, you'll never have to let anxiety, worry and tension lead you to weight gain.

∽ Tip for the Day ∽
*Always have something crunchy available to snack on, such as rice cakes,
air-popped popcorn and fresh fruits and vegetables.*

"Ready money is Aladdin's lamp."

LORD BYRON

A strong incentive to changing bad habits is the promise that it will make your pocketbook fatter. With that in mind, it's important to stop periodically and think about the ways a healthy lifestyle can save you money while it's improving your health.

One woman initially balked at spending money to join a weight-loss program, saying it was too expensive and that she could lose weight by herself. When her solitary efforts failed, she joined and found herself actually saving money because she was no longer buying expensive snack foods or eating at fast-food restaurants. And, like most healthy people, her insurance claims plummeted. Studies show that people who eat healthfully, exercise regularly and avoid smoking have health insurance claims of $190 per year while those with poor habits average $1,550 a year.

When you pay to join a weight-loss program, the nominal weekly fee helps keep you on track because you've made an investment in eating right. Staying with your eating plan makes you feel like you've gotten your money's worth. Whenever your motivation to eat and exercise sensibly needs a boost, attend support-group meetings. Remind yourself of the money you are saving yourself in the short- and long-term. Although your new habits may not give you access to Aladdin's lamp, you'll give yourself a gift even more precious than money—enthusiasm, self-confidence and good health.

Tip for the Day

Add up how much you spend each week on tobacco and alcohol or fast food. Would eliminating these two items make it easier for you to join a weight-loss program?

*"There's folks 'ud stand on their heads and then say
the fault was i' their boots."*

GEORGE ELIOT

There are many excuses people use for being overweight. Some blame it on their parents, saying they inherited an obesity gene or "big bones." Some blame it on their jobs, saying that "if only" they didn't have to sit all day they wouldn't be so heavy. And some blame their weight on their metabolism, convinced that they've gained and lost weight so many times that they've "slowed down" their rate of burning off calories.

Experts say that it's not unusual for the metabolism to be the scapegoat for excess weight. In reality, it can't be blamed for much. One physiologist says that a drop in metabolic rate over a lifetime isn't unusual, but that it doesn't have to be the norm. The biggest component in determining the speed of metabolism is the amount of lean tissue in the body—and you can build lean tissue through exercise, specifically resistance training.

Do what you can to make your body as lean and efficient as possible today by exercising, doing resistance training and moving around as much as possible. If you combine these kinds of activities with sensible eating, you'll feel and look better and will no longer have to blame your body for your problems.

⇌   Tip for the Day   ⇌
*Find several ways to incorporate more activity into your day, such as walking to
do an errand when you might otherwise drive or using the stairs instead of
riding in an elevator.*

"Simplicity is the peak of civilization."
JESSIE SAMPTER

January often marks a time when many people decide to turn over a new leaf and change their lives. They begin to eat and exercise right. Perhaps they begin guilty because they may have overindulged during the holidays, some overdo their new fitness routines and injure themselves by trying to do too much too soon. Consequently, what began as a good intention may wind up in injury, disappointment and a sense of failure.

One word to keep in mind as you start your new regimen is *simplicity*. Instead of drastically limiting your calories, adopt a well-balanced food plan. Gradual changes in your eating behavior are more likely to become long-term ones. Instead of creating an all-or-nothing exercise plan, ease into a more active lifestyle. Try putting more energy into household tasks, for example, or walking with hand weights. If you can make these types of small changes a regular part of your life, you'll find that your January resolutions stay with you all year, and you'll have created the foundation for making other important changes in your life.

Tip for the Day
Instead of making elaborate plans for the new year, keep your resolutions simple and consistent.

Index

A

B

C

E

F

L

M

N

O

P

S

T

V

W